IMAGES
of America

EARLY ONTARIO

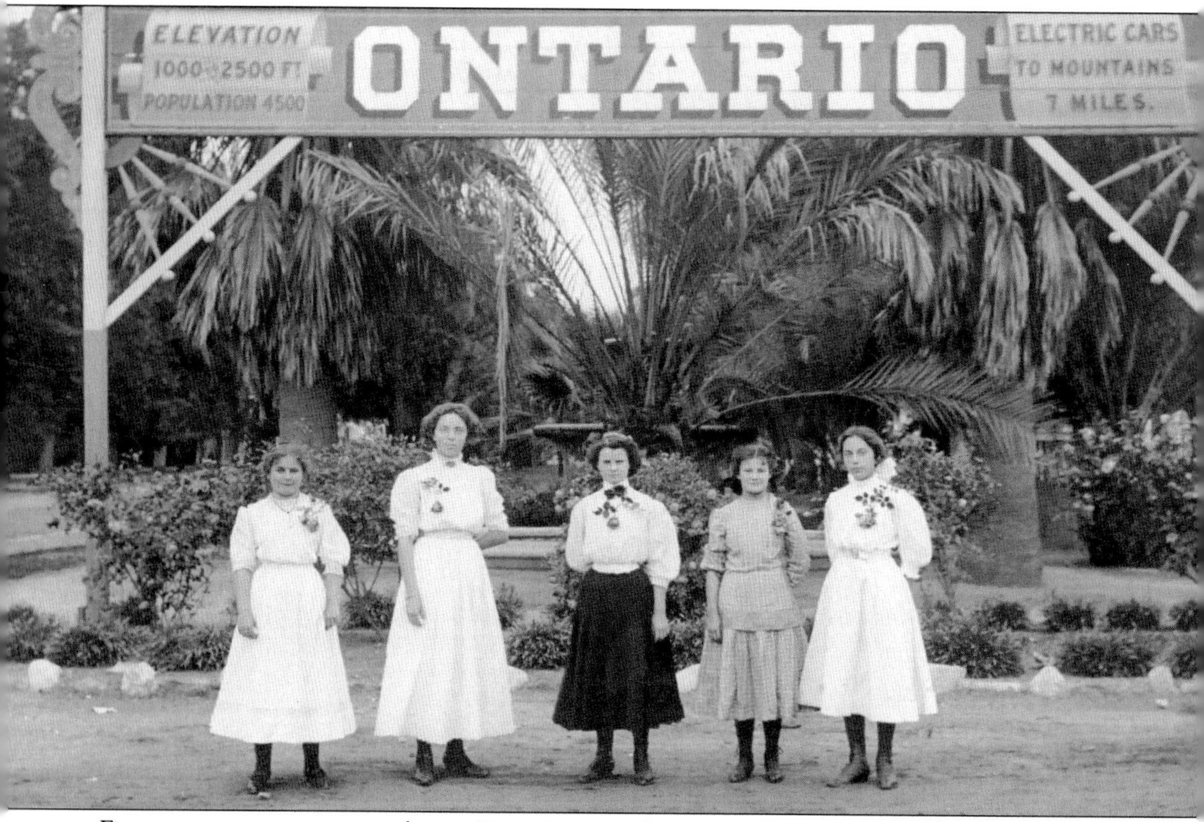

Five young women pose under an Ontario sign advertising electric cars to the head of Euclid Avenue around 1912. Behind them is the Chaffey Fountain, in the original garden on the Euclid Avenue median, which touted the abundance of water to train passengers when the colony was established. The Frankish Fountain, constructed in 1886, sits behind the palm tree.

On the Cover: Ontario's famous gravity mule car, designed by Ontarian J.B. Tays, transported residents and visitors up and down the beautiful Euclid Avenue median from 1888 until it was electrified in 1895.

IMAGES
of America

EARLY ONTARIO

The Ontario City Library

ARCADIA
PUBLISHING

ISBN 978-1-4671-3240-4

Published by Arcadia Publishing
Charleston, South Carolina

Printed in the United States of America

Library of Congress Control Number: 2014936329

For all general information, please contact Arcadia Publishing:
Telephone 843-853-2070
Fax 843-853-0044
E-mail sales@arcadiapublishing.com
For customer service and orders:
Toll-Free 1-888-313-2665

Visit us on the Internet at www.arcadiapublishing.com

This book is dedicated to the people of Ontario,
who continue to keep our history alive.

Contents

Acknowledgments

This book has been over 130 years in the making. The people of Ontario have always exhibited a strong interest in their history, and only through generous donations and support from our fellow Ontarians have we been able to compile this book. Because Ontario has such a story to tell, for this volume, we have narrowed our focus to Ontario's first 40 or so years, highlighting specific people who made a great impact on the city during that time. Considering the vastness of Ontario's rich history, we are unable to include all of the people, places, events, and businesses that helped shape our history, for to do so would require a much larger volume than this; however, we hope that we have created a well-rounded overview of Ontario's early history.

This book is the product of a two-year project organized by the staff of the Robert E. Ellingwood Model Colony History Room at the Ontario City Library. To compile the book, we utilized the many treasures, photographs, and information collected by the history room over the past several decades. The project was managed by Kelly Zackmann, local history librarian, who also wrote the bulk of the text. Additional text was written by Joanne Boyajian, Solie Daza, Helen Fisher, and Shawn Thrasher. Research and technical support was provided by Alana Forbes, Martha Rodriguez, and Solie Daza. The Model Colony History Room would like to thank Cliff Graber and Connie Hernandez of Graber Olive House for providing historical information and numerous images, and for their suggestions and support. We extend special appreciation to Diane Ayala and Rudy Zeledon of the Ontario Planning Department for their input, suggestions, and feedback. Additional thanks to Theresa Hanley of the Ontario Museum of History and Art for providing well-respected guidance and analysis.

All images appear courtesy of the Ontario City Library and Graber Olive House. The library would like to thank the City of Ontario and the Ontario City Council for continuing to support our efforts to preserve and promote local history and historic preservation.

We invite our fellow Ontarians to continue to help our history grow. Please share your stories, family histories, photographs, and local treasures with us in the Robert E. Ellingwood Model Colony History Room at the Ontario City Library.

INTRODUCTION

Ontario celebrates a rich history and heritage, which has shaped what it is today. The land that was to become Ontario in the 1880s was home only to the Tongva Indians until the Franciscans arrived in 1768, developing the Spanish mission system. Mission San Gabriel Arcángel was founded in 1771, which was a pivotal point in the European settlement of the Inland Empire. The Tongva were lured into religious conversion whether they were willing or not, becoming the mission's labor force, working the land as cattle was raised and grapes and citrus were grown, making San Gabriel Arcángel one of the most prosperous missions in the system.

Mexico gained independence from Spain in 1821, and the missions were secularized in 1833. Soon, the Mexican government began awarding land grants to the Californios who were willing to work the land formerly held by the Spanish missions. The Cucamonga Rancho was granted to Tiburcio Tapia, and the Rancho Santa Ana del Chino was granted to Don Antonio Maria Lugo. Portions of these two ranchos would later comprise the area we now know as Ontario. Over the next 50 years, the ranchos would disappear and the land would be carved up and sold.

Ontario was founded in 1882 by George and William Chaffey, brothers from Brockville, Ontario, Canada, who had come to America and settled in Riverside, California. George Chaffey was an engineer and was fascinated by the challenge of irrigating the arid region once known as the Cucamonga Rancho. On Thanksgiving Day in 1881, the Chaffey brothers made an offer to Capt. Joseph Garcia, a Portuguese mariner who left the sea behind to raise sheep in the area, to purchase his large rancho. The brothers purchased 560 acres of land from Garcia with full water rights. A small portion of that land was divided up, and each lot was provided with irrigation from the nearby canyons. George Chaffey named this area Etiwanda and sold the lots, each complete with its own water rights, to settlers. Etiwanda was such a success that the brothers decided to repeat the project on a grander scale, and purchased another 6,216 acres from Garcia along with over 2,500 acres of land from others, most importantly from the Southern Pacific Railroad, which brought their new colony landholdings down to the Southern Pacific tracks. Their model colony was born. It was named Ontario after the brothers' home province in Canada.

George Chaffey developed four principles for the new town site:

(1) To distribute water by concrete pipe to each lot, with each landowner provided an equal share of water rights;
(2) to construct a beautiful thoroughfare from one end of the settlement to the other;
(3) to establish a college to provide agricultural education to the residents and general education for their children; and
(4) to forbid the sale of intoxicating liquor in order to guarantee the highest class of settlers.

The Chaffeys' Ontario Land Company developed brochures and maps boasting of the sunshine and healthy climate in Ontario, sending them back east to lure new settlers. They built a land office complete with a fountain that was used to publicize the abundance of water to potential land buyers who stopped in or passed by the colony by rail. Their strategies worked, and the colony quickly grew, with most settlers coming either from Canada or the Midwest, and many of them coming to sunny Southern California for health reasons.

In 1885, seeing the Chaffeys' advanced principles at work in Ontario, Australians asked the Chaffeys to come to Victoria to develop similar irrigation settlements there. So, in 1886, the brothers sold their entire stake in Ontario to a group of Los Angeles investors, headed by Charles Frankish, an Englishman who came to California by way of Canada and the Midwest himself. The business was named the Ontario Land and Improvement Company, and improve is just what Frankish did. He was responsible for developing San Antonio Heights, the South Side Tract, and the famous Ontario gravity mule car line. Robert Ely Blackburn created Blackburn's Addition in the 1890s from land that was formerly part of the Rancho Santa Ana del Chino, adding another 1,100 acres to the town. Ontario incorporated in 1891, much to the dismay of Charles Frankish, but, despite losing his foothold in the community, he continued to deal in real estate as well as other local enterprises, and remained an influential figure in the new city until his death in 1931.

In 1887, during the big Southern California land boom, Edmund and Alfred Bedford purchased 200 acres of colony lands at $500 per acre from the Ontario Land and Improvement Company. Together with their four brothers, they formed a partnership to develop their own town site to the north of Ontario, located just above what are now the Santa Fe Railroad tracks, and named it North Ontario. It was also referred to as Magnolia. They immediately began grading streets and dividing the land into lots, and within four months, a new hotel was built called Magnolia Villa. In late 1887, however, the brothers ran into financial trouble. To make matters worse, two December windstorms nearly destroyed the hotel and the town's orange crop. By May 1888, the Bedford brothers had gone bankrupt and were in foreclosure, and their interests were sold to brothers Charles and Alfred Harwood in 1891. In 1901, Ontario attempted to annex North Ontario, but its residents opposed annexation. In 1902, action was started against Ontario that eventually landed in the Supreme Court in 1906. The fight between Ontario and North Ontario continued, and on May 5, 1906, the residents of North Ontario voted to incorporate as Upland in order to avoid annexation.

In these early days, agricultural enterprises dominated Ontario's economy. Canadians and Midwesterners purchased land and set out their fruit trees, establishing themselves as gentlemen farmers. Primarily Asian immigrants picked fruit in the fields, which was then transported to packinghouses where men, women, and sometimes children packed local fruit to send across the United States. While many of the Californios remained in the area after California's statehood, and several Mexican immigrants arrived through the turn of the 20th century to help build the railroads and work in agriculture, it was not until after World War I that the Hispanic and African American populations quickly began to expand. Migrants came to the area for work after Chinese exclusionary laws, the Alien Land Act of 1913, and the Immigration Act of 1917 were enacted. At first, migrant workers lived in labor camps set up in various agricultural areas of Ontario, Upland, and Cucamonga. Ontario's La Colonia neighborhood, southeast of the city center, was established in the 1920s, when local Hispanic migration was in its infancy.

So goes the development of the model colony, offering a glimpse into Ontario's first few decades. Its early history is rich with people, businesses, industry, clubs, churches, schools, events, and architectural gems that have helped to create what Ontario is today.

One

A Colony is Established

The town of Ontario was developed on land granted to Tiburcio Tapia by Mexican governor Juan B. Alvarado in 1839. Over the next 40 years, the Cucamonga Rancho changed hands and was divided among individual land owners and land companies. Some of this land was owned by Capt. Joseph Garcia, and other land was owned by Isaias W. Hellman and his Cucamonga Company, among other individual owners. To the south of the future site of Ontario was the Rancho Santa Ana del Chino, which, by the 1880s, was owned by Richard Gird, the founder of the town of Chino and owner of a large sugar beet factory.

George Chaffey Sr. was born in Ohio but resided permanently in Ontario, Canada, where he engaged in various enterprises, including building ships designed for use on the Great Lakes. He retired in 1878 and moved to Riverside, California, bringing his daughter Emma and sons Charles and William Benjamin. William, who was 22 and fascinated with horticulture, was quick to become popular within the community for his knowledge of soils and plants. In 1880, 32-year-old George Chaffey Jr. visited his father and siblings in Riverside and never returned to Canada.

Between William's knowledge of horticulture and George's knowledge of engineering, the brothers entered a 15-year partnership, developing irrigation colonies in California and Australia. For Ontario, they created four guiding principles used to develop their model colony: water distribution to each land owner, the construction of a beautiful main thoroughfare, the establishment of a college, and drawing the "best class of settlers" by forbidding the sale of liquor.

To Canadians, the Iroquois word *ontario*, which means "beautiful waters," would evoke a ready supply from the local canyons, brought by gravity to the top of each settler's plot of land. Parcels were set out along Euclid Avenue, the beautiful street that ran from the railroad tracks up to the foothills. Lined with pepper trees, it also fronted Chaffey College, which was founded in collaboration with the University of Southern California in 1883.

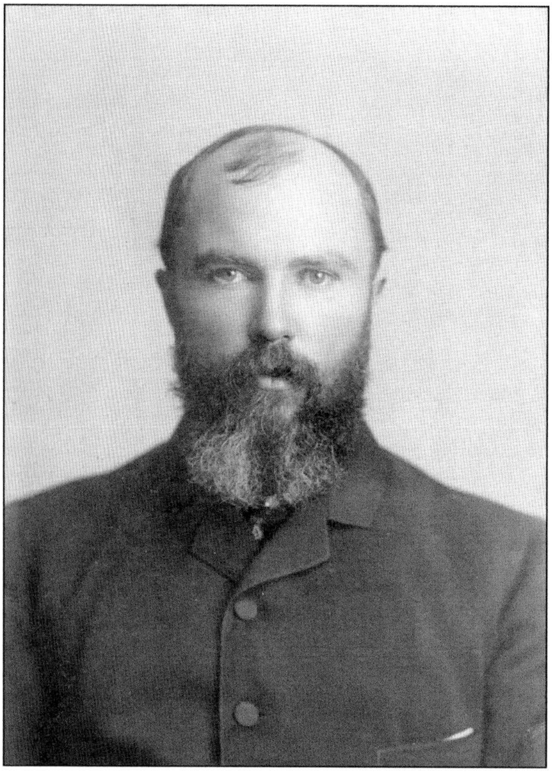

George Chaffey Jr. was born on January 28, 1848, in Brockville, Ontario. Chaffey had little formal education, but, as a teen, he began working for his father's freight business. By age 20, he had earned an engineer's certificate and worked as a tugboat captain, and went on to design steamships for use on the great lakes. During this time, he married Annette McCord and the couple had three sons.

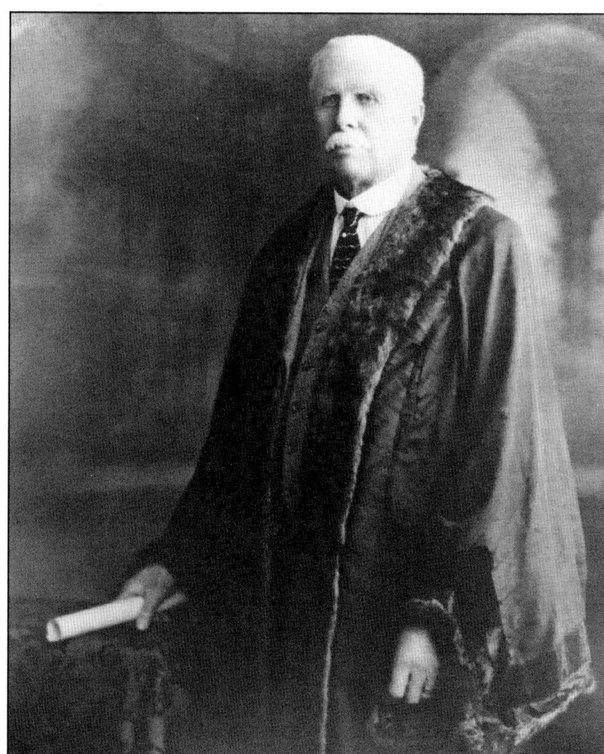

William Benjamin Chaffey was born on October 21, 1856, also in Brockville. In 1878, George Chaffey Sr. retired and moved to Riverside, California, bringing William along with him. William was fascinated with horticulture and became known for his expertise with soils and plants. In 1880, his brother George Jr. joined the family in Riverside and began working with Matthew Gage, bringing water to Riverside's citrus groves. Soon, the Chaffey brothers would embark on new adventures.

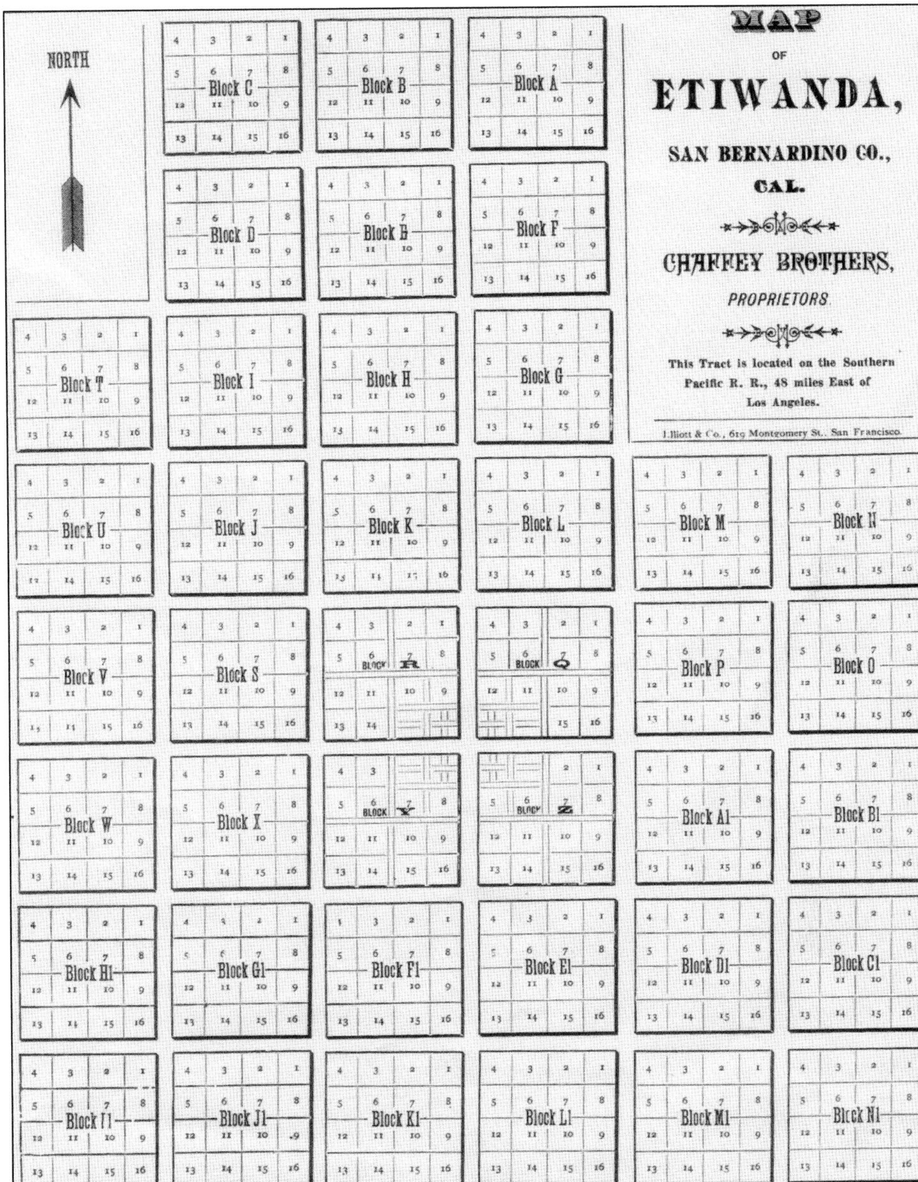

The Chaffey brothers' first business endeavor began on Thanksgiving Day, 1881, when they and surveyor J.C. Dunlap rode by horseback from Riverside to a ranch owned by former Portuguese sea captain Joseph Garcia and shared a Thanksgiving meal. Afterward, George offered to purchase 560 acres of Garcia's land with full water rights. Garcia accepted the offer, and the Etiwanda colony was born. The brothers divided the land into 10-acre blocks. Water was brought to the highest point of each lot from Day, Young, and Middle Canyons through cement pipes. The challenge of irrigating the colony brought with it the formation of one of California's earliest mutual water companies, created by the Chaffeys and Luther M. Holt, a local newspaper publisher who had experimented with mutual water companies in Pomona and Artesia. The colony was named Etiwanda, apparently after an Iroquois Indian chief who was a friend of the brothers' uncle Benjamin. George hoped that the name and its affiliation with Canada would draw his fellow Canadians to settle in the colony.

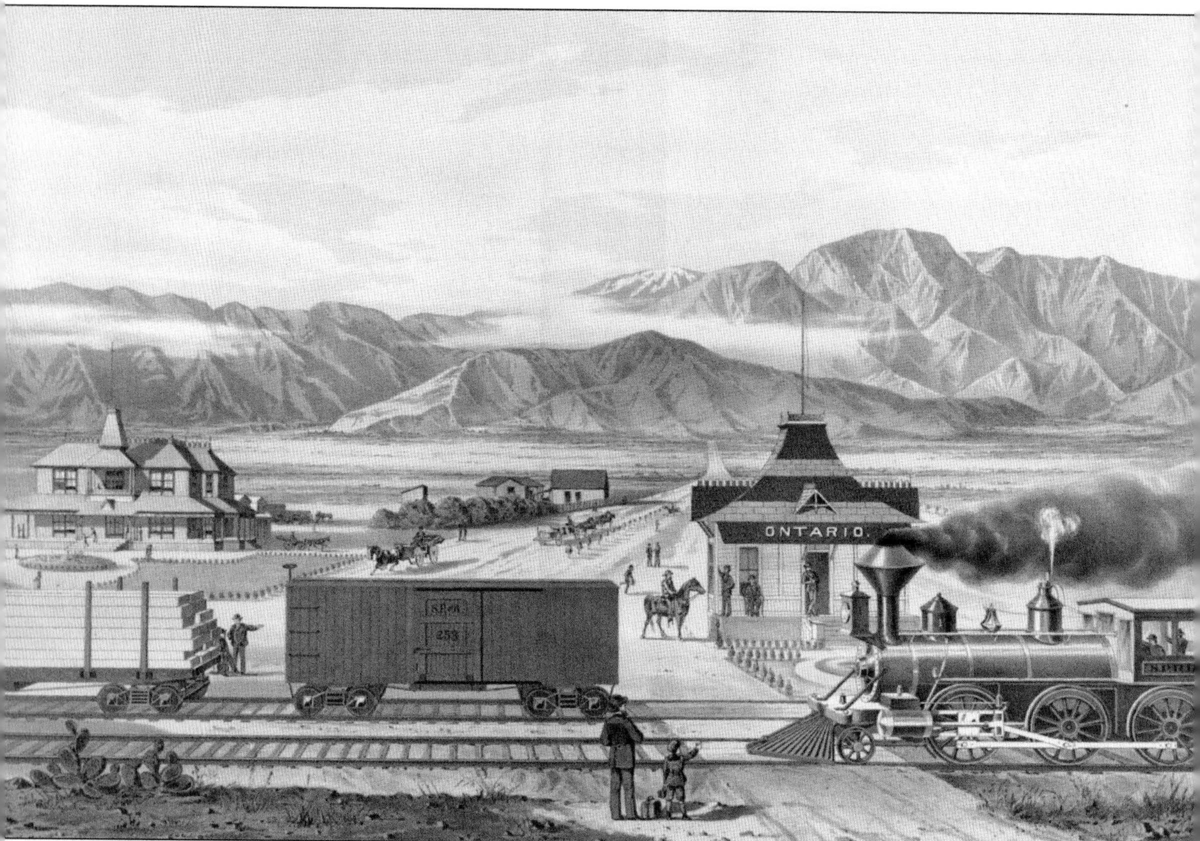

The success of Etiwanda provided the Chaffey brothers with the financial leverage they needed to create Ontario, their model colony. Before the Chaffeys founded Ontario, Joseph Garcia was offered an option on some land from the Cucamonga Company, much of which would later become part of the Ontario Colony. When the Pomona Land and Water Company found out about the option, they quickly offered to buy the land from Garcia, but the Chaffey brothers offered Garcia more money and won the bid. They purchased 6,216 acres from Garcia for $60,000. The Chaffey brothers purchased additional land from the Southern Pacific Railroad Company and from individual land owners, extending their future colony from the foothills of the mountains to just below the existing Southern Pacific tracks. The town center was created just north of the Southern Pacific, and, soon, the railroad would make Ontario one of its stops, bringing prospective buyers directly to the colony.

The name Ontario, meaning "beautiful waters," was likely used to lure Canadians to settle here, and also highlighted the availability of water in the colony. However, water did not come without a fight between the Chaffey brothers and the Pomona Land and Water Company. Both claimed the water that flowed through the San Antonio Canyon, but George Chaffey instinctively knew that water could be found underground. The two groups negotiated and settled on sharing the surface water.

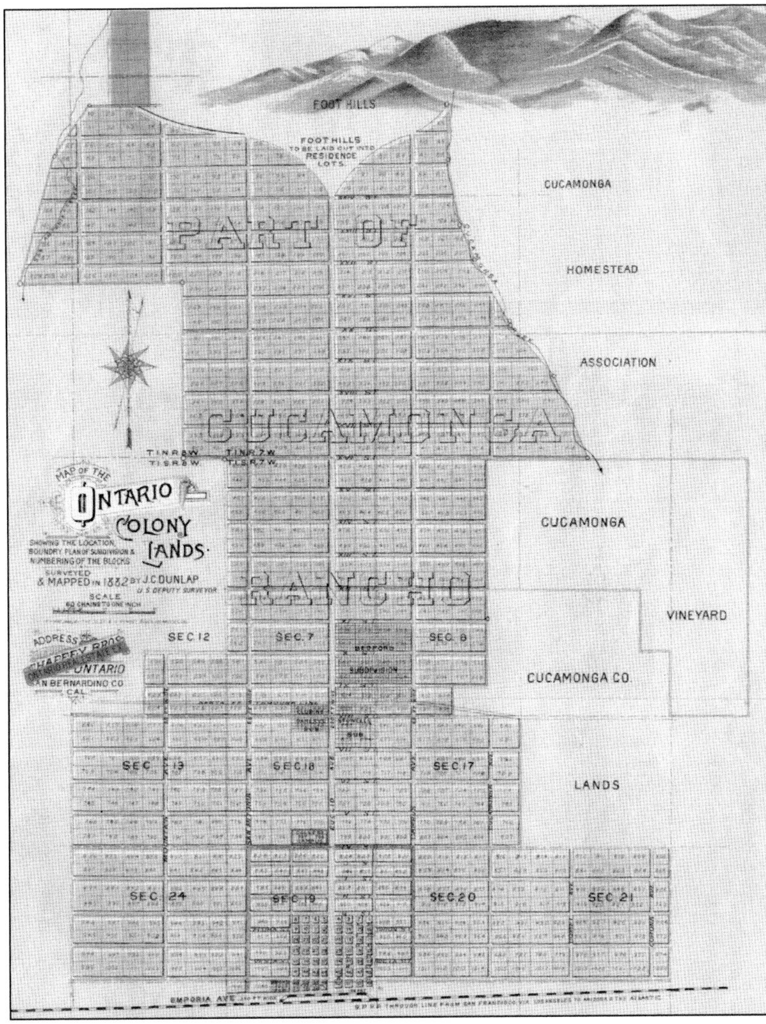

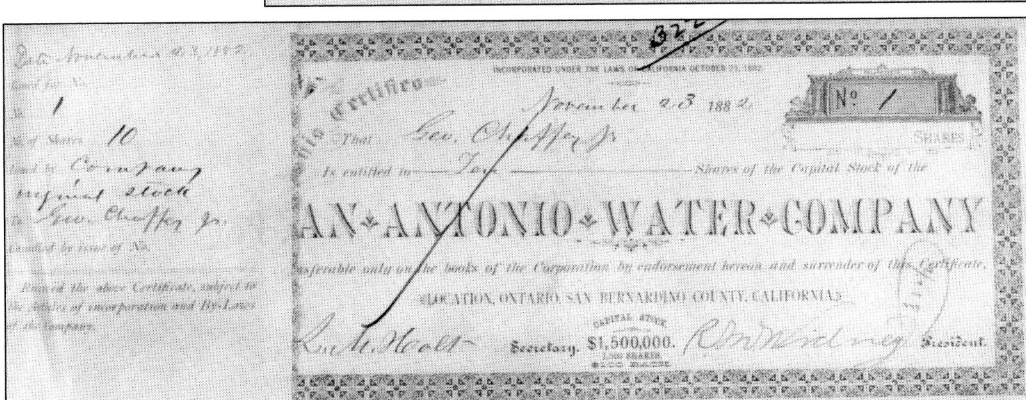

The Chaffey brothers established the San Antonio Water Company in October 1882, and the first 10 shares were sold to George Chaffey that November. Each land purchaser was provided water rights at one share per acre, and each property owner had a say in the business dealings of the San Antonio Water Company, which revolutionized how water companies ran in California.

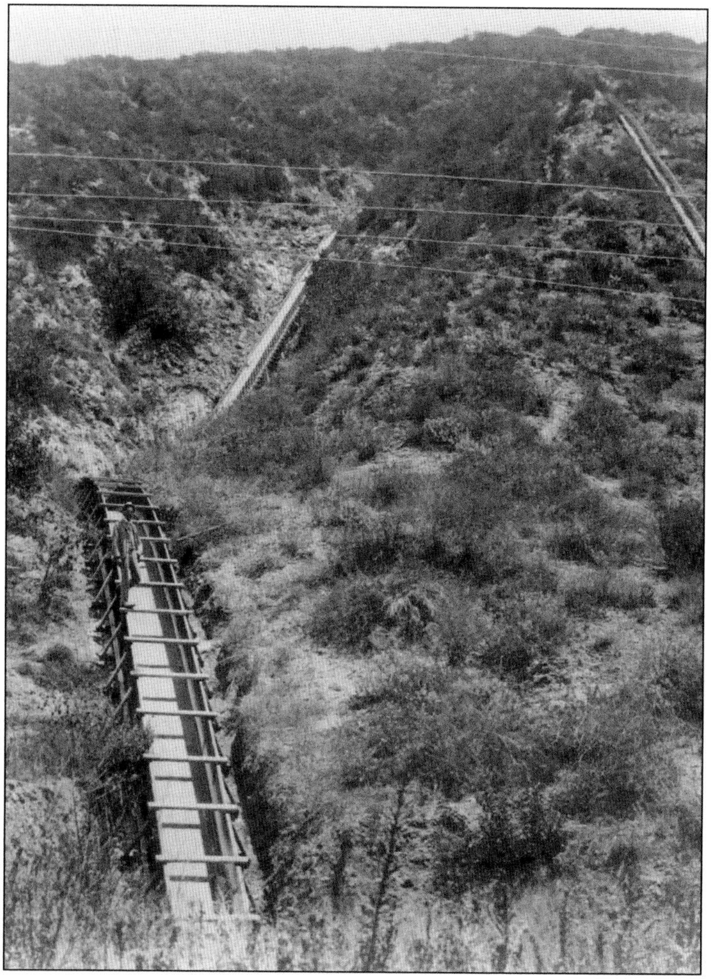

Water was brought down from the canyon through wooden flumes such as these. The water flowed into reservoirs for future distribution to land owners. Concrete pipes were constructed throughout the colony, and water was delivered by these pipes to the highest point on each parcel of land, at specific intervals. George Chaffey had a tunnel constructed in the San Antonio Canyon in order to tap the subterranean water to supplement the surface water. The flumes, pipes, and tunnels were built, owned, and maintained by the mutual water company. Since the colony was located just below the foothills, it allowed gravity to do most of the work, saving money on the delivery of water.

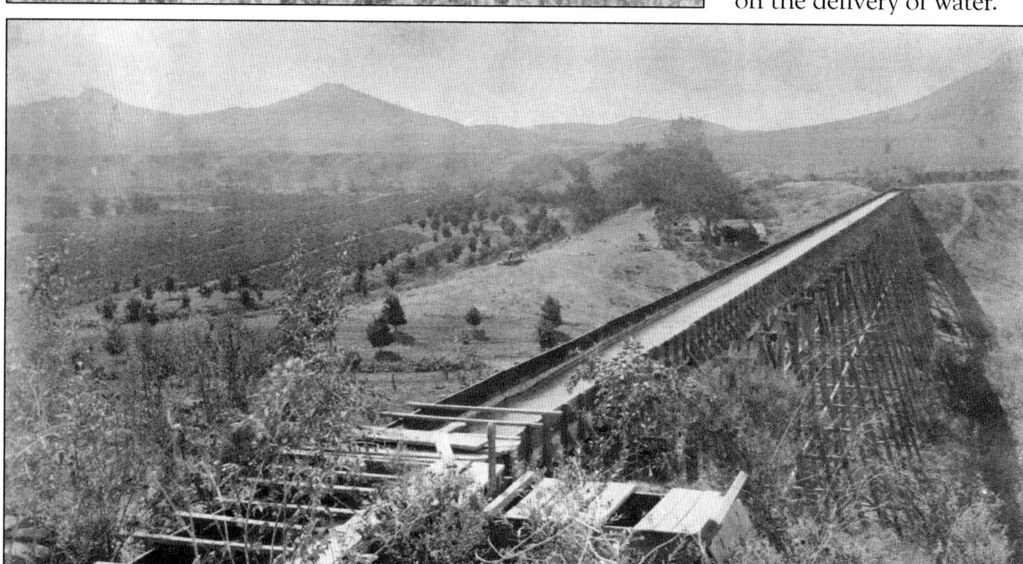

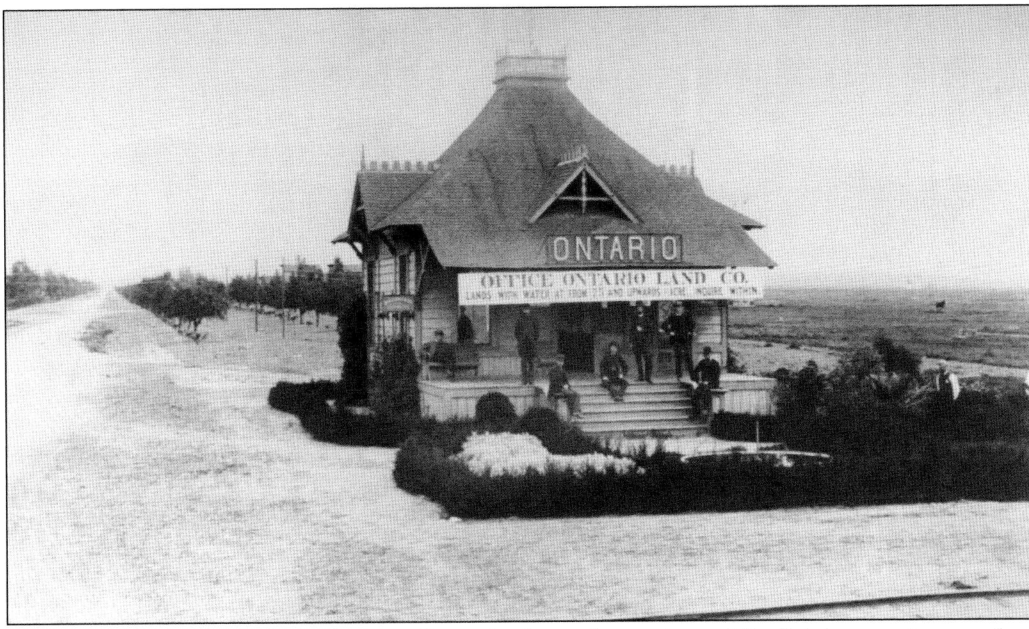

The Ontario Land Company (pictured) was built on the median of Euclid Avenue just north of the railroad tracks, and served as Ontario's train depot until 1887. Potential buyers would exit the train here and be taken to the Ontario Hotel for accommodations. George Chaffey had a small fountain constructed just in front of the land company building to show off the availability of water when the trains came through.

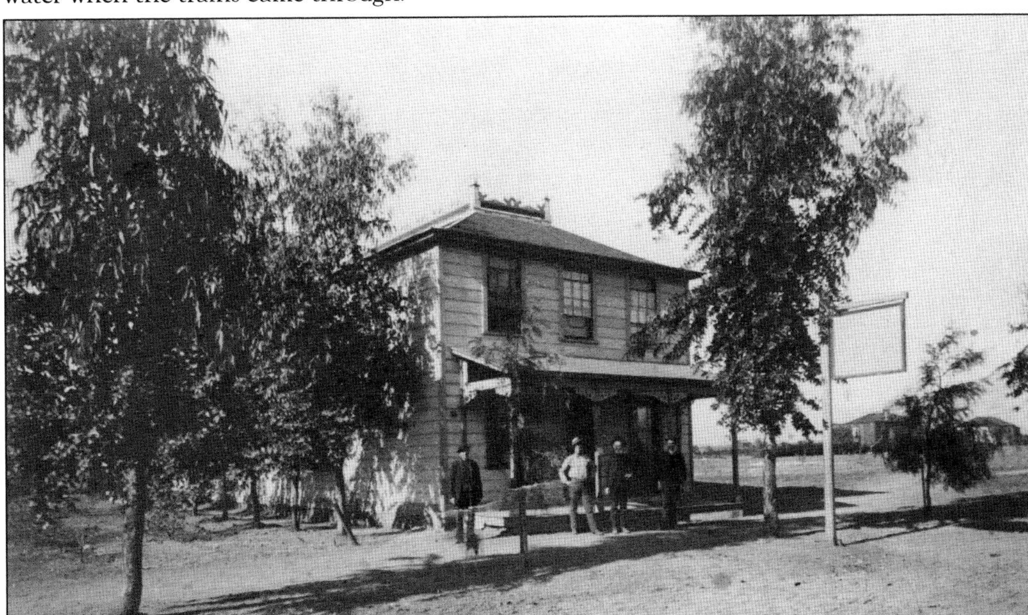

The Avenue Boarding House was one of the first buildings constructed in the new colony. Built in 1884, it housed the men hired to build the colony. It was originally located at 307 North Euclid Avenue but was moved to Princeton Street in 1925 and became a private residence. Famous children's author Beverly Cleary lived in the house while she attended Chaffey College in the 1930s. The house still stands today.

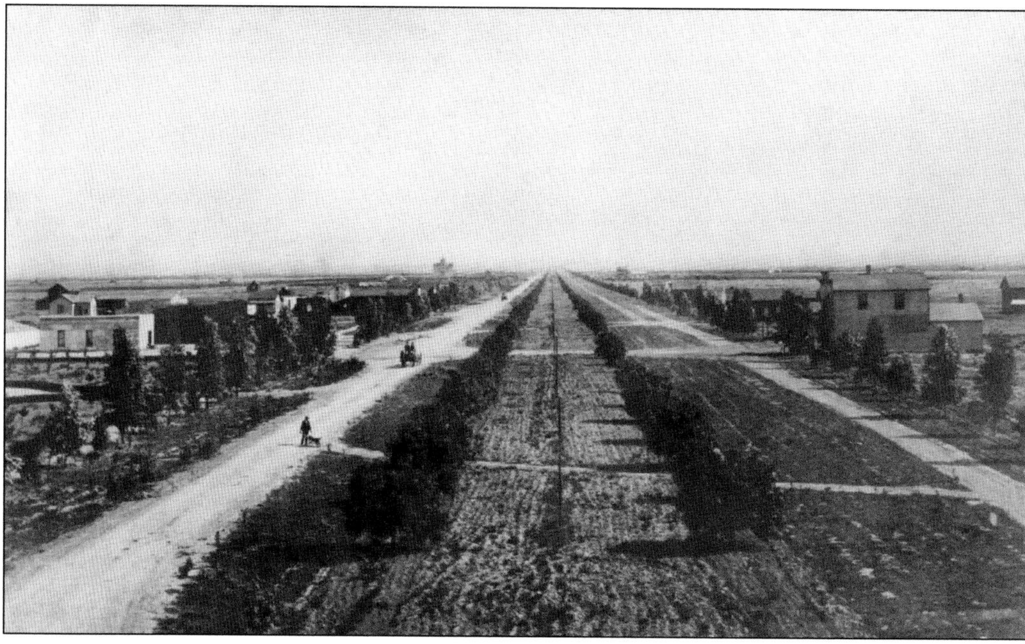

Euclid Avenue was modeled after Magnolia Avenue in Riverside, and George Chaffey named his 200-foot-wide thoroughfare after his favorite mathematician. Swiss immigrant Edward J. Jacquet was hired to oversee the planting of trees on the grand avenue beginning in April 1883, and the project was completed in 1886. George Chaffey visited Ontario in 1894 and stated in a newspaper article that he regretted the decision to plant pepper trees on the avenue, and that he had only intended to keep them for a few years in order to quickly create a showy spectacle for prospective buyers. His intention was to have the avenue permanently lined with palm trees.

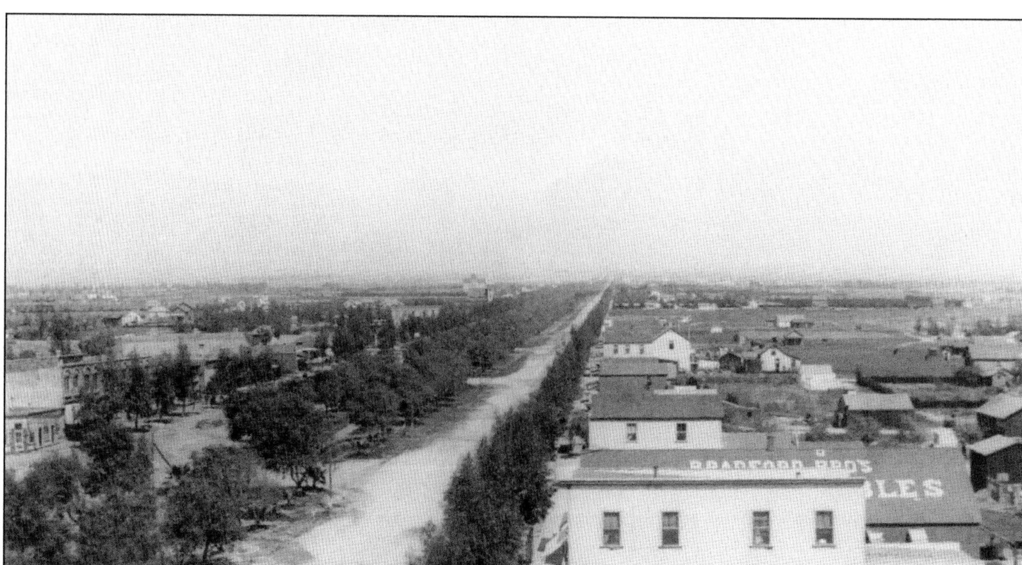

Two

THE COLONY BECOMES A CITY

A delegation from Australia's Royal Commission on Water Supply and Irrigation visited George Chaffey in 1885. Seeing his advanced principles at work in Ontario, the delegates asked him to come to Victoria to work similar irrigation wonders. In 1886, the Chaffey brothers sold their whole stake in Ontario to a group of Los Angeles investors, who created the Ontario Land and Improvement Company. British immigrant Charles Frankish served as manager of the new land company, developing San Antonio Heights, the South Side Tract, and the mule car railroad linking downtown Ontario to the head of Euclid Avenue in San Antonio Heights. The railroad was electrified in 1895, drawing power from San Antonio Creek. E.H. Richardson was hired to run the power plant, and in 1904, he founded the Pacific Electric Heating Company, more commonly known as Hotpoint.

In 1891, Ontario was incorporated as a city, but it took several years into the new century for Ontario's fire department, police, and wandering library to become city departments with permanent buildings. The Bedford brothers started a development in 1887 named North Ontario. After a years-long annexation fight with Ontario, the citizens of North Ontario incorporated in 1906 as Upland.

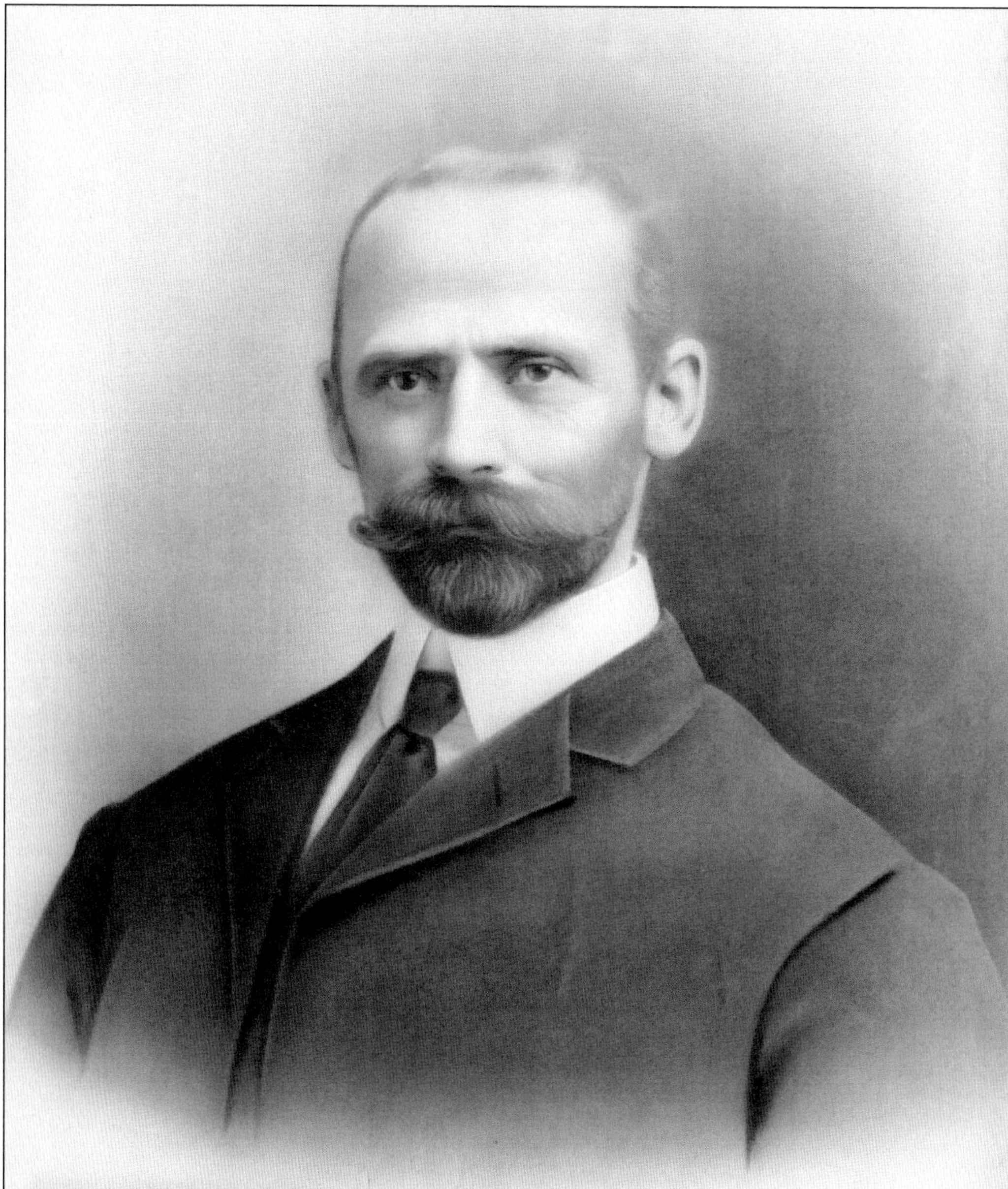

After the Chaffey brothers accepted their invitation to Australia, they sold their interests in the Ontario Land Company to a group of investors from Los Angeles. The company was named the Ontario Land and Improvement Company, and Charles Frankish served as manager and was also a stockholder. Frankish married his first wife, Ruth, in Kansas, and moved the family to Riverside, where his brother was living. After accepting the position of manager for the land company, he, Ruth, and their children finally settled in Ontario. While he is less known than Chaffey, Frankish was largely responsible for the success of the Ontario Colony. The development of San Antonio Heights, the South Side Tract, and the Frankish Building, and the establishment of the gravity mule car are just a few of his accomplishments. He was not well liked by all and was often chided by the editor of the *Ontario Record*, who once referred to him as "Czar Frankish," for his business practices and his regular protests against Ontario's incorporation.

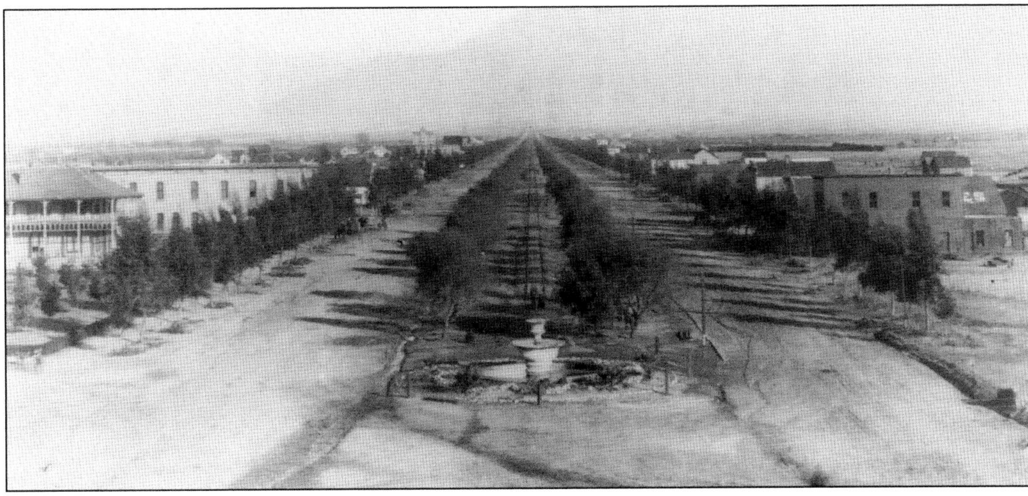

Frankish constructed a new fountain on the Euclid Avenue median to serve as a focal point to potential land buyers. The land office building had to be moved to the west side of Euclid Avenue to accommodate the fountain. Completed in 1886, the Frankish Fountain was grandiose, equipped with a compound sprayer with jets that proudly showed Ontario's abundance of water to every person traveling through town. By the 1950s, though, the fountain had fallen into disrepair and was threatened with demolition. After protests from the community, the city paid $300 to have the fountain painted and new landscaping installed. When the Euclid Avenue underpass was constructed in the 1980s, the fountain was moved to the east side of Euclid Avenue onto the grounds of the Ontario Museum of History and Art, where it stands today.

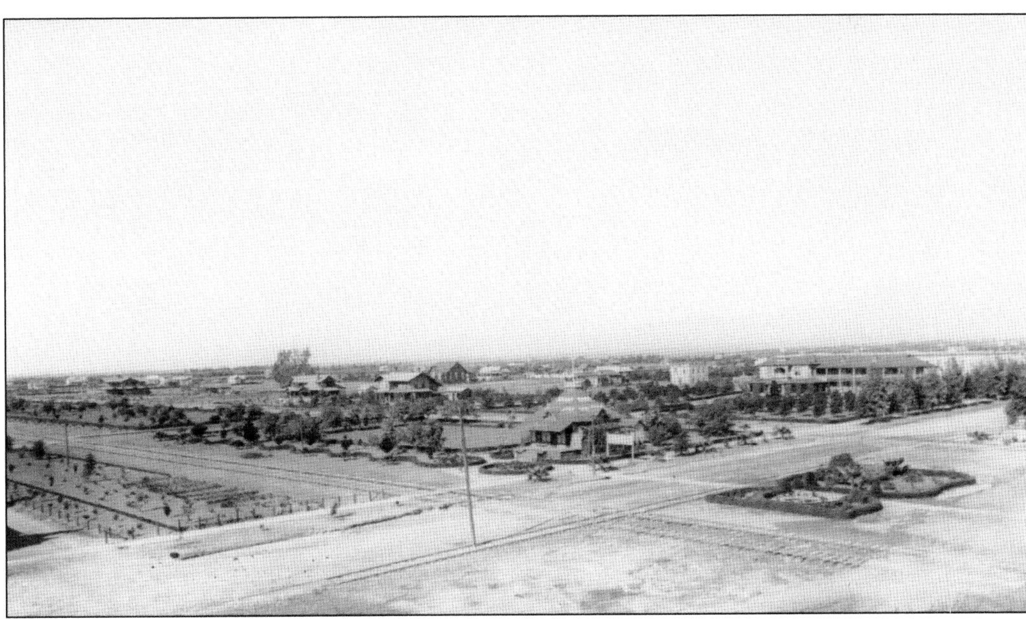

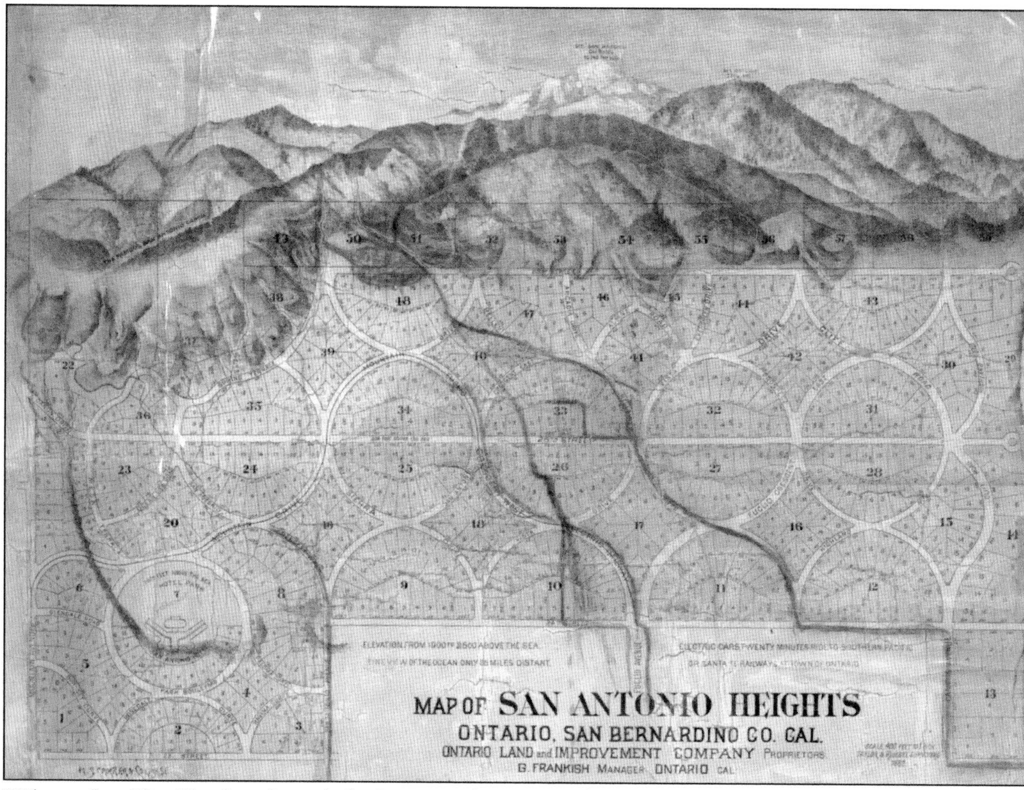

When the Chaffey brothers left Ontario for Australia, San Antonio Heights had yet to be developed. Determining its layout was one of Frankish's first accomplishments, completed in 1887. He designed the foothills landscape into circles and crescents in order to make the most efficient use of the hillsides. The development was marketed as a "haven of rest and joy" and claimed to have ocean views.

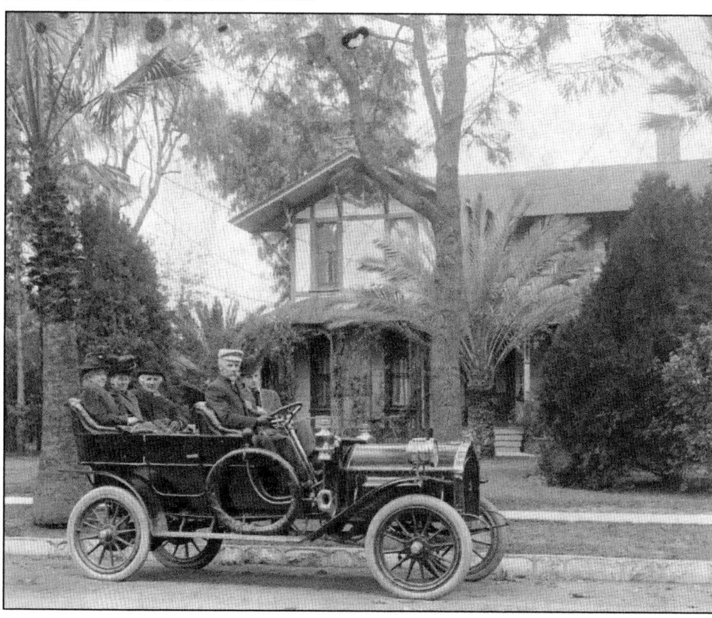

Charles Frankish, his second wife, Eliza, son Hugh, and two other unidentified people sit in the family's Northern automobile in 1909 in front of the Frankish home on West Emporia Avenue. In 1887, Frankish developed the South Side Tract, envisioning the area as Ontario's new metropolitan town center. The South Side Tract begins at Holt and extends south to California Street, with Sultana and Vine Avenues serving as the east and west boundaries.

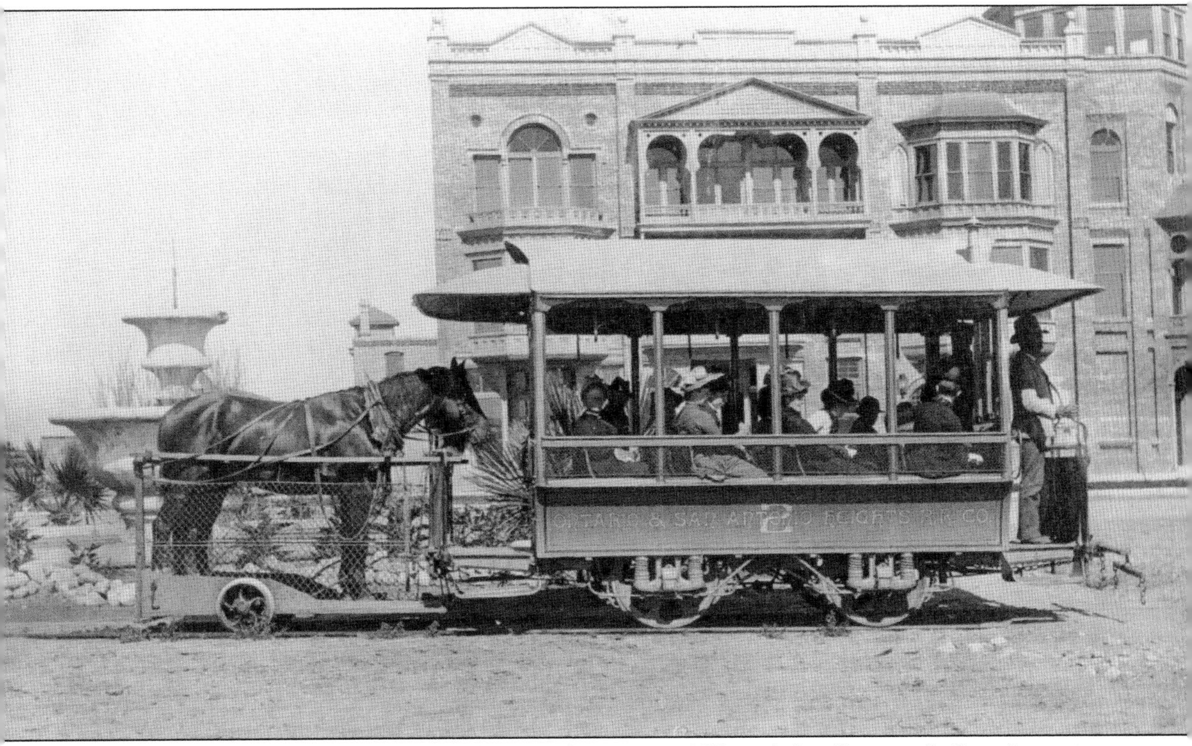

Construction of the gravity mule car line was begun in 1887, and the Ontario & San Antonio Heights Railroad Company commenced in 1888. Charles Frankish was a major stockholder in the company, as were his son Charles Goodwin Frankish and George T. Stamm. What made the mule car unique compared to other mule-drawn cars was the fact that while the car was pulled uphill by two mules, it returned from San Antonio Heights solely by gravity. The mules were provided with a platform on the back of the car where they stood for the ride south, ending in front of the Southern Pacific Hotel, seen here. The mule car line was electrified in 1895. Today, the folk tale goes that after the line was electrified, the mules were retired and sold to a local farmer to help plow his fields. The farmer was disappointed in the mules because they would only pull the plow in one direction and then stop and expect to be given a ride back to the starting point.

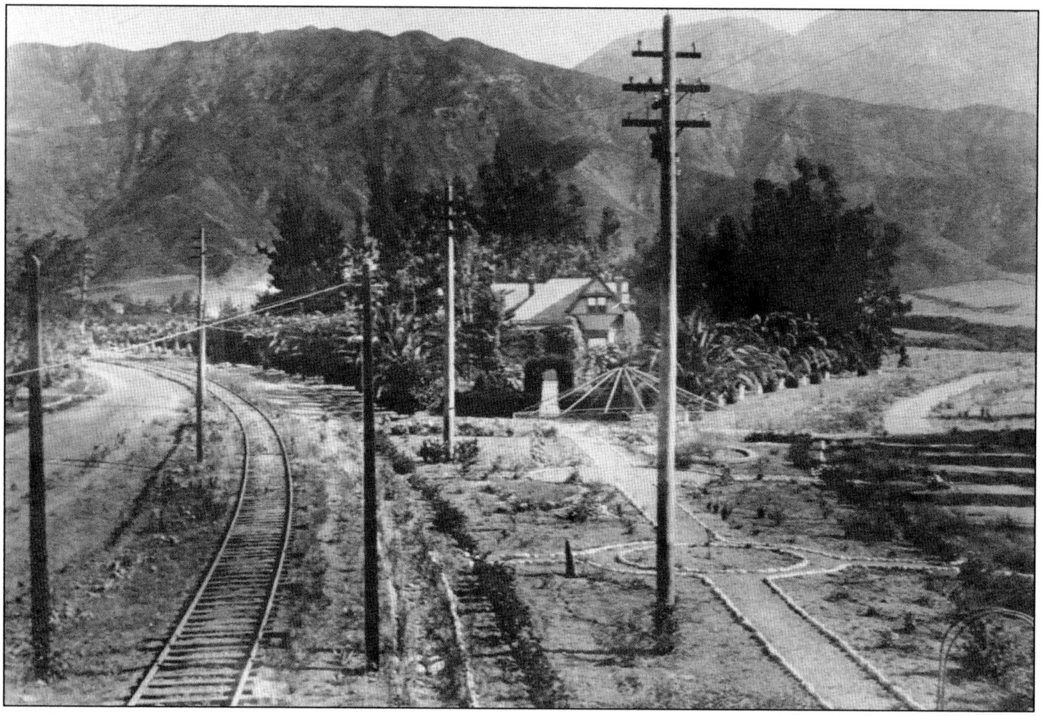

To electrify the line, poles were installed along Euclid Avenue. The power lines brought electric lighting to Ontario as well as an electrified rail line. The Ontario Electric Company installed the system at a cost of $100,000. The power for the electrified rail line was generated in San Antonio Canyon, and each 40-person car could travel at 20 miles per hour. In 1903, William Kerckhoff, president of the Pacific Light & Power Company, controlled by Henry Huntington, purchased the Ontario & San Antonio Heights Railroad Company. The line then became part of the Pacific Electric Railway.

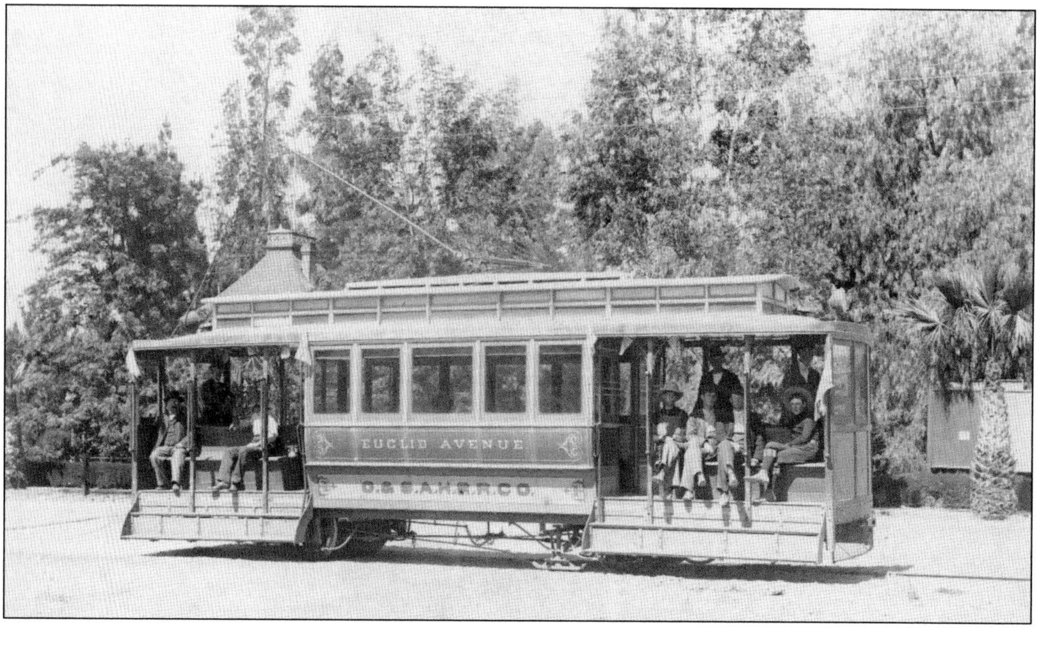

When the line was electrified in 1895, a new powerhouse was built at the mouth of the San Antonio Canyon to generate the power needed for the electric railway and the residents of Ontario. The building, seen here, was constructed of local fieldstone and nicknamed the "Stone Castle." E.H. Richardson, who later invented the Hotpoint iron, was hired to run and maintain the power plant.

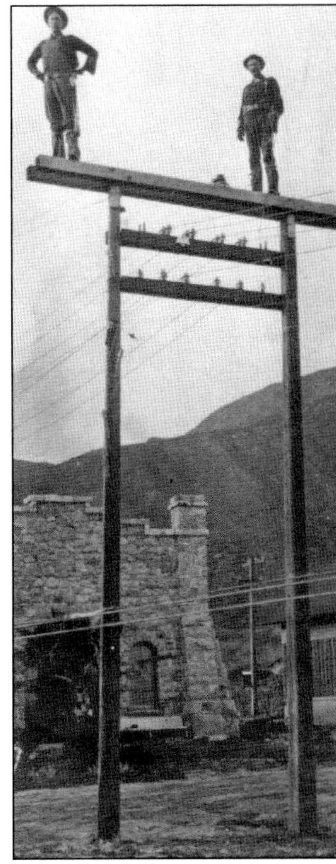

In 1902, the power company built this substation on Euclid Avenue near the Santa Fe Railroad tracks in what is now Upland, and Richardson and his family moved into an adjoining apartment. In 1904, Richardson left the power company to start his own electrical appliance business, the Pacific Electric Heating Company.

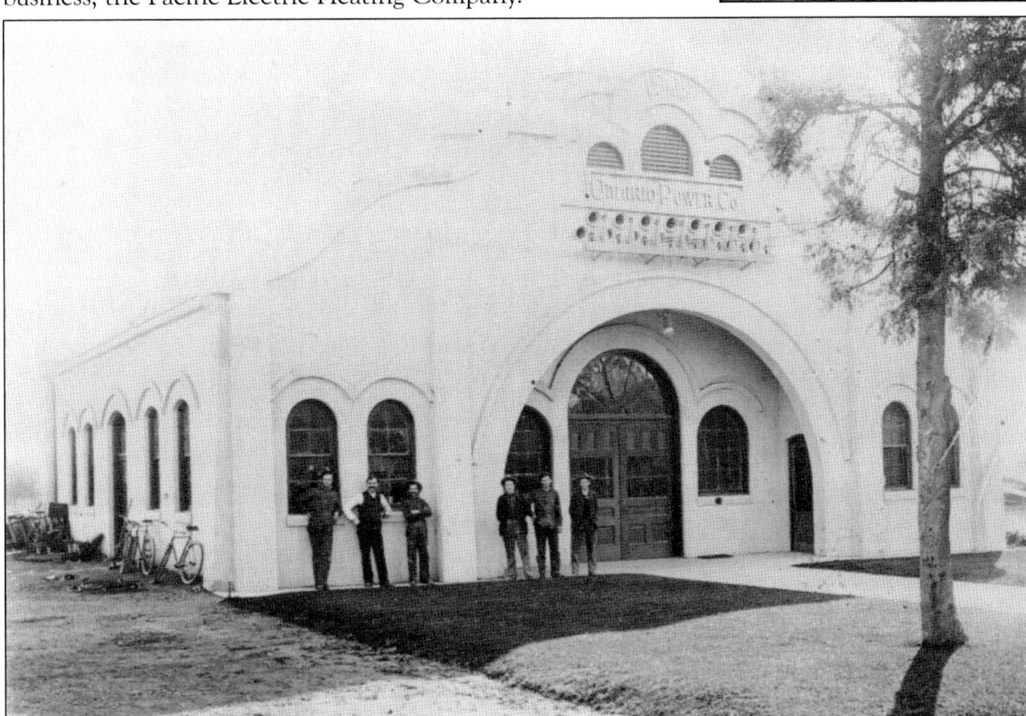

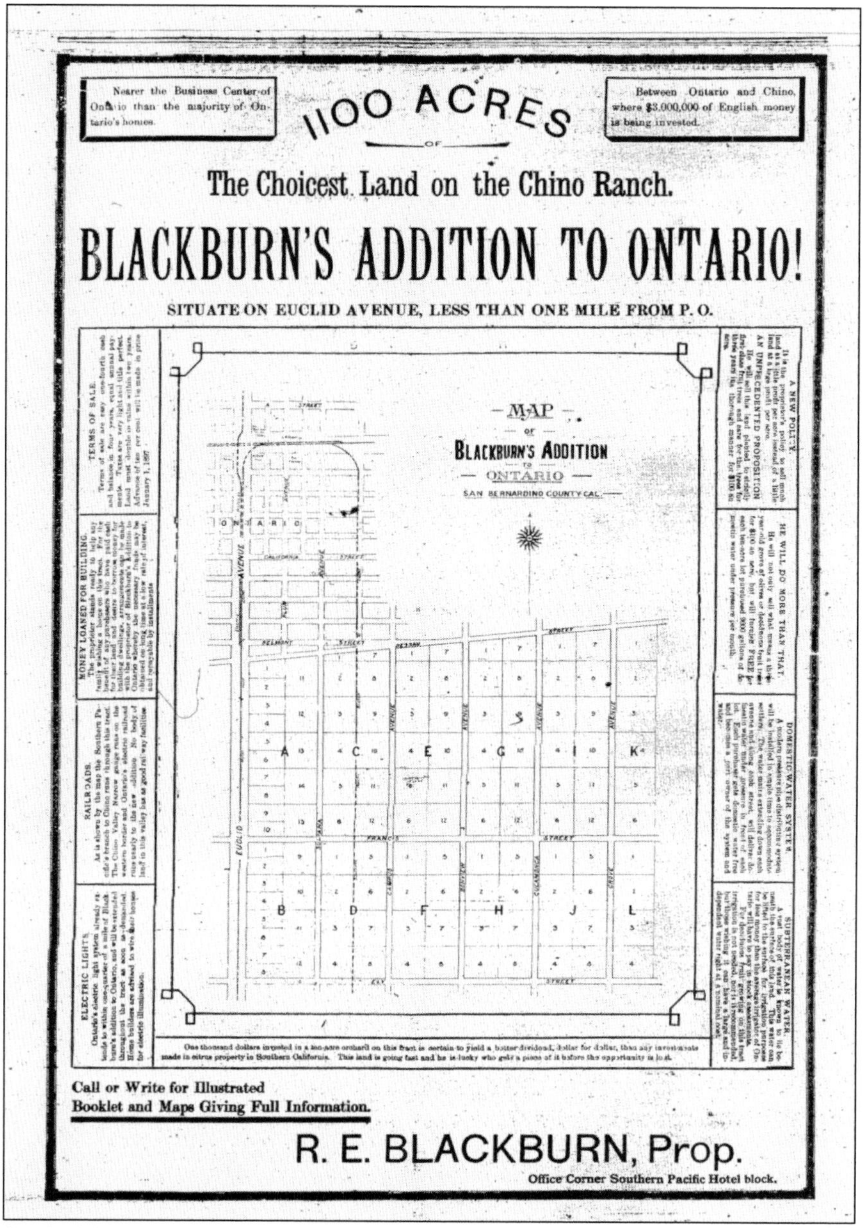

Robert Ely Blackburn, a native of Missouri, moved to Ontario in the late 1880s. In the early 1890s, Blackburn purchased 1,100 acres of the Chino Rancho lands southeast of Ontario. In June 1896, he began selling the land, offering lots complete with mature fruit trees and up to 9,000 gallons of water a month. The land, known as Blackburn's Addition to Ontario, begins on the east side of Euclid Avenue and travels east to just past Grove Avenue. The south boundary is located on the north side of Philadelphia Avenue, and the north boundary is just south of Philips Street. Philadelphia Avenue was originally called Ely Street, Blackburn's middle name, and Philips Street was originally called Dessau Street, his wife's maiden name. The street names changed in the 1950s when they were extended to the existing streets in Pomona. Blackburn also owned the *Ontario Observer* newspaper from 1888 to around 1898, which he used to advertise his real estate enterprise, as seen in this image.

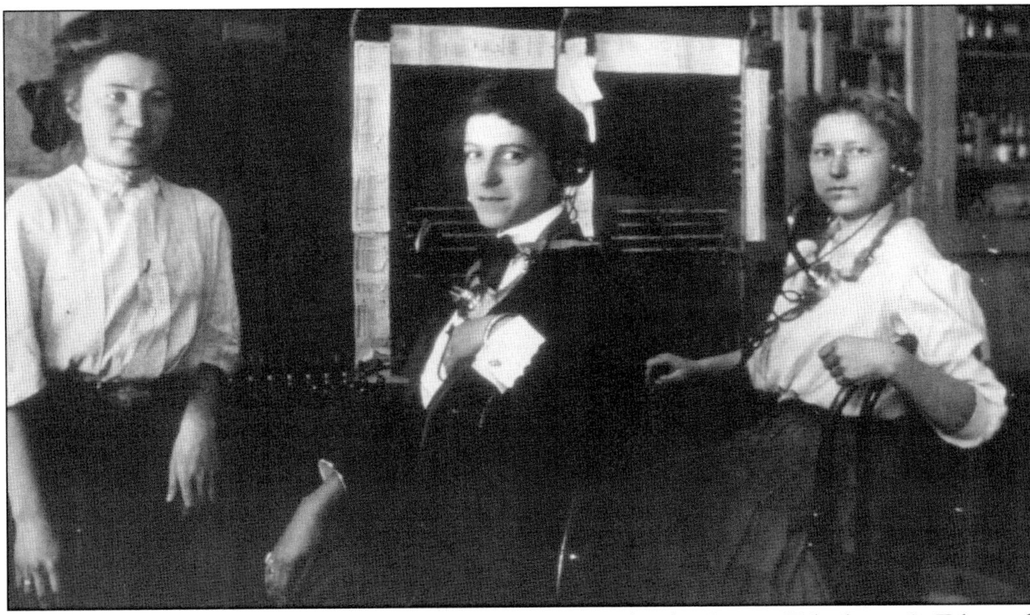

The first pay telephone was installed in Ontario in 1886 by the Sunset Telephone & Telegraph Company, probably in Henry Rose's drugstore. In 1891, Sunset installed Ontario's first exchange, with a magneto switchboard set up in Jacob Jesson's drugstore, at 105 North Euclid Avenue. As the population grew, so did the desire for residential and business telephone service. Sunset Telephone & Telegraph Company dominated the Ontario market until 1905, when the San Bernardino Valley Telephone Company was franchised by the city to compete with Sunset. In 1907, the Pacific Telephone & Telegraph Company took over Sunset's Ontario operations; it then merged with the San Bernardino Valley Telephone Company in 1912. In 1928, Pacific Telephone sold the Ontario operations to the Pomona Valley Telephone & Telegraph Union, which was acquired by Associated Telephone in 1929.

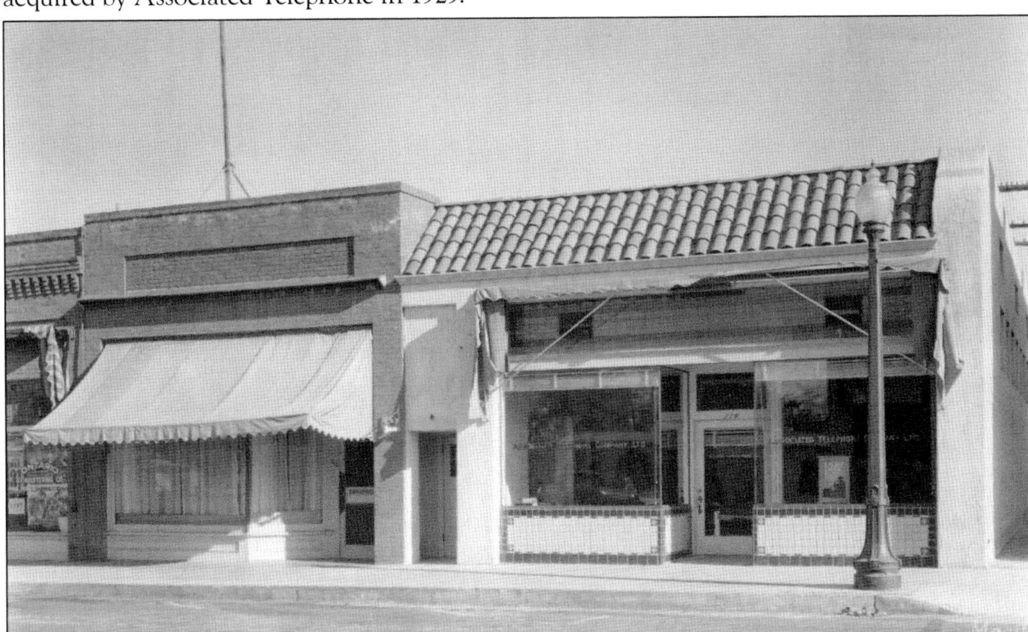

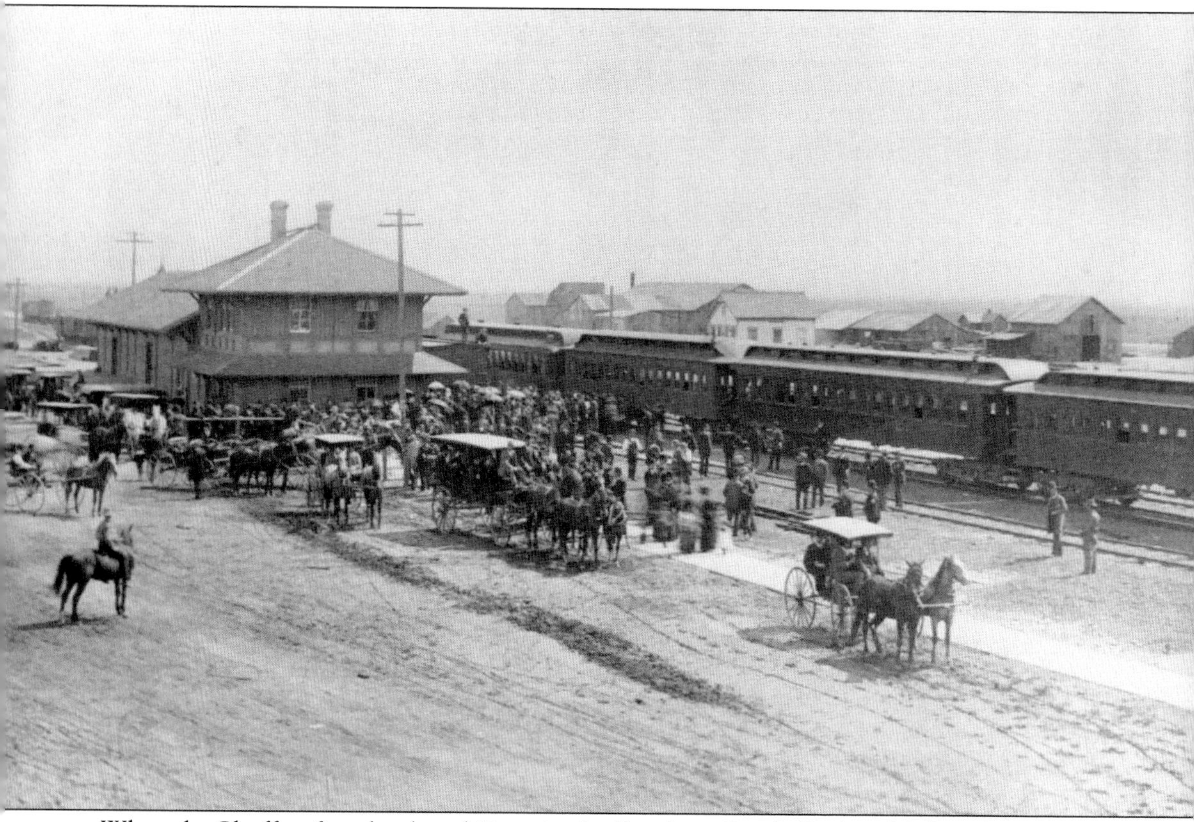

When the Chaffeys first developed Ontario, the Southern Pacific Railroad did not have a stop in town. Instead, the train would stop in Cucamonga and George Chaffey would pick up potential buyers at the Cucamonga depot and provide them with a tour of both Etiwanda and Ontario. The Chaffeys had the handsome Hotel Ontario built to accommodate potential buyers, and the land office was set up to double as a train depot in anticipation of a train stop. The Southern Pacific set a stop in Ontario in 1883. In 1887, a new, larger depot, seen here, was built on East Main Street. In 1917, the depot was completely remodeled. The building was demolished in 1971.

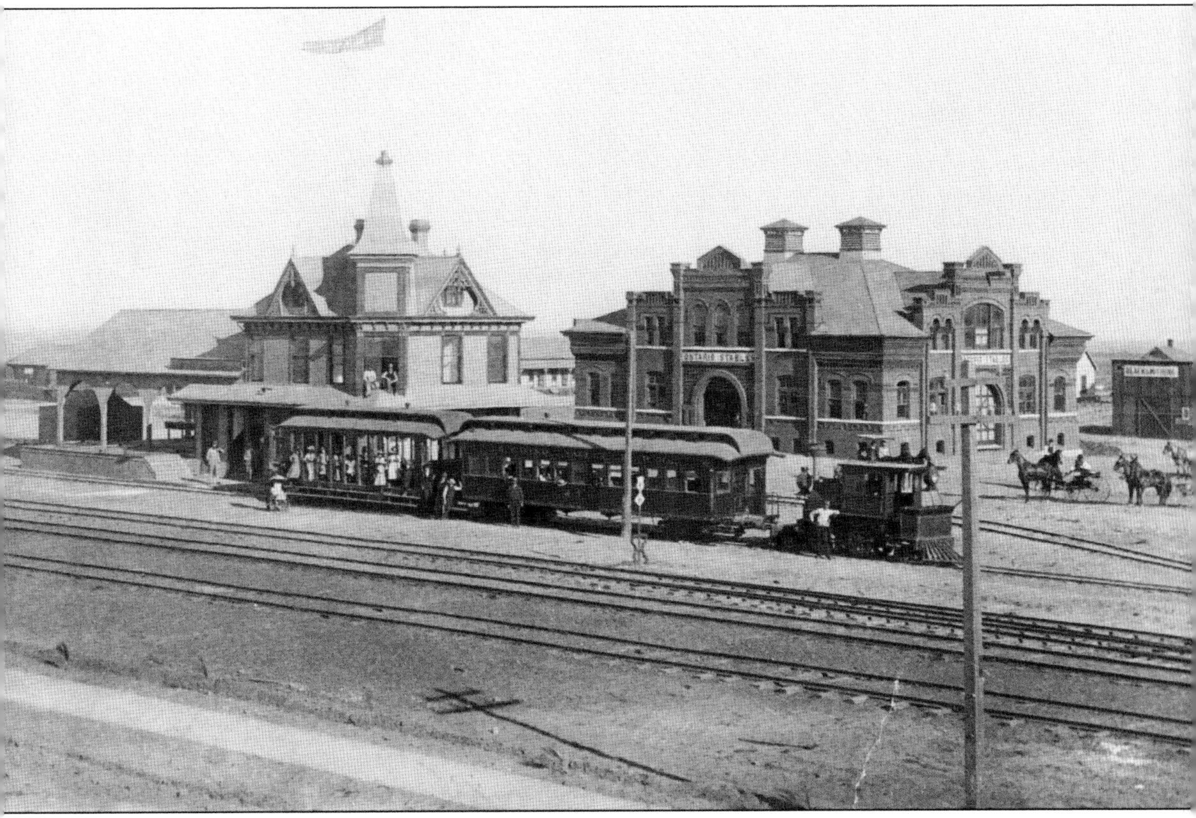

In the 1880s, Chino founder Richard Gird built a private railway between Chino and Ontario in order to transport sugar beets from area farmers to his sugar beet factory. The railway was a narrow-gauge line that extended from East Main Street in Ontario south along Euclid Avenue for two miles and then turned west to end in the center of the town of Chino. A Porter locomotive pulled one passenger coach and an open-air passenger car, which is shown in this photograph. A depot was built sometime around 1889 south of the tracks from the Southern Pacific depot. Gird sold the line in 1895, and new owners converted the tracks to standard gauge. However, competition with the Southern Pacific Railroad put the railway out of business in 1901, and the tracks were removed. The depot building (at left) was moved from this site in 1906 and converted into a residence. The building on the right is a livery stable that later became the Hotpoint factory.

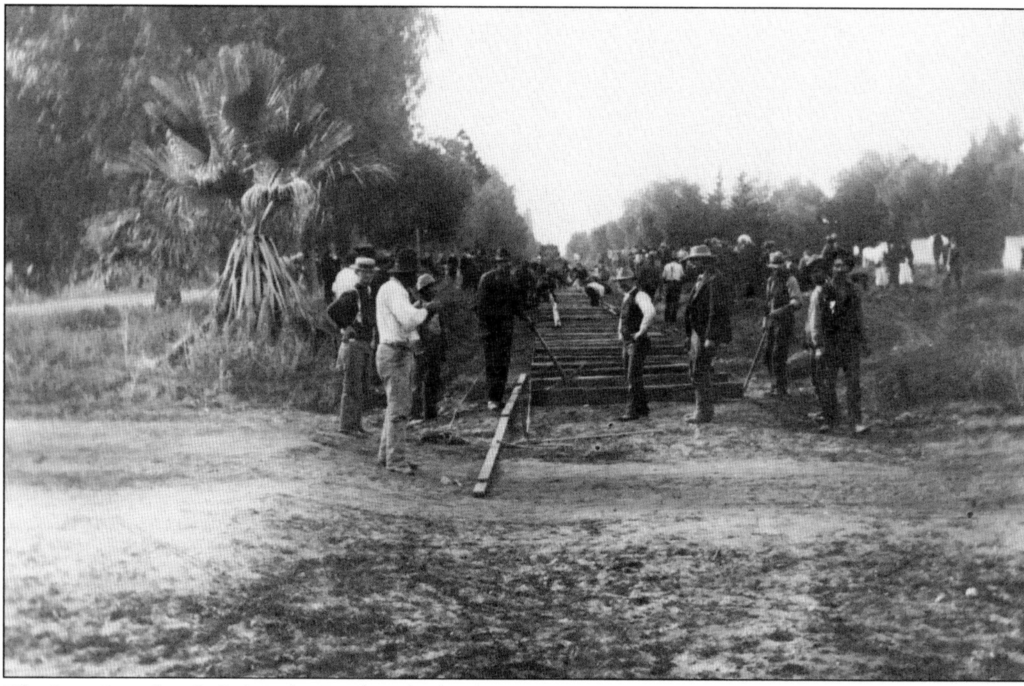

The Los Angeles & Salt Lake Railroad, also known simply as the Salt Lake Route, was organized in 1901 to build a railway from Los Angeles to Salt Lake City, providing Southern California with a transcontinental rail link. This became an important artery for citrus and freight shippers, and in January 1903, construction of the railroad reached Ontario (above). That same year, a depot was constructed on East State Street (below). The Salt Lake Route was acquired by the Union Pacific Railroad in 1921, and is still in operation today. The train depot was demolished in 1977.

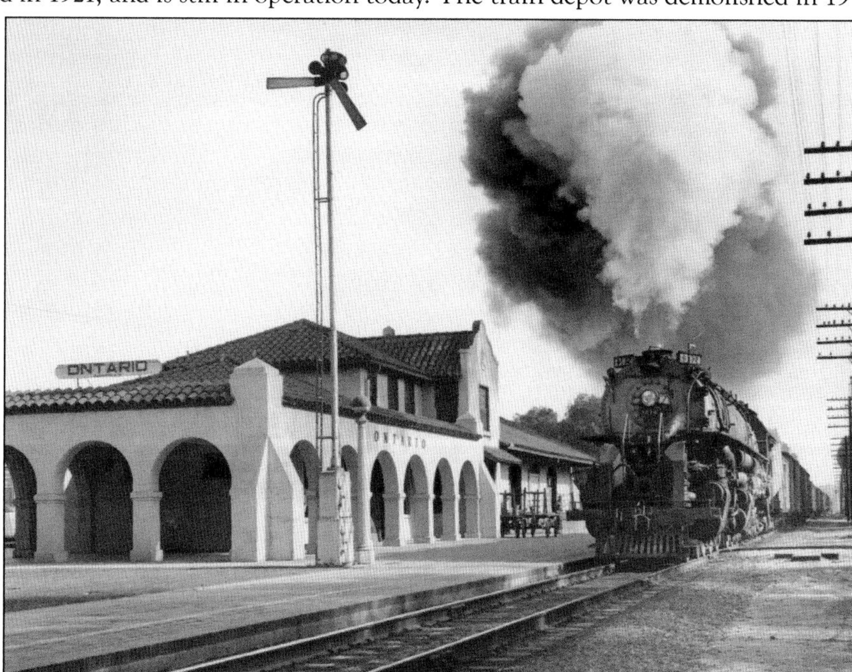

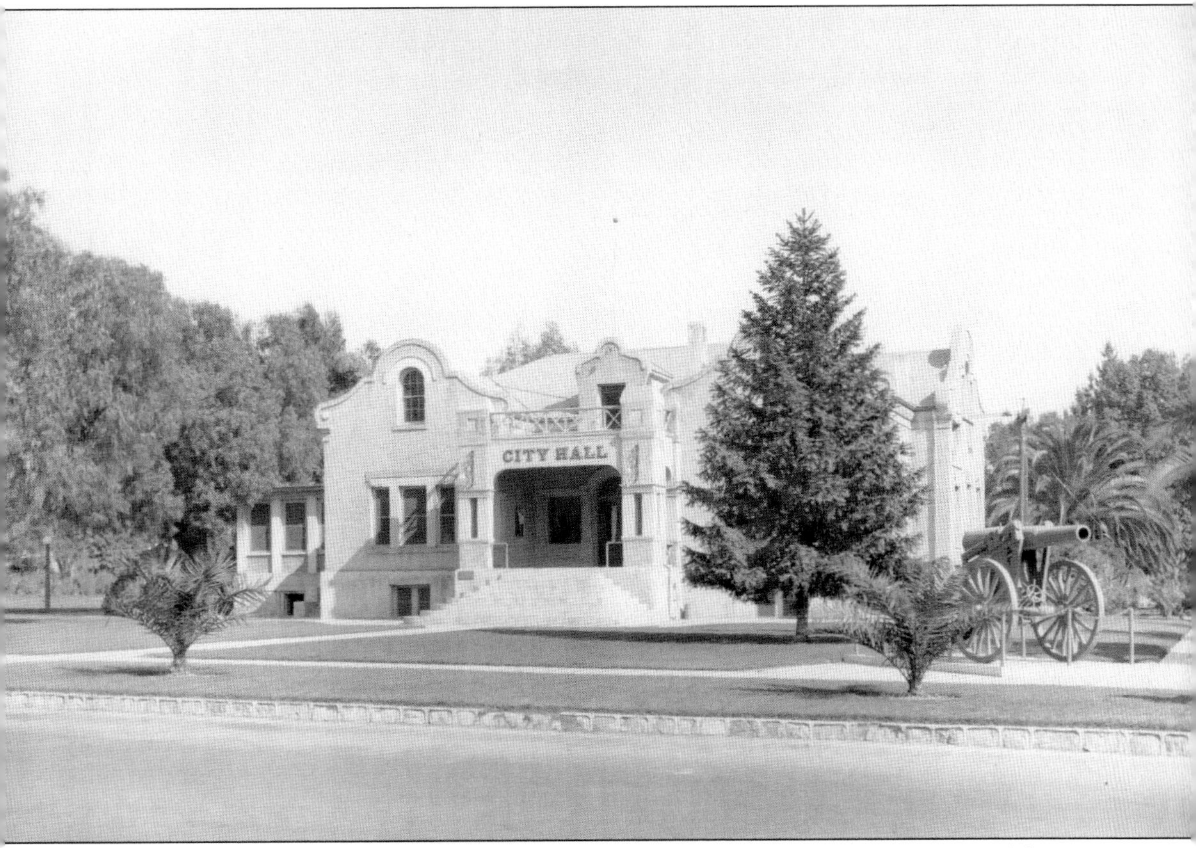

On December 10, 1891, Ontario incorporated as a city of the sixth class under the California constitution. It adopted a city council–city manager form of government. Initially, the city did not have a city hall building, so meetings were held at various sites until it was able to purchase the defunct Ontario Country Club building (pictured) in 1910 for $10,000. This mission-style building was constructed in 1903 as an unsuccessful community country club and was located on the southeast corner of Euclid Avenue and Emporia Street. This building served as the city hall until it was demolished in 1936 to make way for a new city hall, which is now the home of the Ontario Museum of History and Art.

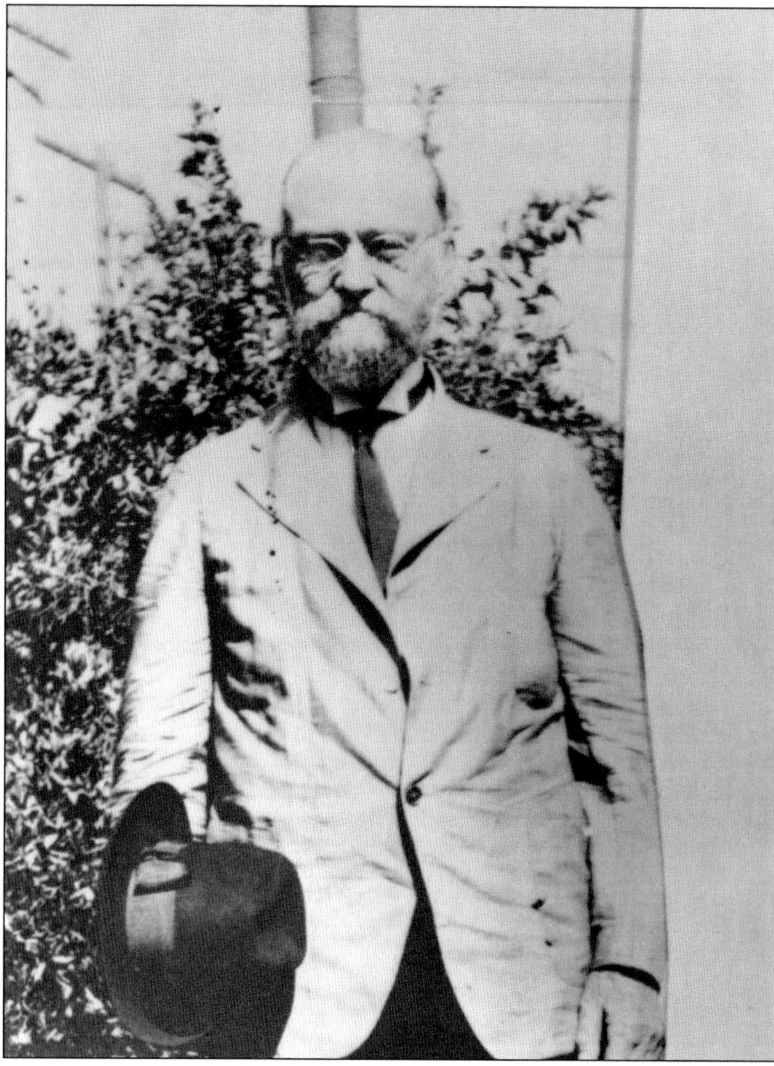

Ontario's mayor was originally called the president of the board, and was chosen by the council, or the board of trustees, as it was then called, from among their number. Subsequently, the law was changed to allow the people to elect the mayor directly. David T. Jones, the owner of a successful general store, was elected the first president of the board, making him Ontario's first mayor.

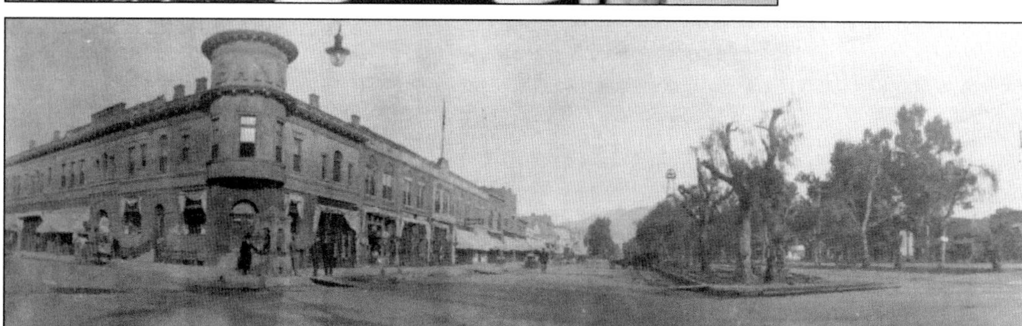

Ontario's fire department dates to 1893 as a volunteer brigade. It was reorganized by the city in August 1905 when a new fire chief was appointed. In the early days, fire calls were received through the telephone exchange at the drugstore, and the store clerk would then ring the fire bell that hung on a steel tower on the Euclid Avenue median between A and B Streets, visible here in the distance.

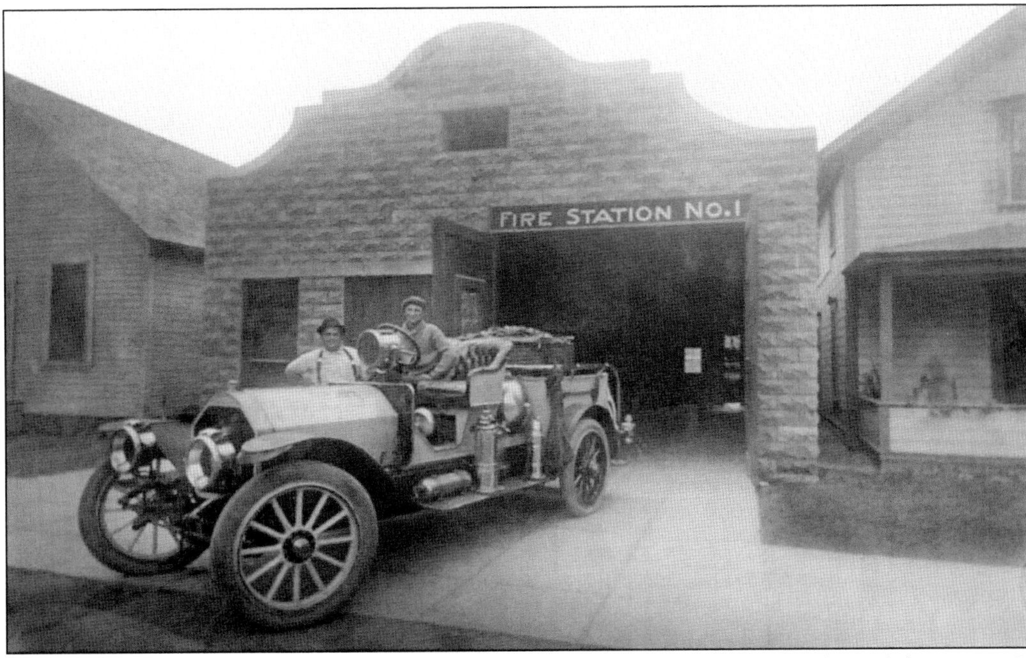

A fire hall building was constructed of concrete block in 1907 at 316 North Euclid Avenue. In 1911, a new, six-cylinder Mitchell fire truck was purchased. Two full-time employees were hired to operate the truck during its calls, one to work during the day and the other at night, while the firefighters remained volunteers. In 1918, the volunteer firefighters were compensated $2 for each call.

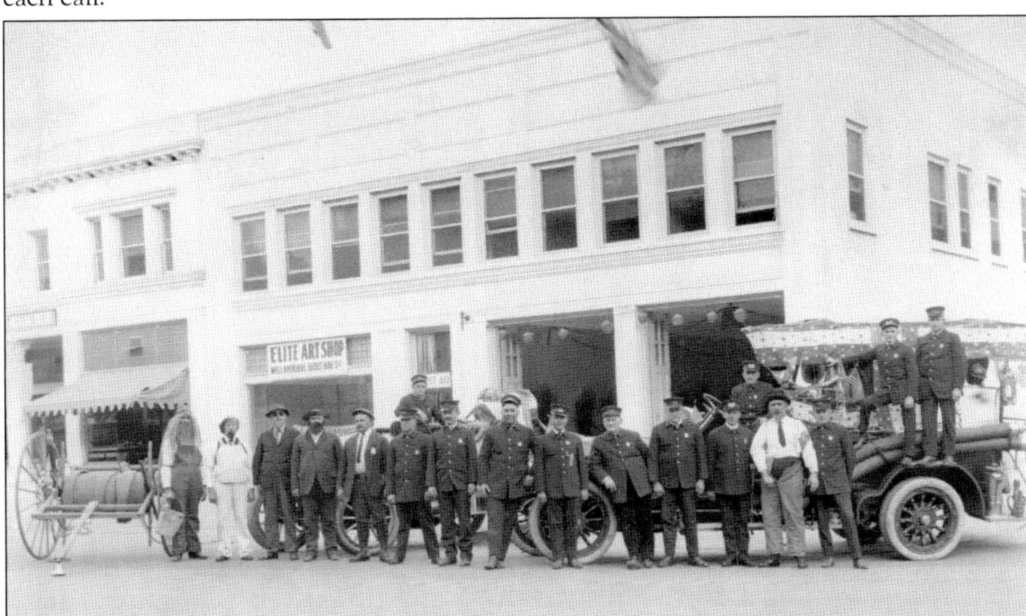

In 1916, the fire department adopted its constitution and bylaws. In 1922, a new fire station was built on the northeast corner of Euclid Avenue and Transit Street. While new electrical bells were used, it was reported that the original fire bell was moved to the top of this new building to be used in case of emergencies, and was later sold for scrap metal.

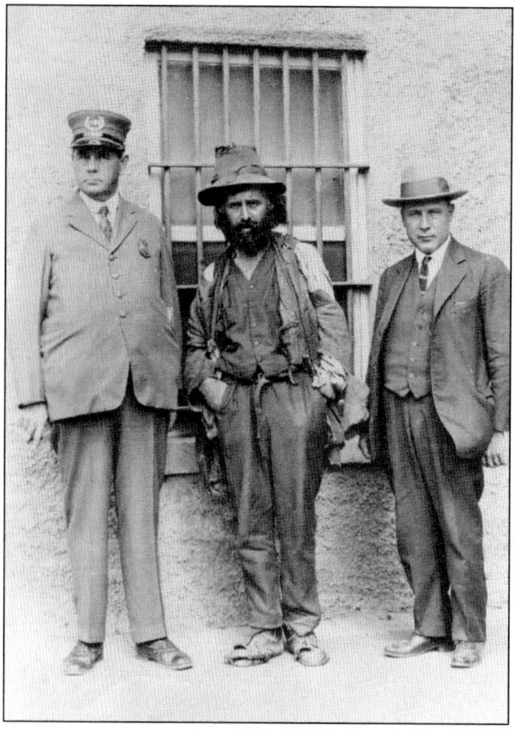

Before Ontario had its own police department, law and order was provided by a town marshal. In 1907, the city elected Walter O. Hardy, pictured on the left, as its township constable. Hardy's title was later changed to chief of police, and he served in this position until he retired in 1927. He was replaced by Arthur Axley, pictured on the right with a local vagrant.

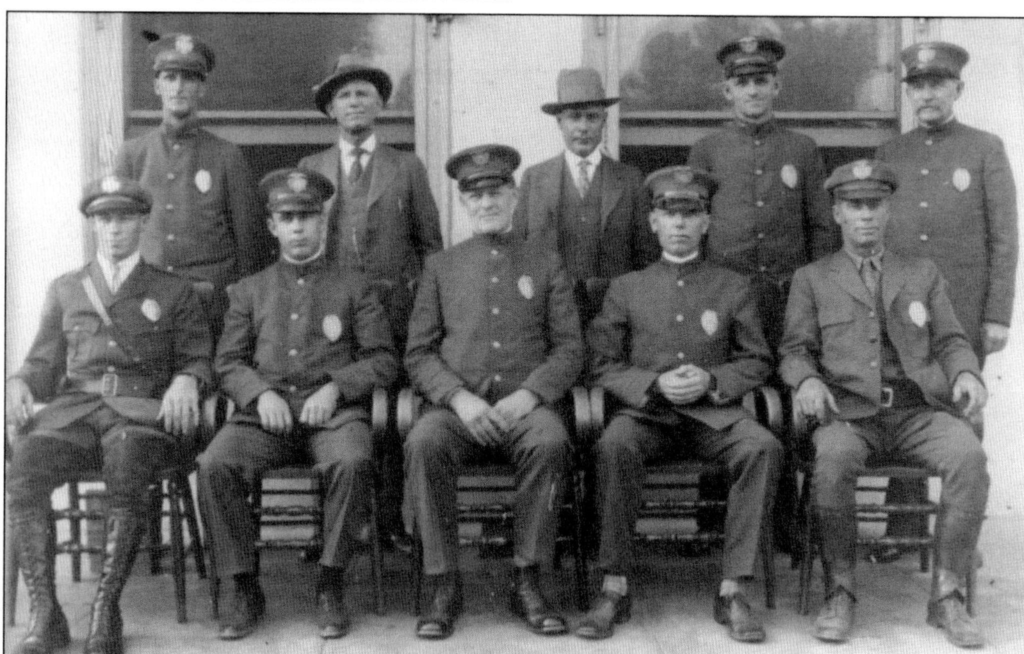

In the early days, the police department was located at city hall, but it shared quarters with the fire department between 1922 and 1937. The jail was located just behind, on Transit Street. Pictured in this 1930 image are, from left to right, (first row) William H. Hammond, Robert Sydenstryker, E.P. Onderdonk, George Brumfield, and Frank Clark; (second row) Harry Smith, Arian G. Figgins, chief of police Arthur Axley, George Brown, and Johnny Clark.

The Ontario City Library was founded on November 15, 1885, by community members. The next month, a social benefit was held that resulted in the collection of 200 books, $40, and a large bookcase. The group formed a library association, and William Chaffey served as its first president. The Chaffey brothers provided space for a reading room, and Alfred Piddington, pictured here, served as the first librarian.

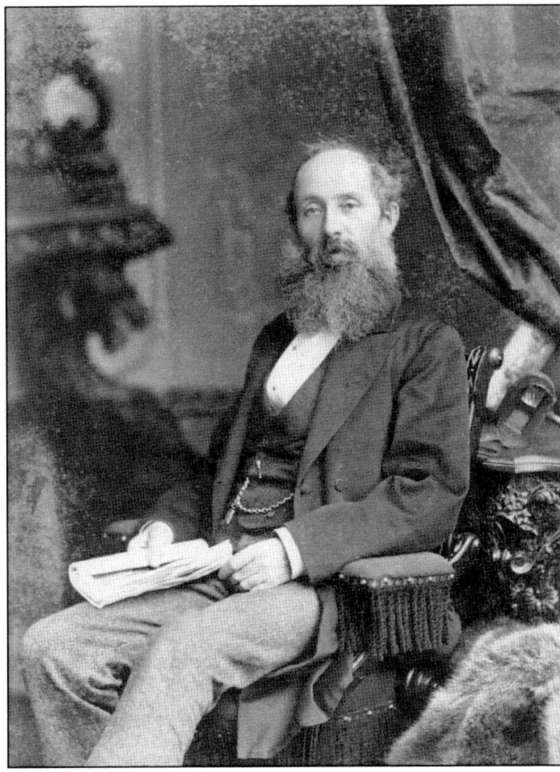

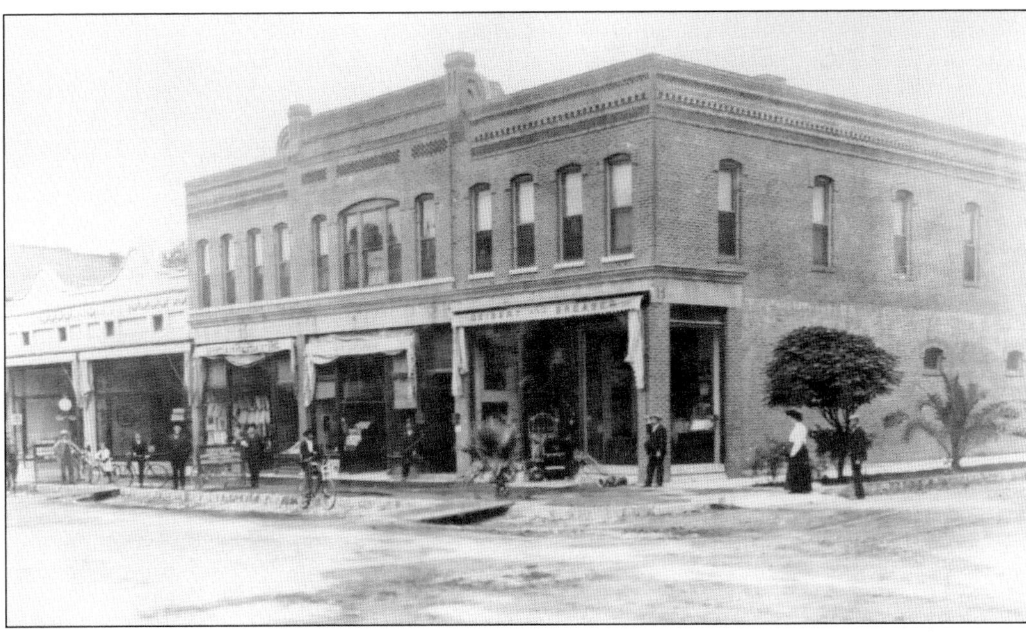

Because the Chaffeys left Ontario for Australia in early 1886, the library lost its reading room. For the next several years, the library moved around town, at one point even sharing space with a funeral parlor in the Sweet Block, seen here, which today is Gemmel's Pharmacy. In 1894, the library was put under the control of the city, but it would be 13 years before the library would have its own building.

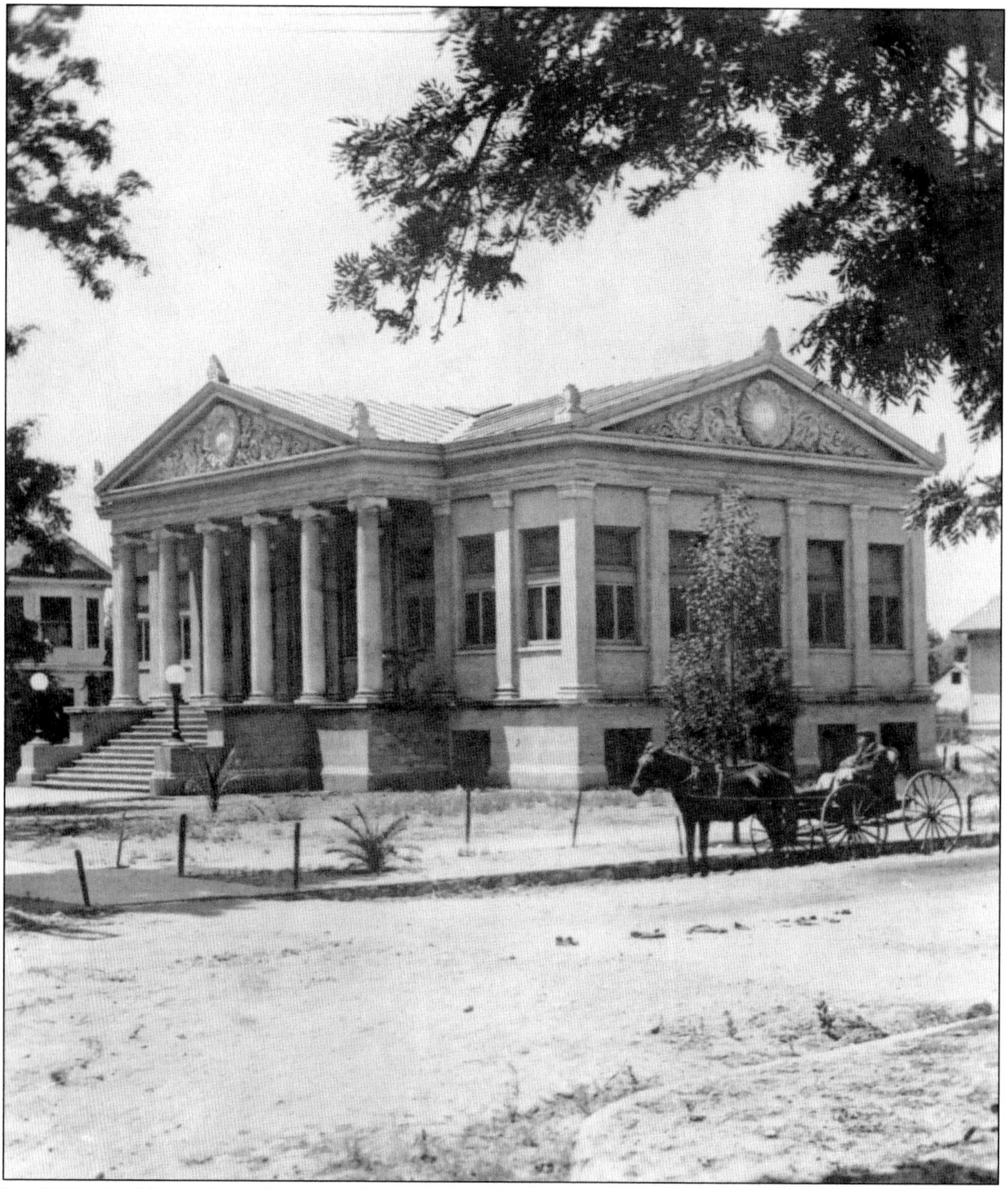

In 1902, the library board wrote a letter to Andrew Carnegie asking for funds to erect a library building, and the residents of Ontario raised $700 to buy land on the southwest corner of Euclid Avenue and D Street in anticipation of a grant from Carnegie. However, years passed with no word. Finally, in 1906, the board received a letter from Carnegie agreeing to provide $10,000, with the stipulation that the city must agree to spend 10 percent of the grant each year for maintenance. The building was designed by Franklin Pierce Burnham, and S.L. Bloom of Corona was contracted to construct the building at a cost of $9,187. The city's board of trustees wanted to use the library basement as a temporary city hall, so the cost of the building escalated. The library board asked Carnegie to donate additional funds, and he agreed to provide another $2,000. The building, while still not completely finished, was dedicated on April 12, 1907. Unfortunately, it was later deemed unsafe in the event of an earthquake and was demolished in 1959.

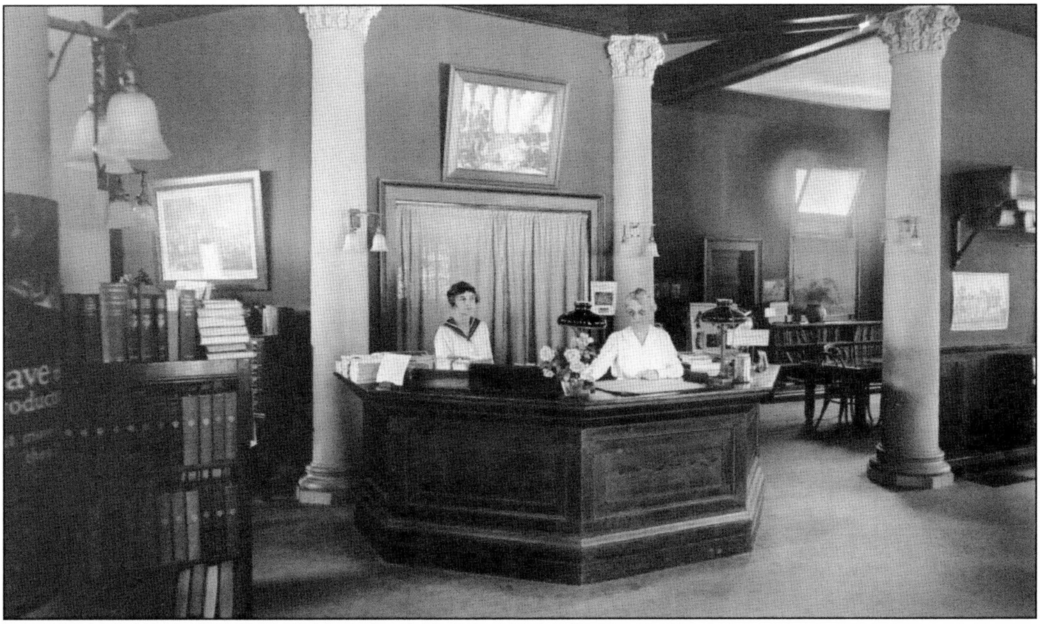

Kezzie Monroe (right) served as librarian from 1899 until 1928. The new library was considered innovative for its time, with a semicircular checkout desk and a fumigation closet for sanitizing the library's books each day. Circulation at the new library increased 30 percent in its first year, and the library's hours were expanded to include Sundays.

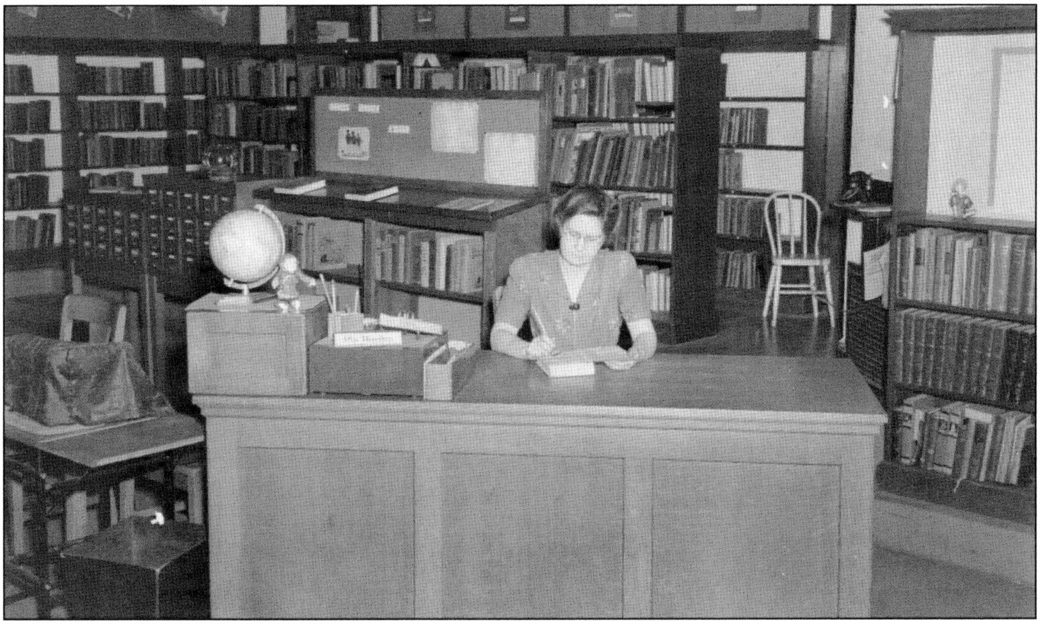

By 1915, the library was already nearing capacity, but a request for additional funds from Andrew Carnegie to expand the library was denied, and a few years later, the city also denied funds for expansion. The library board finally proposed converting the basement into a children's area, which was approved. The children's collection was also expanded, and the new department opened on April 24, 1924. Margaret Hamilton, longtime children's librarian, is pictured here in the children's area.

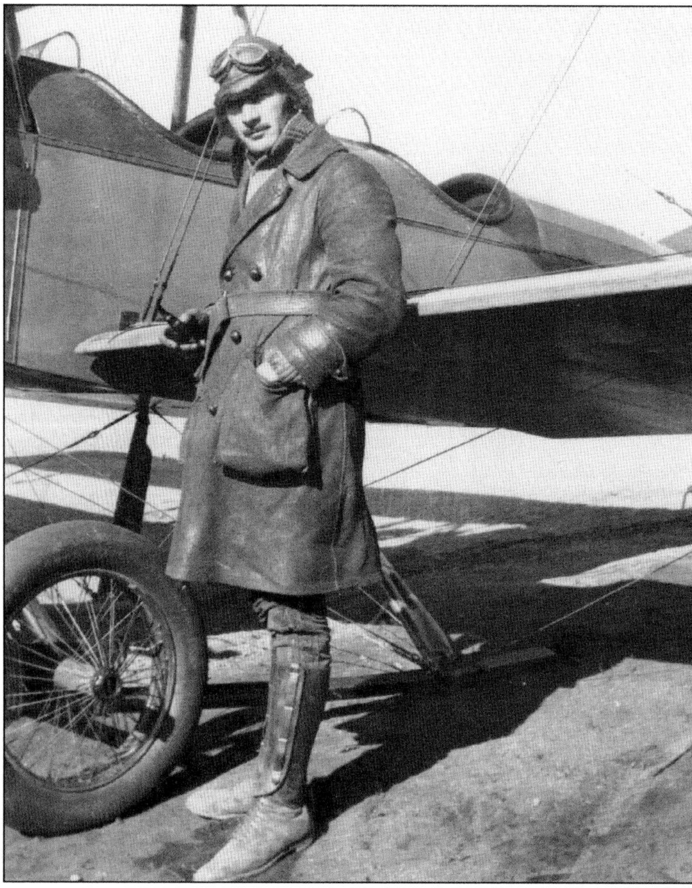

The founding of an airport in Ontario started when friends and aviators Waldo Waterman (left) and Archie Mitchell (below) established the Ontario Aircraft Corporation in 1923. They leased a parcel of land near San Antonio Avenue and the Union Pacific railroad tracks called Latimer Field and flew passengers in their Curtiss JN-4 "Jenny" aircraft. In 1929, the City of Ontario purchased a 30-acre tract of land about three miles east of Latimer Field to use as an airport, and Latimer Field was abandoned. Waterman, the grandson of California governor Robert Waterman, went on to design several unique flying machines, and Mitchell, an Ontario native, became a local attorney and judge.

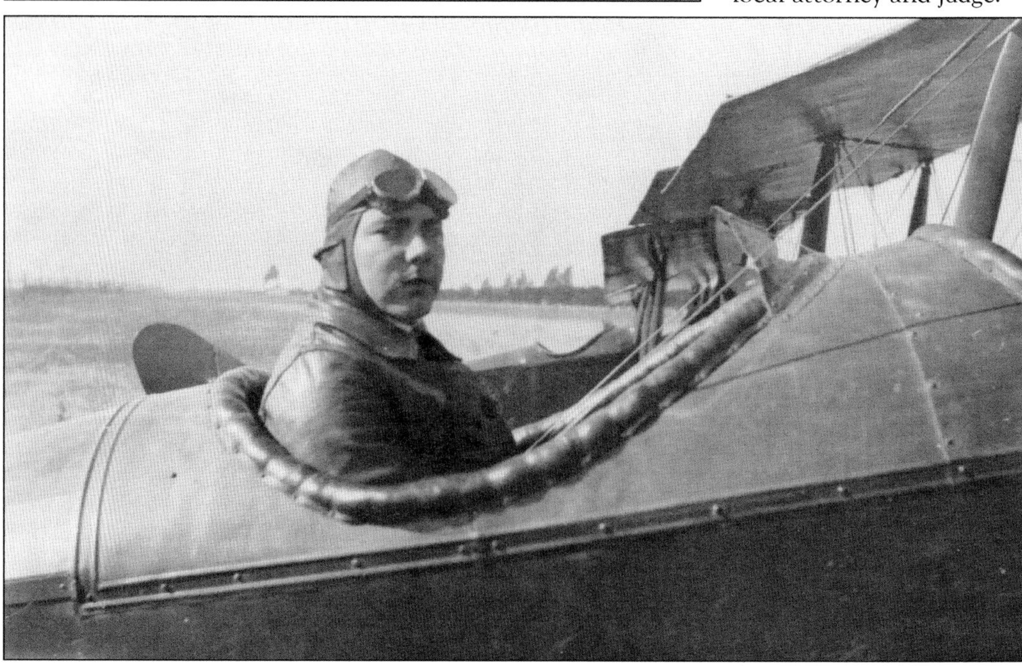

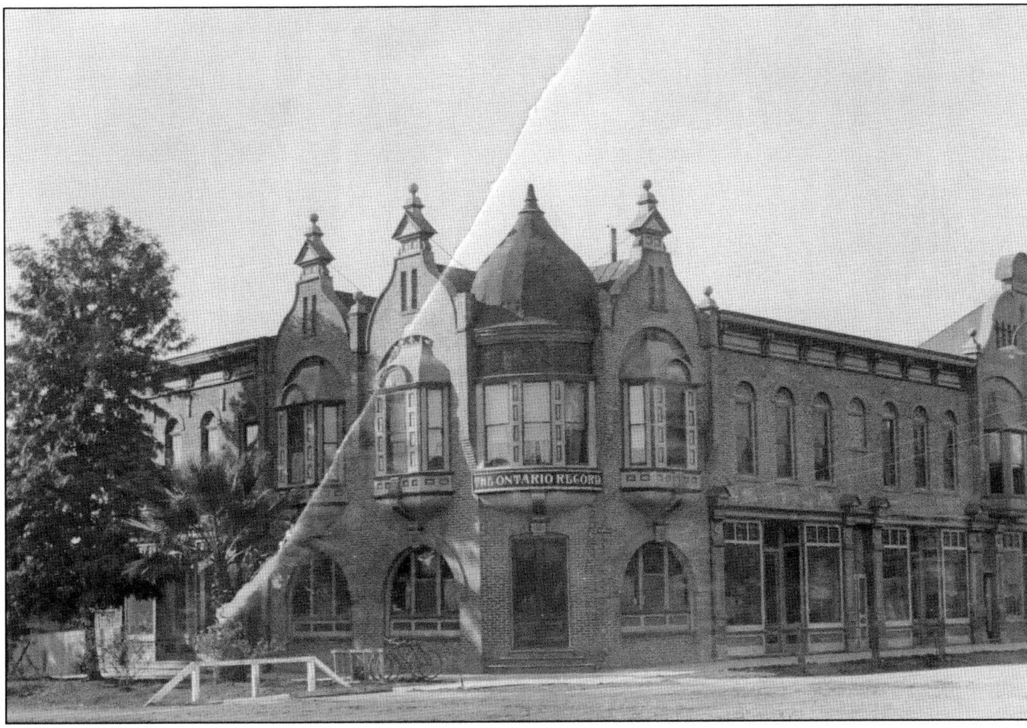

Ernest P. Clarke (right) came to Ontario in 1885 from Alna, Maine, and founded the *Ontario Record* newspaper. The first newspaper published in Ontario, it was originally operated out of the Bank Block (above). The *Record* was sometimes in competition with the *Ontario Observer*, established by S.J. Holsinger in 1888 at the request of Charles Frankish and later sold to Robert Blackburn, the developer of Blackburn's Addition. The *Ontario Record* was very critical of Charles Frankish, and one might have thought that Frankish expected the competition would put the *Record* out of business. This did not happen, however, and the *Observer* ceased publication in 1897. Clarke ran the *Ontario Record* until the mid-1890s and then went on to be the editor of the *Riverside Press*.

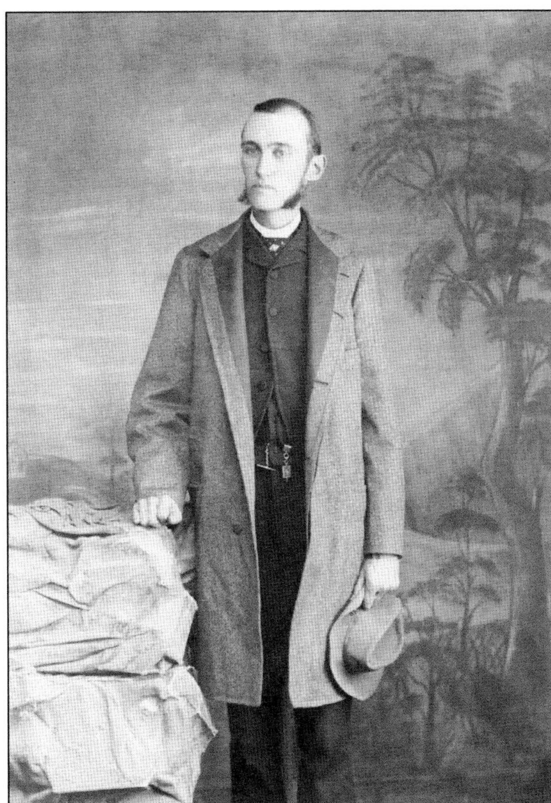

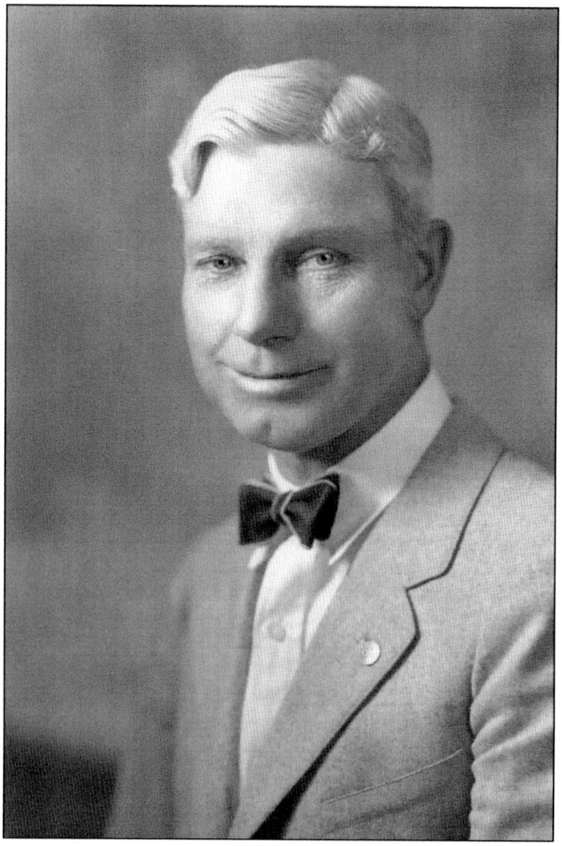

Crombie Allen came to Ontario in 1912 and bought the *Ontario Daily Republican*, established in 1910 by F.E. Unholz, and renamed it the *Ontario Daily Report*. The first issue was published on January 1, 1912, and Allen remained publisher until September 1930, when it was sold to Frank Appleby. Allen, pictured here, was very active in the community and served as the first president of the Ontario Rotary Club.

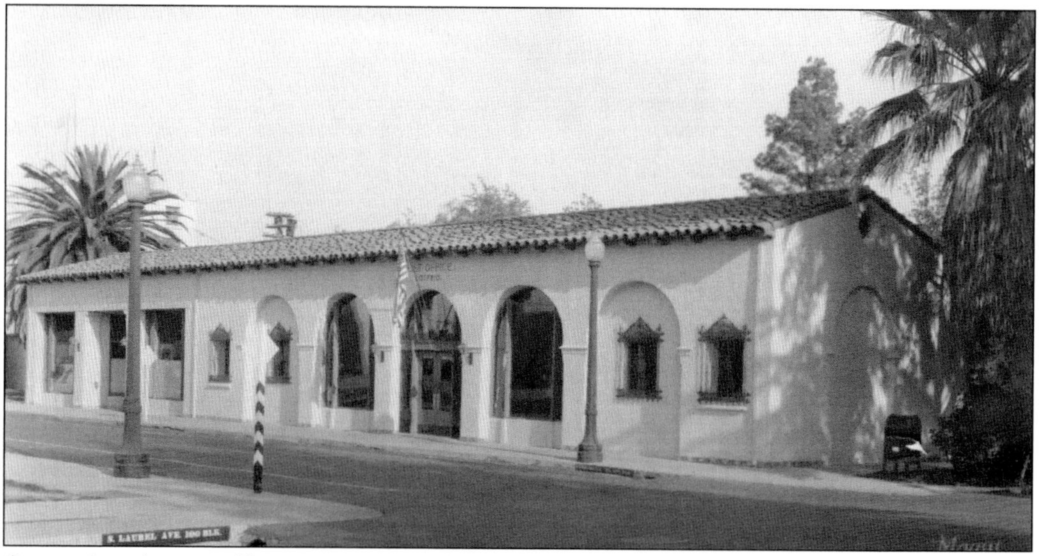

Ontario's early post office was run out of various buildings around town until a dedicated post office building was erected in 1926. This beautiful building, located on West Transit Street, was designed by renowned African American architect Paul Revere Williams and served as the city's post office until 1941, when a larger building was constructed on Holt Boulevard. The building, now converted into artists' lofts, still stands today and is one of the city's historic landmarks.

Three

The Development of the Citrus Industry

The first orange trees in California were planted in 1769 at the Mission San Diego de Alcalá, and at the turn of the 19th century, the first orange grove was planted at Mission San Gabriel Archángel. Luther and Eliza Tibbets of Riverside are credited with planting the first Washington navel orange trees in Southern California in 1873. Called the Washington navel because it was brought to California from Washington, DC, it is said that all such trees in California can be traced back to two parent trees, one of which still grows today. These particular trees became quite popular, spurring the industry throughout Southern California.

With the colony growing, agriculture drove its economic engine. The first Washington navel orange tree was planted in Ontario in 1883 by Isaac Whitaker near Fifth Street and San Antonio Avenue. The first grove in Ontario was planted in the same area by L.S. Dyar, and it was so successful that others tried their hands at citrus ranching. By the end of the 19th century, Ontario was said to have the second-largest acreage dedicated to citrus ranching in the state.

Starting in the 1880s, views of flourishing citrus orchards surrounded by palm trees and snow-capped mountains were depicted on postcards, in brochures, and in magazines, summoning people to Southern California to claim their own bit of health and wealth. It often worked, and many of those who came to Ontario were wealthy Midwesterners and Canadians, flocking to the area to start their own ranches and become gentlemen farmers. By the 1920s, there were citrus orchards as far as the eye could see.

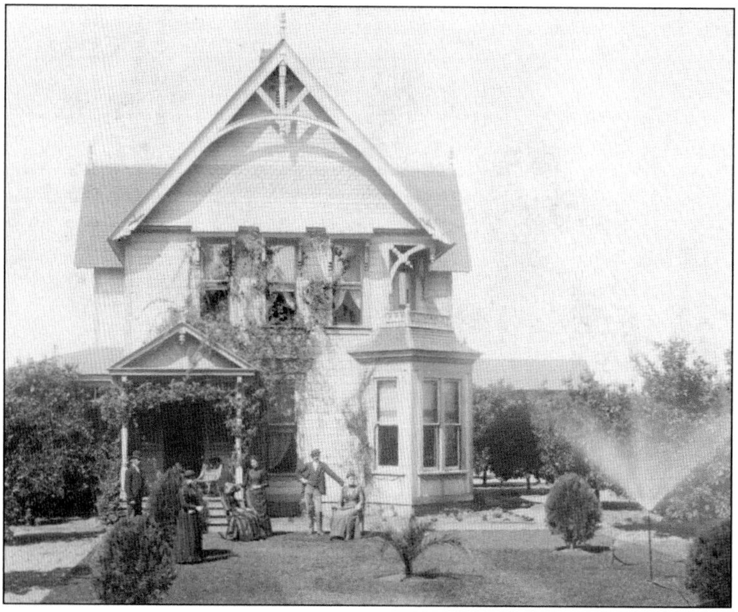

The Oakley family were prominent pioneers from Ontario, Canada. Abraham Oakley purchased land and began ranching citrus in Ontario in 1884, and his son Herbert Clubine Oakley was involved in the real estate business with his young uncle Andrew Franklin Clubine. This image shows gentleman farmer Herbert, his brother J.W., and the Oakley family in front of their 1887 Stick-style home, which still stands today on Euclid Avenue.

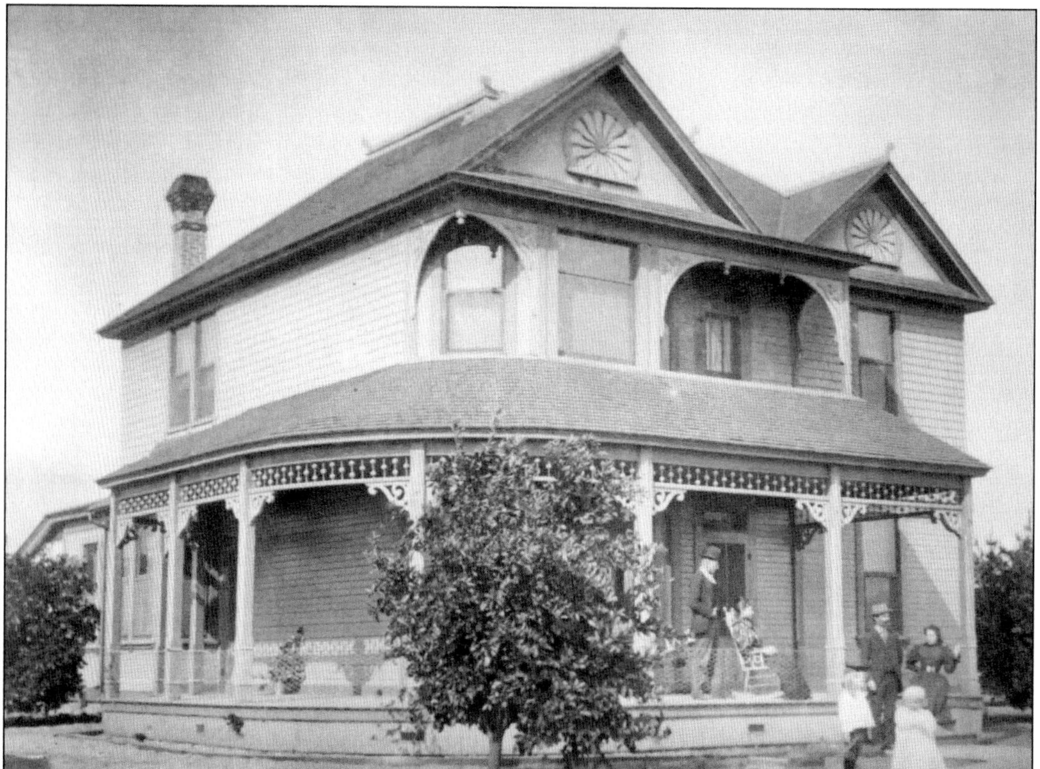

In the late 1880s, William Stewart, along with his brothers Milton and Lymon, planted 200 acres of citrus groves in North Ontario. By the end of the 19th century, they were ranching 800 acres of citrus in the area. In 1901, the brothers formed the Stewart Citrus Association. William and his wife, Mary, built this Queen Anne–style home surrounded by groves on West Sixth Street in 1895, and the Stewart family remained prominent within the citrus industry until the late 1980s.

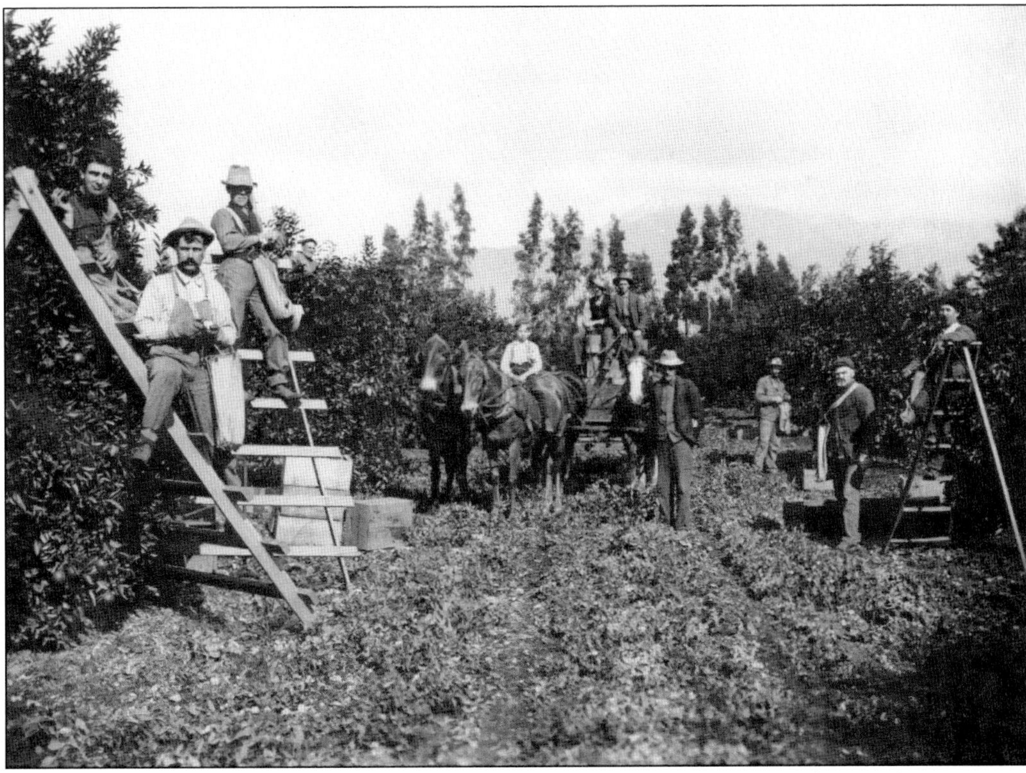

By the end of the 19th century, books were being published instructing ranchers on best practices for picking and packing citrus fruit in the field. For instance, pickers were trained to clip the fruit close to its "button" rather than pulling the fruit from the branches, so the skin remained intact and prevented citrus oils from being released, which would spoil the fruit. Gloves were worn to protect the fruit, which was packed gently into field crates to avoid bruising. Most of the techniques for picking and packing the fruit were learned from Chinese workers who, by that time, had been ranching citrus for hundreds of years.

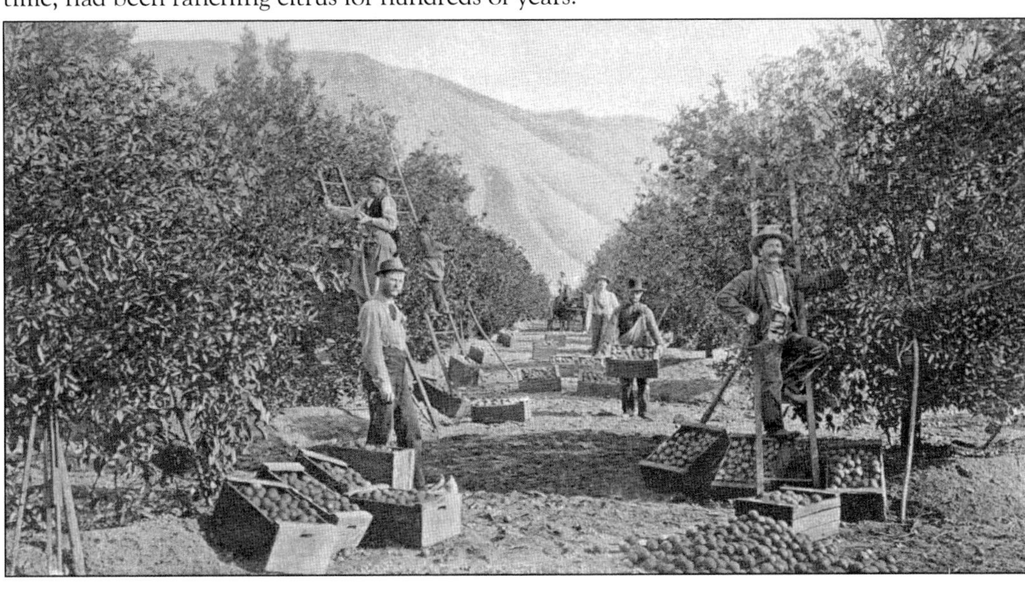

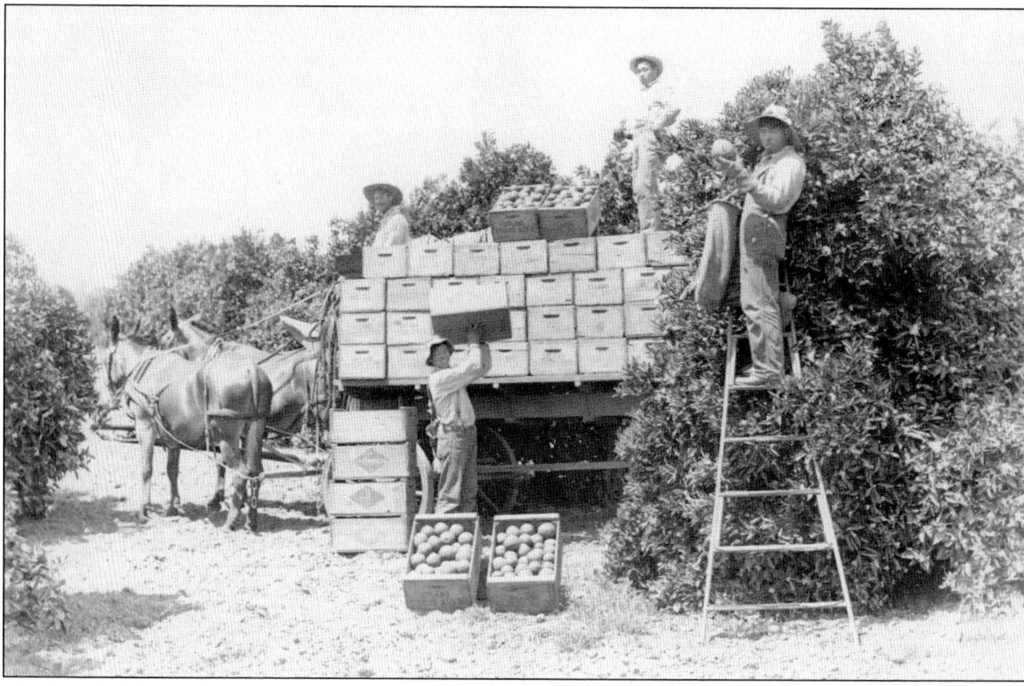

During California's mission era, most field labor was done by local Native Americans. The development of the transcontinental railroad and the California gold rush brought Chinese immigrants to California. By the 1870s, Chinese workers made up the majority of the area's field labor, and small Chinatowns formed in citrus growing areas. However, by the early 1900s, the Chinese were pushed out of the labor force as a result of Chinese exclusionary laws. Japanese, Filipino, and Korean immigrants replaced Chinese workers and lived in labor camps set up throughout the region. Later, Japanese workers began purchasing and farming their own land, which led to the Alien Land Act of 1913, barring further immigration by the Japanese. The Immigration Act of 1917 barred immigration of people from Asia and the Pacific Islands. By 1920, most field labor was done by local Mexican Americans and Mexican nationals who were transported to the area as guest workers during the picking season.

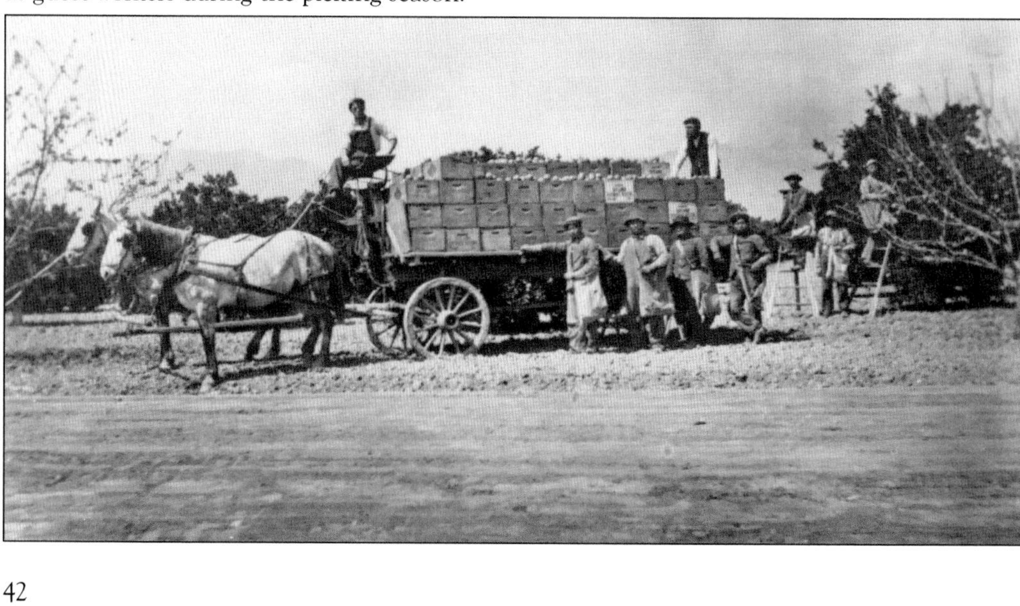

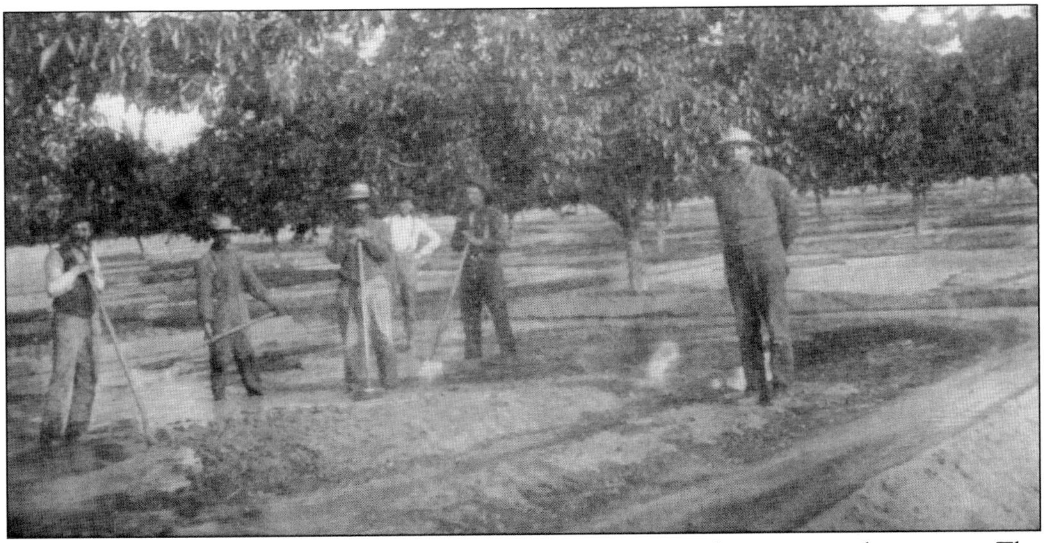

Allotments of water were released to growers about once a month to irrigate their groves. The water was released through a gate and would arrive at a grove through cement pipes to its highest point. Growers dug trenches to move the water by gravity throughout the grove to irrigate individual trees.

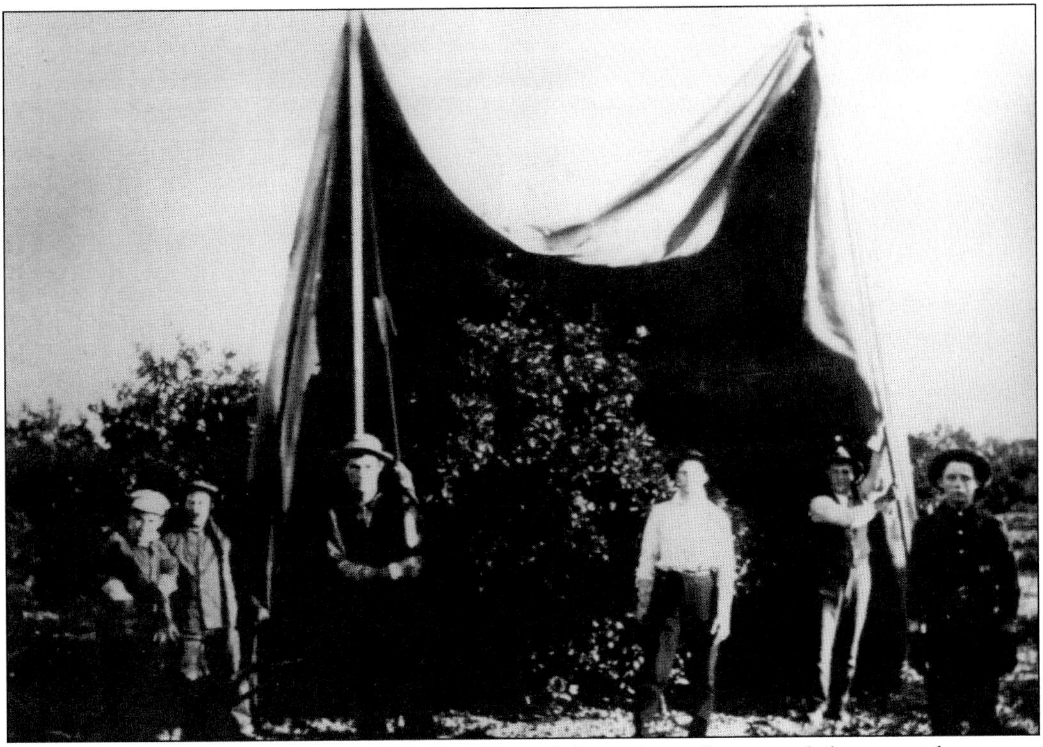

In 1886, D.W. Coquillett of the US Department of Agriculture discovered that cyanide gas was the most effective product against scale insects. Tents made of cotton duck were pulled over individual trees with tall poles. Liquid cyanide gas was then pumped into the tent, and the tree would be treated for about one hour. If any gas escaped the tent during treatment, workers could die from cyanide poisoning.

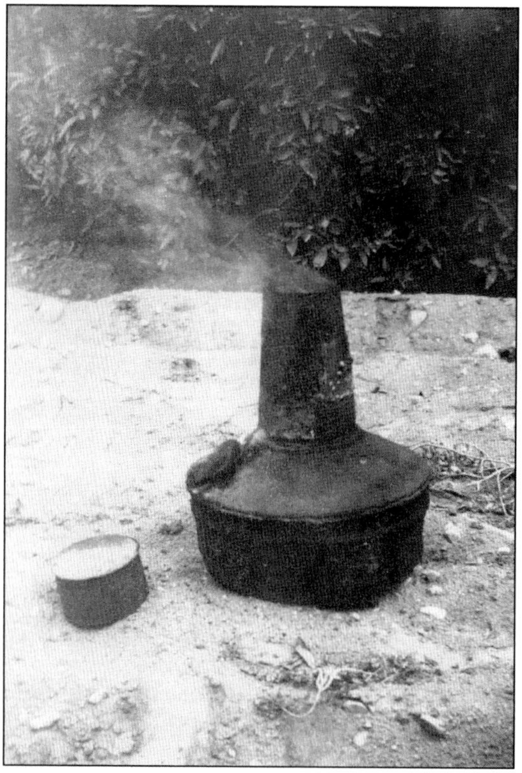

Smudge pots have been used to warm orchards during seasonal freezes for many years. Pots are placed within an orchard at a rate of about one pot per every two trees, and also along the perimeter of the orchard. The heat warms the lower-lying areas where the air is colder. While the practice is relatively effective, the smoke created by their use not only causes visibility problems, but, during the heyday of their use, it also incited uproar among non-growers due to the heavy layer of smoke and sooty residue it produced. In September 1937, Ontario City Council approved an ordinance banning oil-burning heaters that produced smoky matter in excess of one gram per minute, with compliance to a half-gram per minute required by October 1940. The ordinances were a result of residential and industrial development and the influx of non-growers to the region.

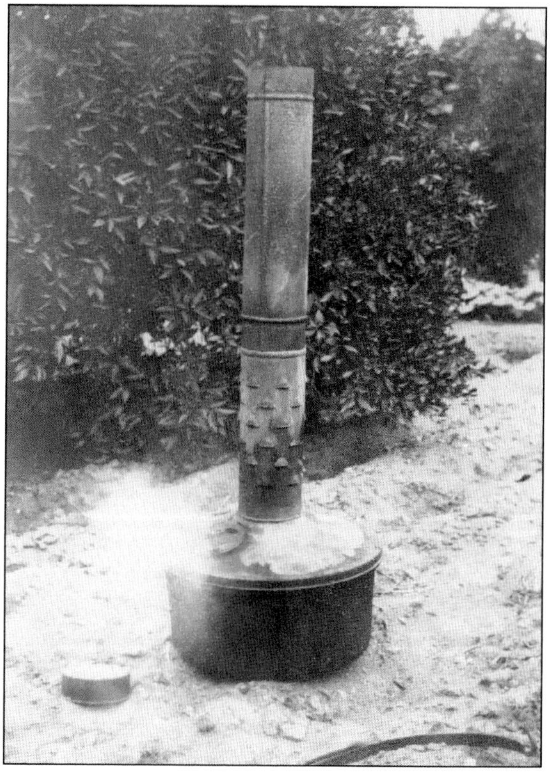

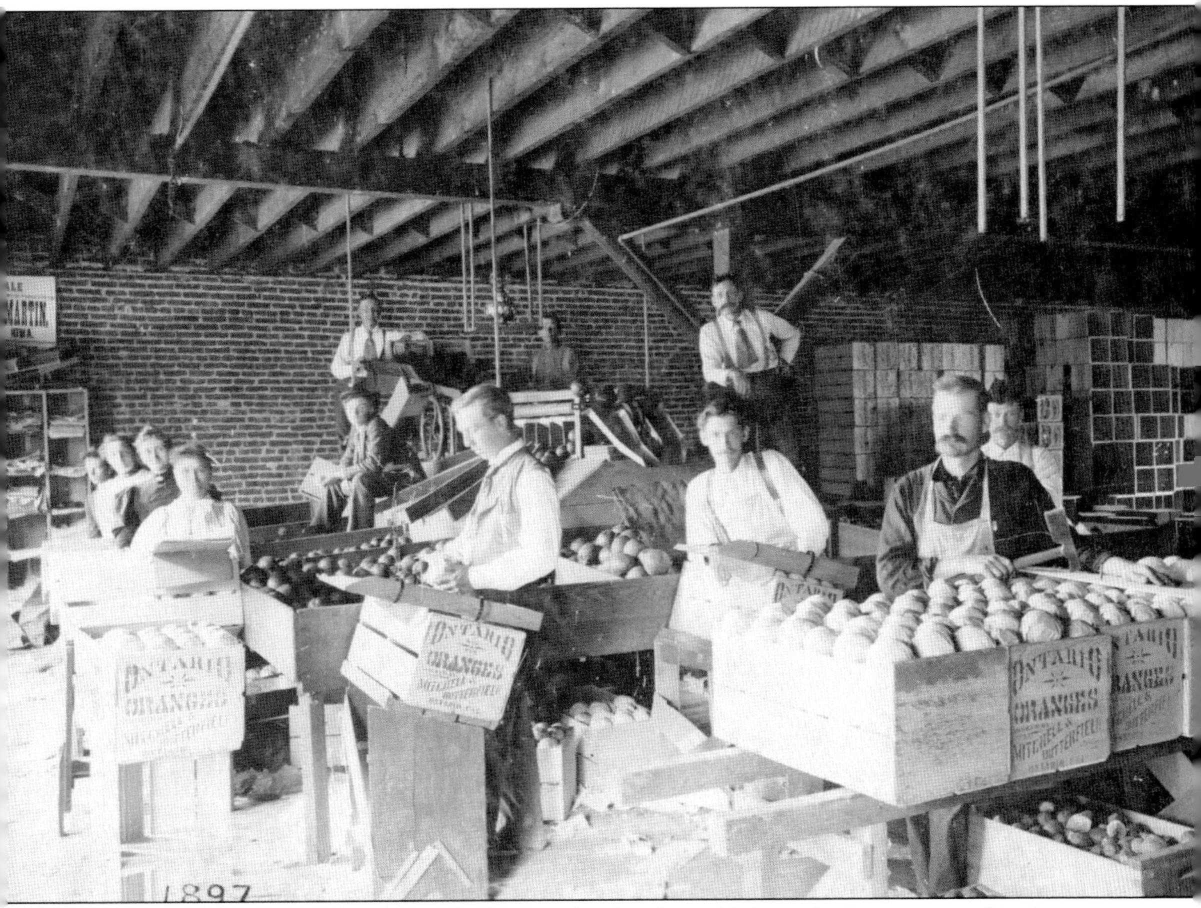

Grocers N.L. Mitchell and G.T. Butterfield are credited with establishing the first citrus packinghouse in Ontario in 1891. Mitchell, a native of Kansas, arrived in Ontario in May 1890. In the spring of 1891 he opened a grocery store, and soon after started the packinghouse. Butterfield joined the business shortly thereafter. The packinghouse was located in a former livery stable on the southeast corner of Euclid Avenue and Main Street, which later became the Hotpoint plant. Mitchell and Butterfield sold fruit grown by local ranchers for $2 a box and paid $30 a month in rent for the building. The packinghouse moved to East Main Street by 1904 and was in business until 1907.

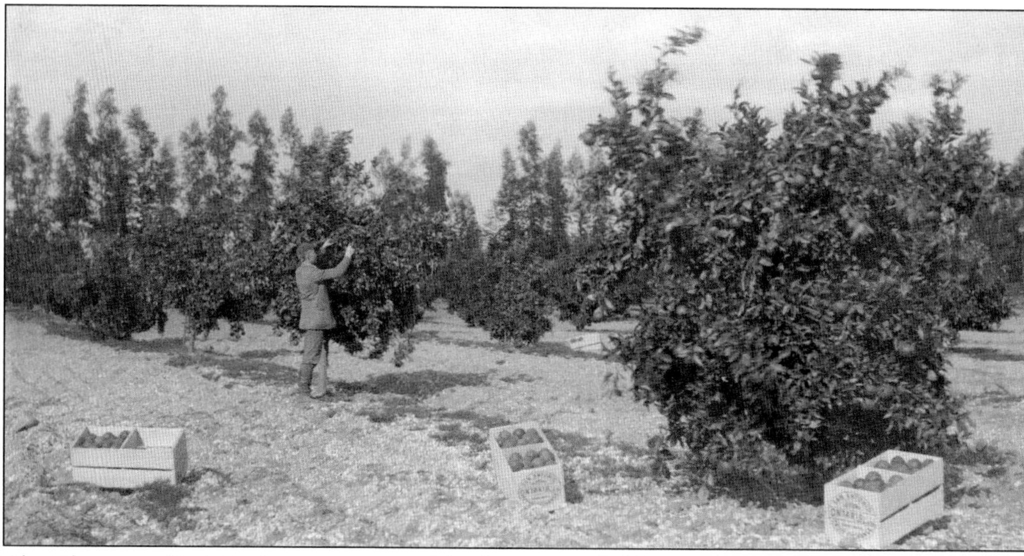

The Claremont Fruit Exchange was one of the first successful fruit exchanges in Southern California and served as a model for future exchanges. In 1893, the exchange united with three other local exchanges: the Pomona Fruit Exchange, the Azusa-Covina-Glendora Citrus Association, and the Ontario Fruit Exchange. Together, they formed the San Antonio Fruit Exchange. This type of early exchange system led to the development of Sunkist in 1908.

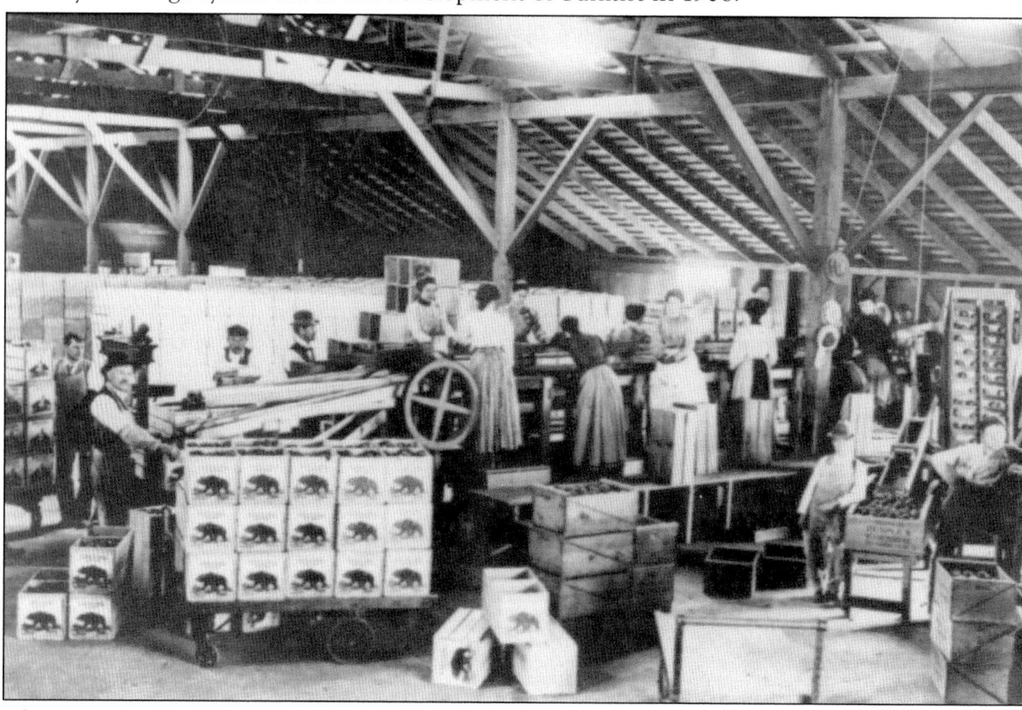

The Ontario-Cucamonga Fruit Exchange, also known as the O-K Fruit Exchange, represented several local fruit associations, including the Ontario Fruit Exchange, the Upland Citrus Association, the Cucamonga Citrus Fruit and Growers Association, and the Citrus Fruit Association. The latter, based in Ontario, packed the Special Bear brand of fancy-grade oranges and lemons, as seen on the labels in this photograph.

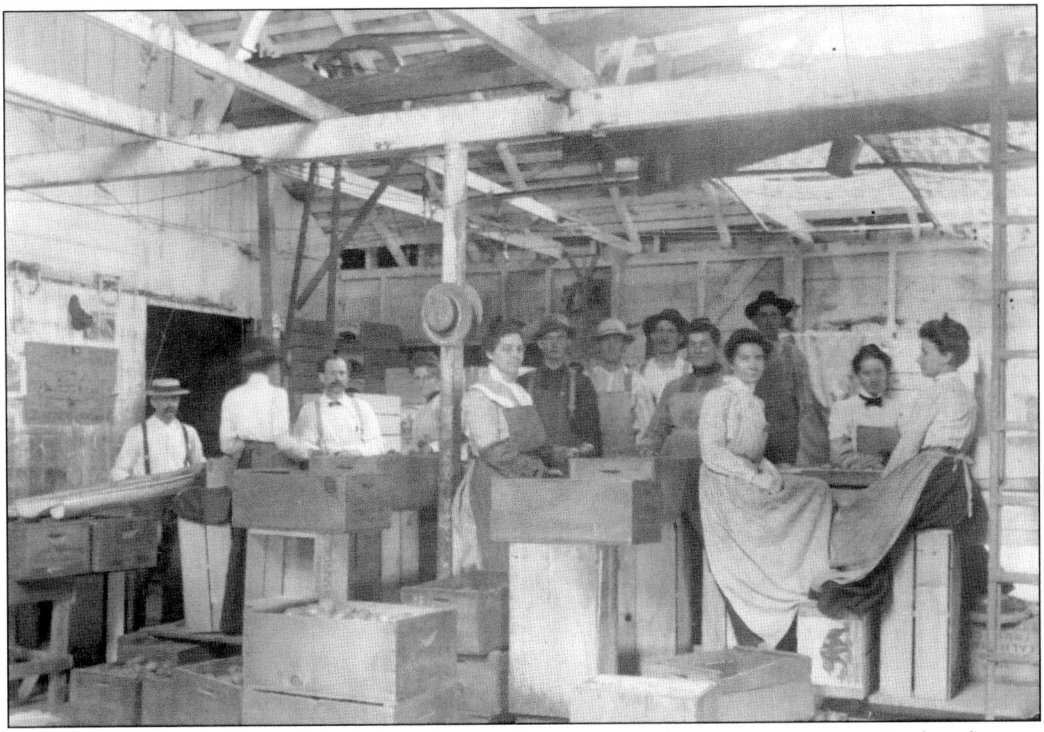

The advent of citrus growers' associations brought more and more opportunity. Packinghouses popped up throughout the area and employed men, women, and sometimes even children during harvest time. Women often worked in packinghouses, even in the early days, while men worked in the orchards.

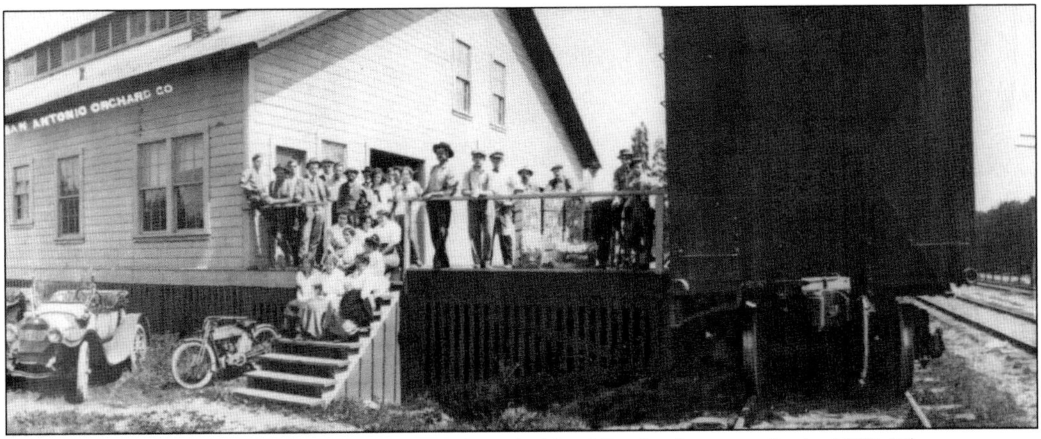

The San Antonio Orchard Company was founded by Charles Latimer Sr. in 1912. The company is noted for its long-held independence, as it was not affiliated with cooperatives such as Sunkist until recent years. The company moved to Northern California in 2001, but continues to sell premium-grown citrus to small international markets. The packinghouse was originally located at 321 South San Antonio Avenue, the current site of O.H. Kruse Milling.

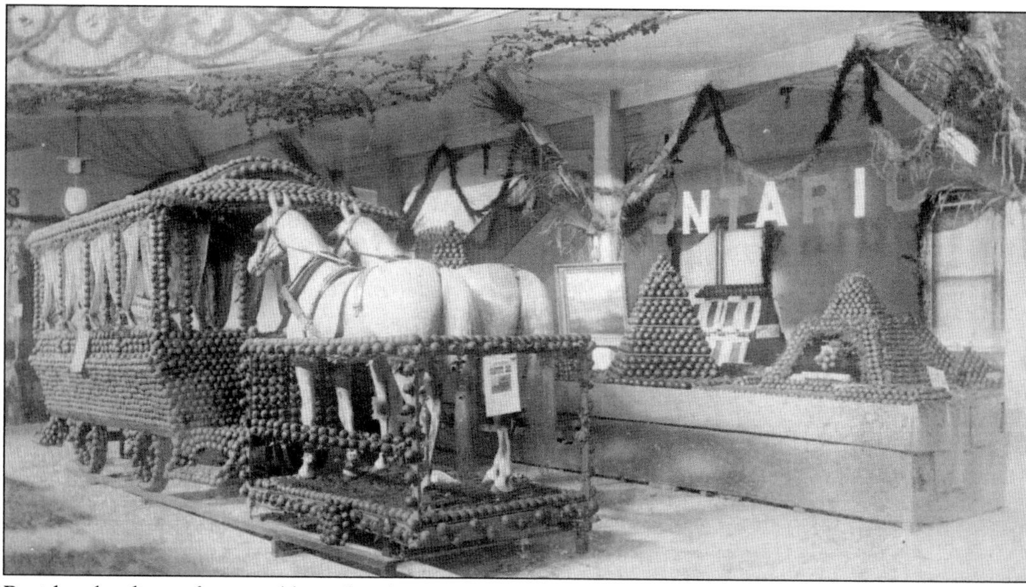

Besides the direct financial benefit of growing citrus, citrus fairs offered an opportunity to publicly boast of the region's economic health and vitality, which in turn often attracted more settlers to the region. A prime example of an exhibit combining citrus with unique aspects of the Ontario community is this gravity mule car display from the 1893 Los Angeles and Chicago Citrus Fair.

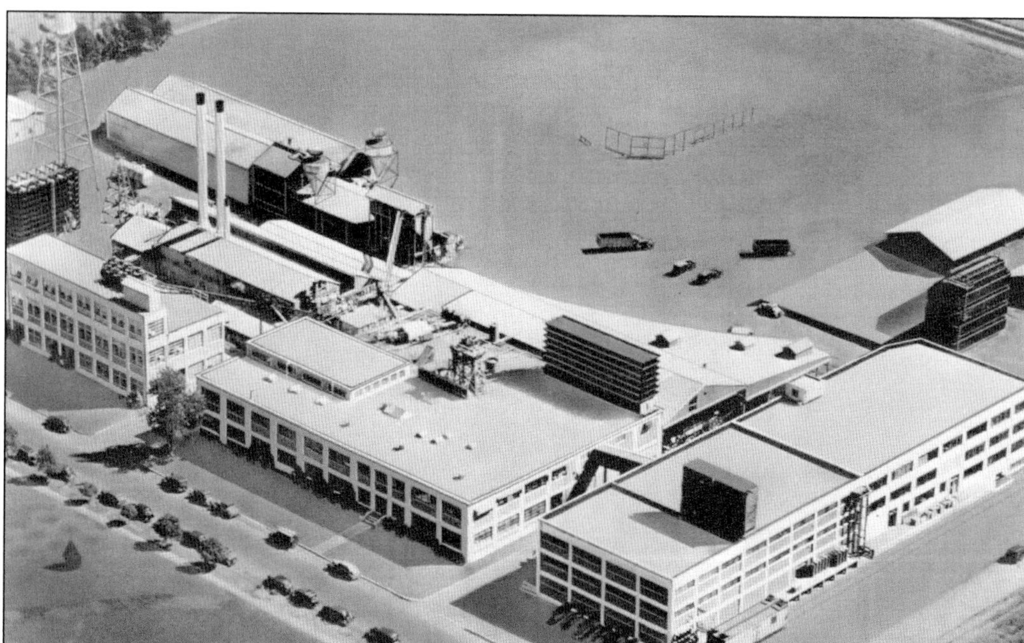

While fresh citrus was a primary force in driving the sale of the fruit, Sunkist developed the Exchange Orange Products Company in 1926. This Ontario plant utilized fruit that was not suitable for the fresh market by making citrus by-products such as juice and aromatic oils. The plant thrived and was a major employer in Ontario for decades. In 2008, Sunkist consolidated its operations, closed the Ontario plant, and moved to Tulare County.

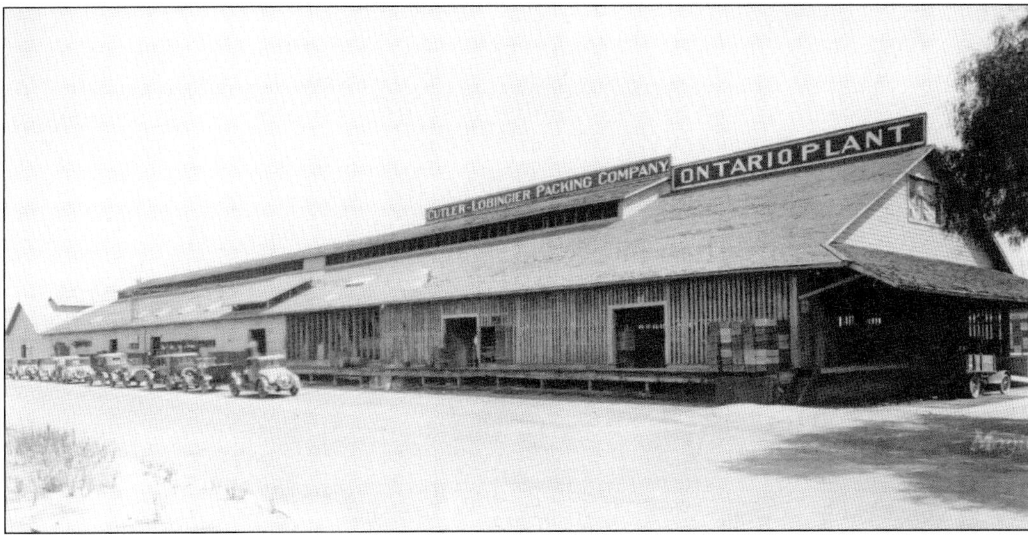

The Cutler-Lobingier Packing Company was located on the southeast corner of Sultana Avenue and Main Street and operated a cannery and packinghouse. This allowed the business to pack citrus and also can peaches, apricots, and other stone fruits. The cannery was formerly known as Golden State Cannery, which was the most successful private cannery in Ontario. Cutler-Lobingier operated the cannery in Ontario from about 1924 to 1935.

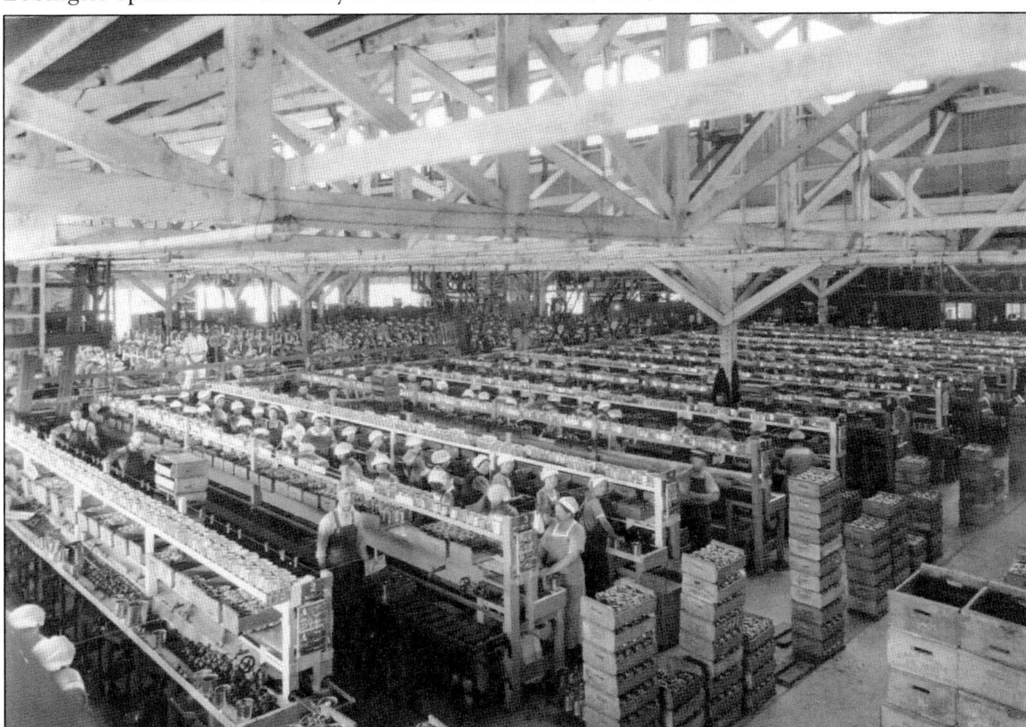

California Cooperative Canneries operated just to the east of Golden State Cannery in the 1920s. While a private cannery packed fruit that was grown on its own orchards, cooperative canneries purchased fruit from several local growers. Cooperative canneries helped support the small ranch that could not afford to can and market its own fruit.

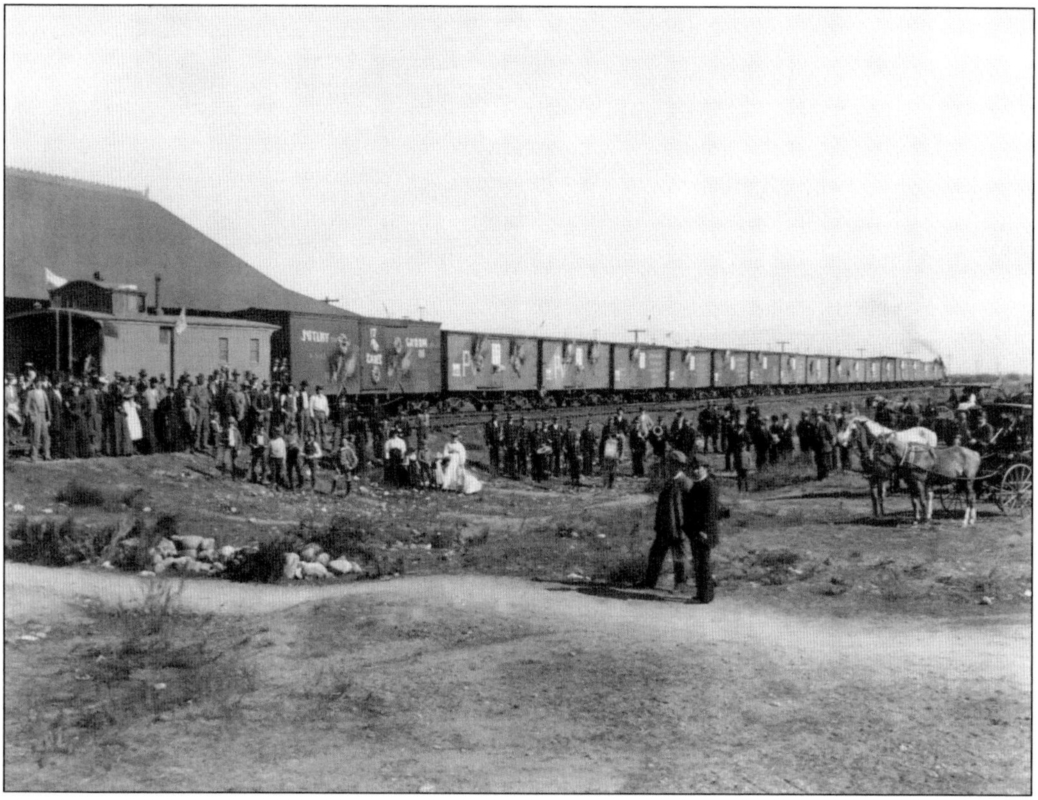

In November 1893, the largest trainload of fruit from the Ontario-Upland area to date was shipped on the Santa Fe Railroad. Here, 17 cars loaded with fruit, weighing over 400,000 pounds and destined for Cedar Rapids, Iowa, was packed by Sutliff and Groom of Iowa, pictured in the foreground, who leased the Ontario Cannery in 1893 for the specific purpose of shipping the fruit east.

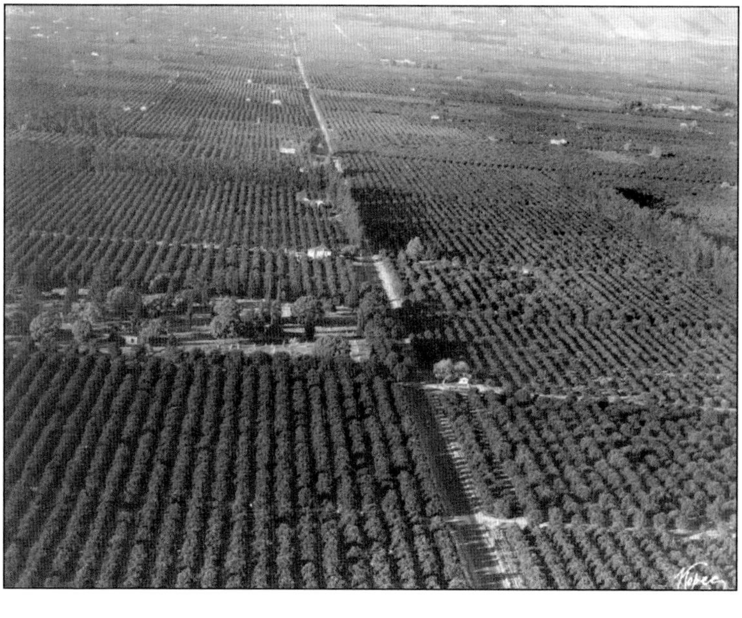

This aerial view looking north on Mountain Avenue in Ontario, dated to around 1920, illustrates how extensive citrus ranching had become during Ontario's first 40 years, with nearly every inch of land covered with citrus trees. At left center is Bellevue Cemetery, at Mountain Avenue and G Street.

Four

The Founding of Armstrong Nurseries

Another settler from Canada to the Ontario model colony was John Samuel Armstrong, who arrived on March 3, 1889, with $6 in his pocket. After convalescing in San Antonio Canyon for a summer due to tuberculosis, he was well enough to start working at local nurseries. By 1893, he opened his own nursery, primarily growing fruit trees.

In 1902 he produced his first mail-order catalog, filled with fruit trees, shrubs, and roses. This mail-order business grew to become worldwide. Over time, the nursery became famous for its hybrid roses, winning awards and increasing business. The Charlotte Armstrong Rose, developed by noted hybridist Dr. Walter Lammerts in 1941, was such a winner, and Ontario named it the city's official flower in 1962.

Armstrong wrote about his life in a manuscript called *The J. S. Armstrong Story*, which is the basis for the information in this chapter. Armstrong died four months before his 100th birthday in 1965.

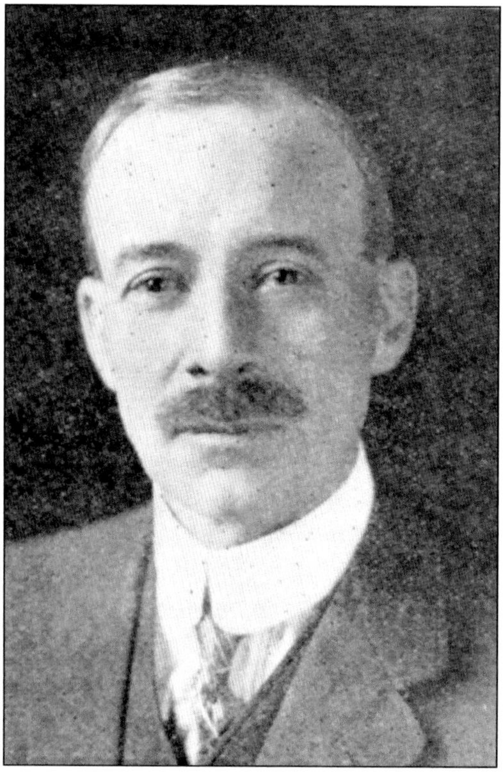

John Samuel Armstrong was a native of Ontario, Canada, born in 1865. He left school at age 14 and went to work learning woodworking, specifically cabinetry and furniture building. While working in Clinton, Ontario, he contracted tuberculosis and was advised to go west for his health.

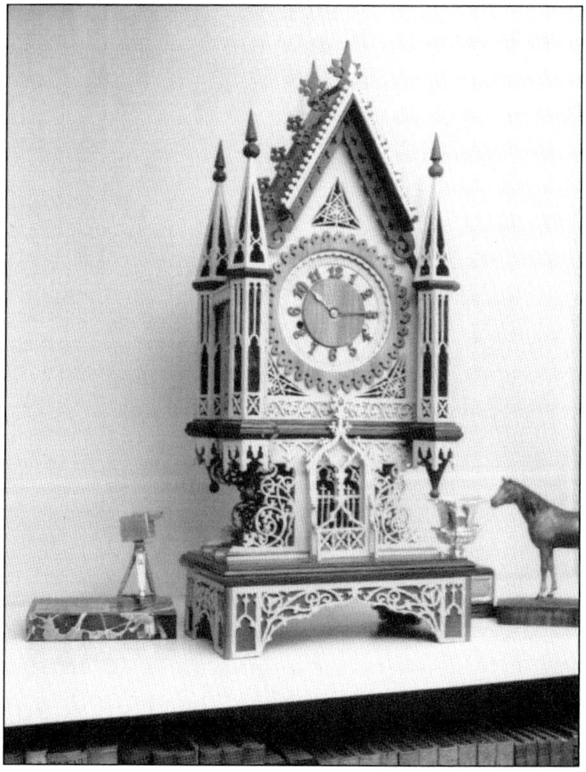

Armstrong often made elaborate items, including this very ornate clock case, which he made from six types of wood. Armstrong sold the clock case for $35 for money to pay for his passage to California. He arrived in Ontario on March 3, 1889, at age 23, with $6 in his pocket. He spent the summer convalescing in the San Antonio Canyon.

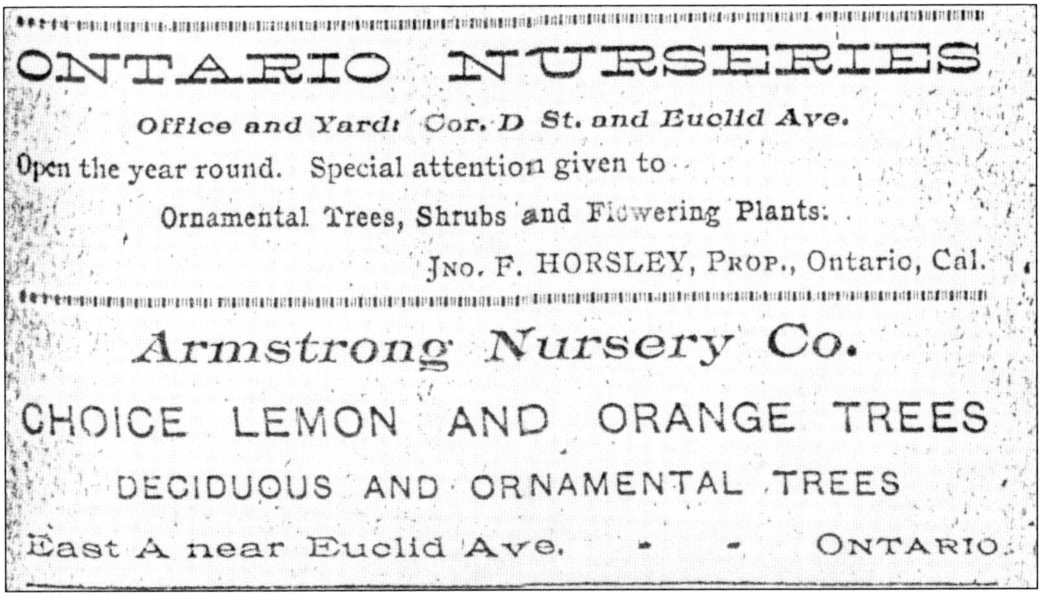

Once he felt better, Armstrong began working for various nurseries, including Ontario Nurseries. Eventually, he felt he had learned enough to open his own nursery. In 1893, he opened his first sales yard on a rented lot on East Euclid Avenue between Holt Boulevard and the Southern Pacific tracks. He originally called it Ontario Nursery, but Ontario Nurseries paid him $16 to rename it. He grew fruit trees on a 10-acre lot he rented on the Chaffey College campus.

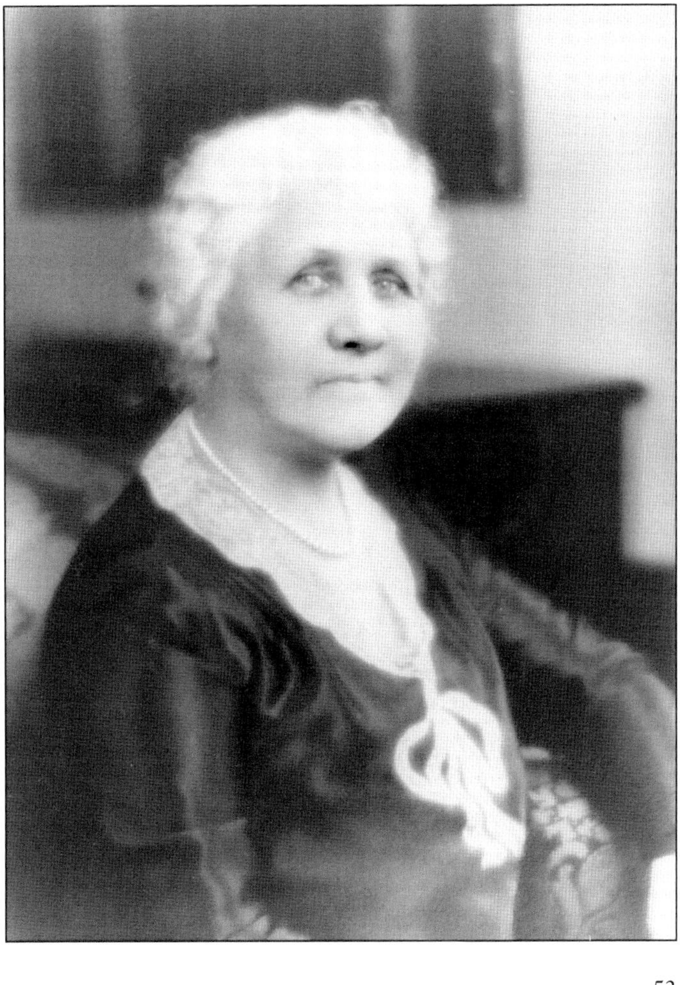

In 1894, J.S. Armstrong became a US citizen, and in 1896, he returned to Canada to marry his sweetheart, Charlotte Cooper (pictured), and bring her to Ontario. For a while, they lived in a small rented house on State Street. Soon after, Armstrong bought his first house, at C Street and Plum Avenue, for $500.

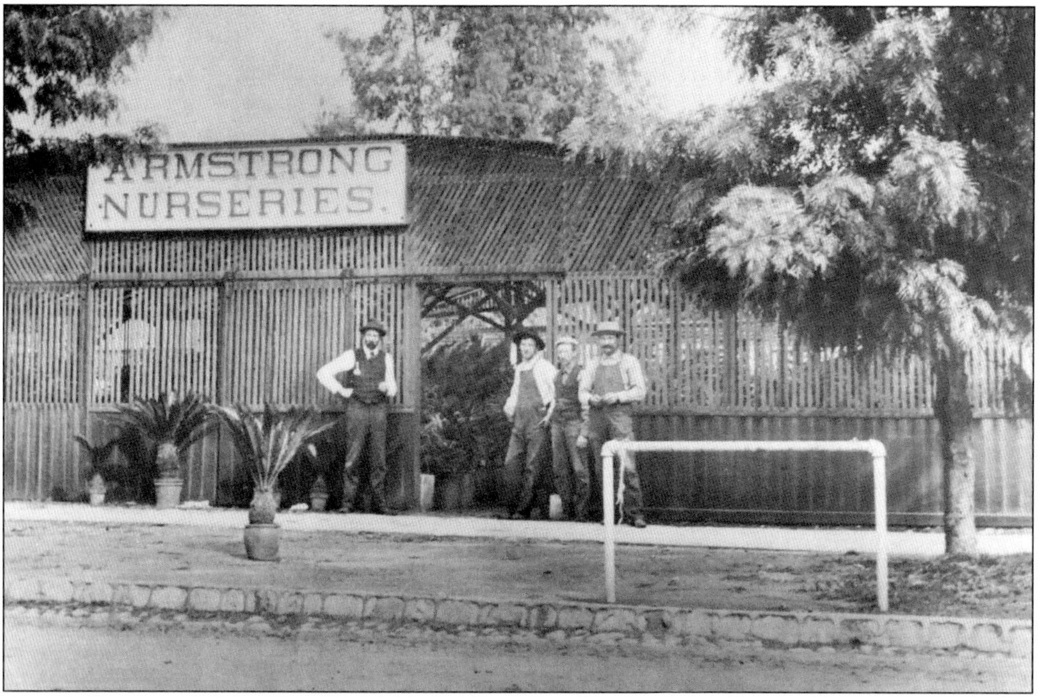

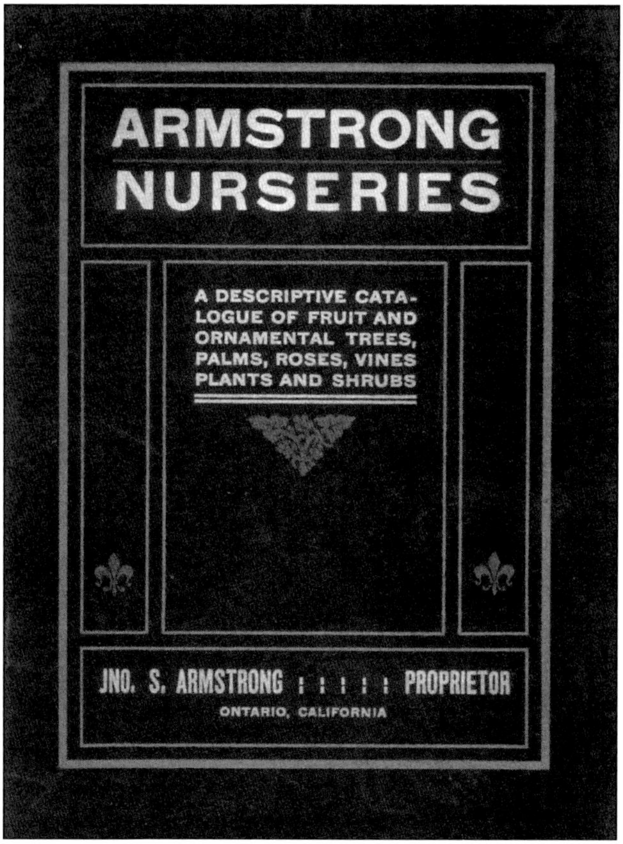

In 1898, Armstrong purchased three lots on the northeast corner of Euclid Avenue and D Street from George Chaffey's son Andrew for $112 each. He then continued to purchase lots until he owned almost the entire block, and built a two-story house on the south corner in 1900. He soon purchased 10 acres of land on Sixth Street just west of Mountain Avenue, and another 20 acres on West Philips Street.

Armstrong purchased a mailing list of 2,500 names from a defunct nursery business and issued his first catalog in 1902. The list consisted primarily of easterners, providing Armstrong with a national mail-order presence. He offered fruit trees, deciduous trees, ornamental shrubs, and roses. Eventually, Armstrong Nurseries grew into a worldwide mail-order business.

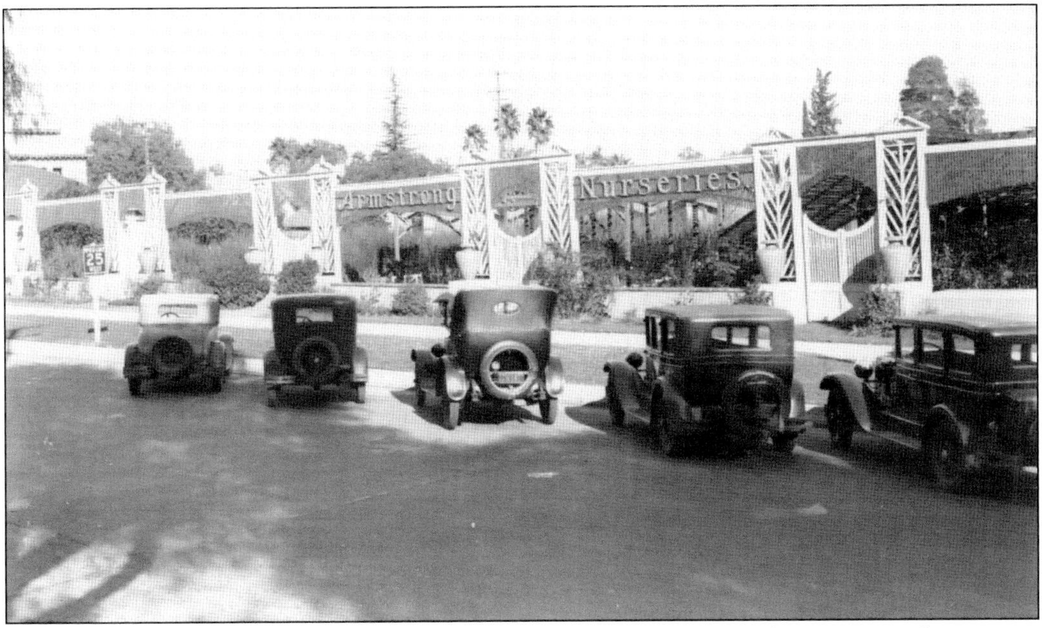

The sales yard continued to grow throughout the 1910s and 1920s, and its presence dominating an entire block of downtown Ontario helped its sales. Armstrong was well known in town, not only for his business, but also for his service within the community. During his life, he served as a member of Ontario City Council and the library board, and was also a member of many local service organizations.

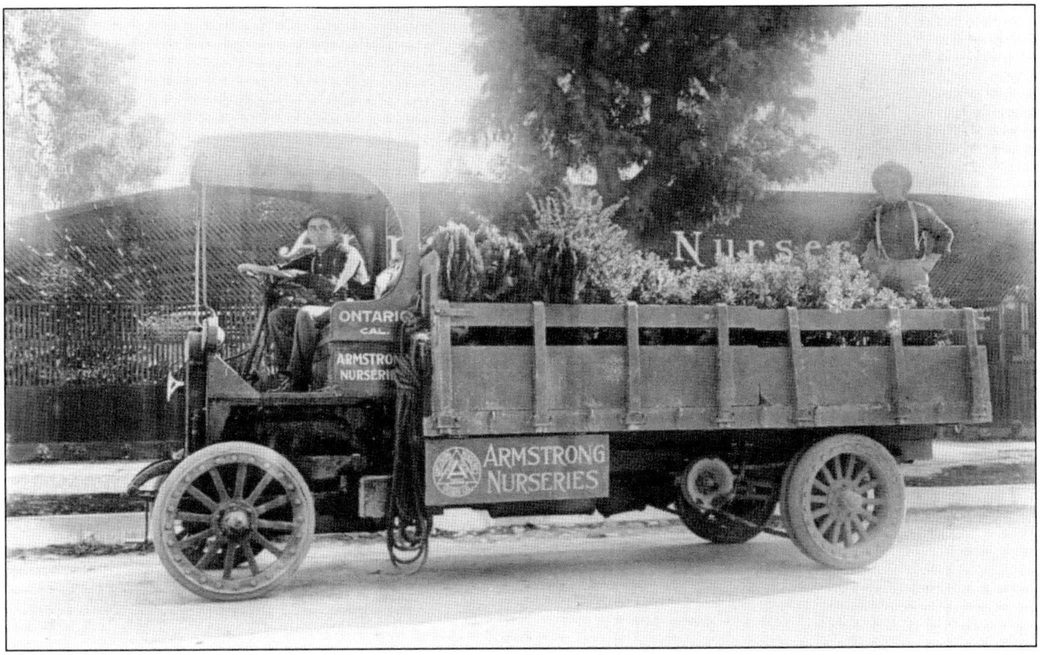

Along with the introduction of its mail-order catalog business, Armstrong Nurseries began delivering orders daily to customers throughout the region by truck. Clients received their orders quickly, and the plants remained fresh. An early delivery truck from about 1915 is seen here in front of the sales yard at Euclid Avenue and D Street.

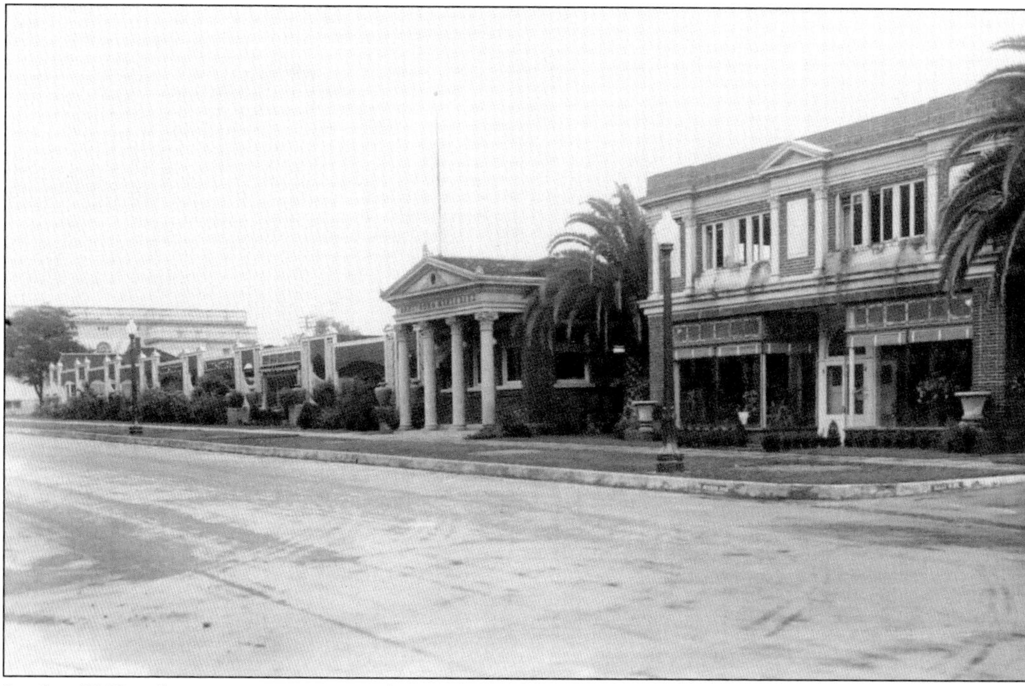

In the 1920s, the nursery continued to expand as more space was needed. Armstrong donated his two-story house on the corner of Euclid Avenue and D Street to the American Legion in exchange for moving it off the property and then built a new office building and flower shop, which opened in 1926. The new building also had club rooms, a social hall, and a kitchen and dining room upstairs for Armstrong employees.

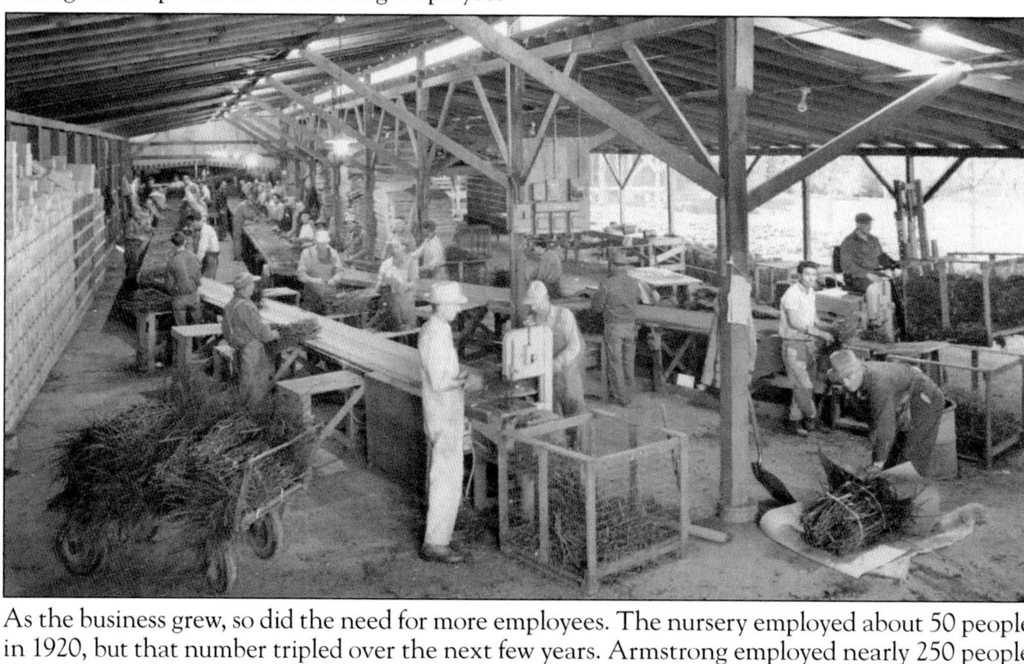

As the business grew, so did the need for more employees. The nursery employed about 50 people in 1920, but that number tripled over the next few years. Armstrong employed nearly 250 people by the mid-1930s, with an annual payroll of $225,000. He was considered a fair employer and provided profit-sharing bonuses to his employees.

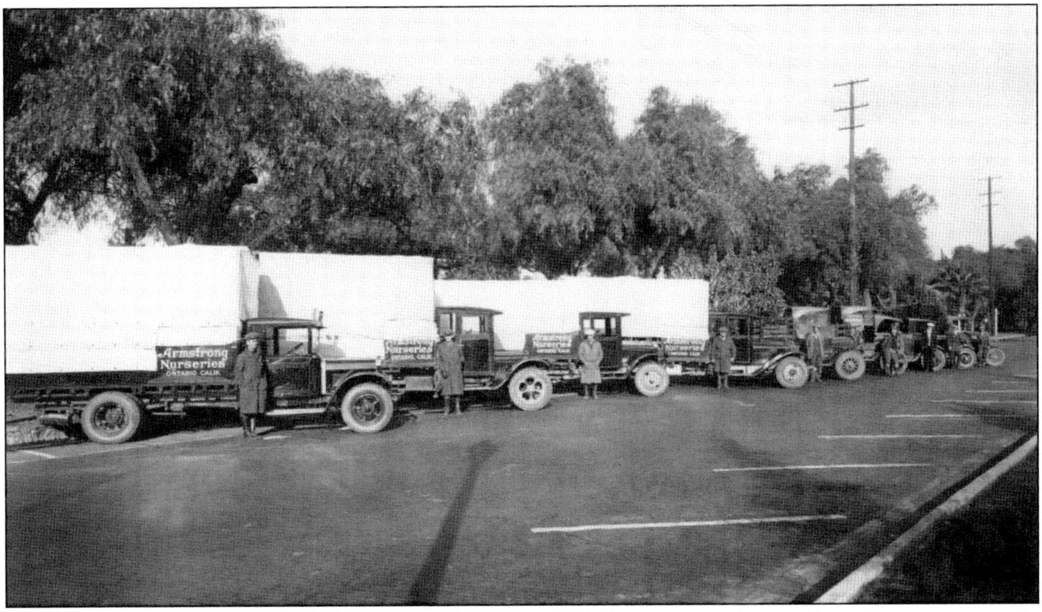

Trucks delivered to customers throughout Southern California every day, and purchases were made all over the world, shipped by automobile, truck, train, and steamship. Armstrong had clients in Spain, Palestine, Great Britain, Mexico, South America, Russia, and Morocco, just to name a few. Armstrong also had some well-known customers, including safety razor magnate King C. Gillette and silver screen legend Clark Gable, who visited the nursery in person from time to time.

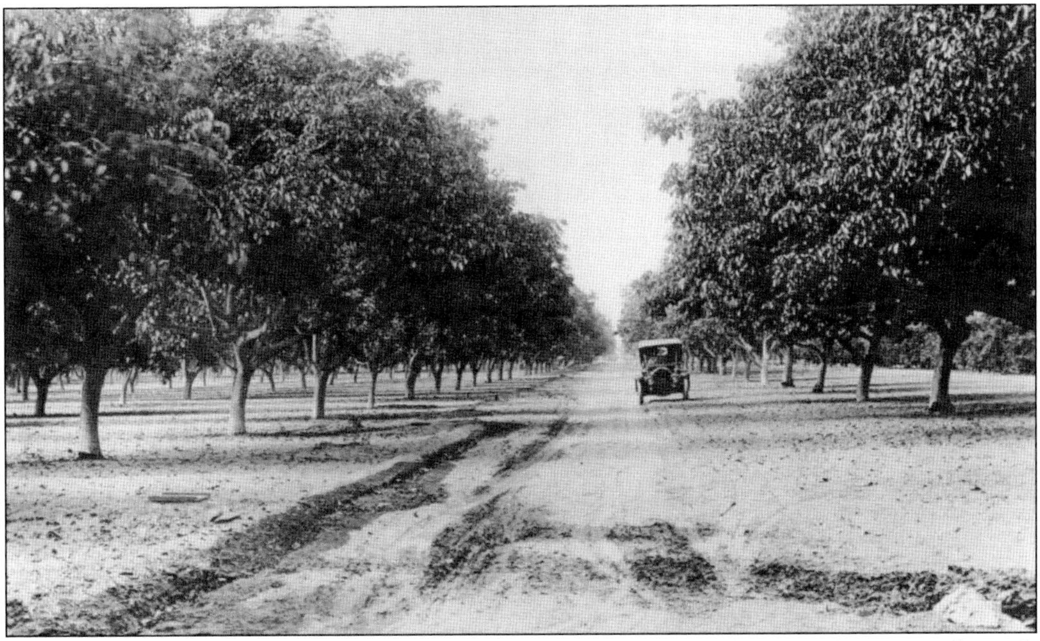

Hybridist Walter Lammerts created Armstrong's research and development division in the mid-1930s. Most associate Armstrong Nurseries with the beautiful roses they invented and patented, but the nursery originally offered fruit trees for sale, such as the peach trees shown here. After their research division was established, Armstrong developed and patented fruit trees, ornamental shrubs, avocado trees, and many other plants.

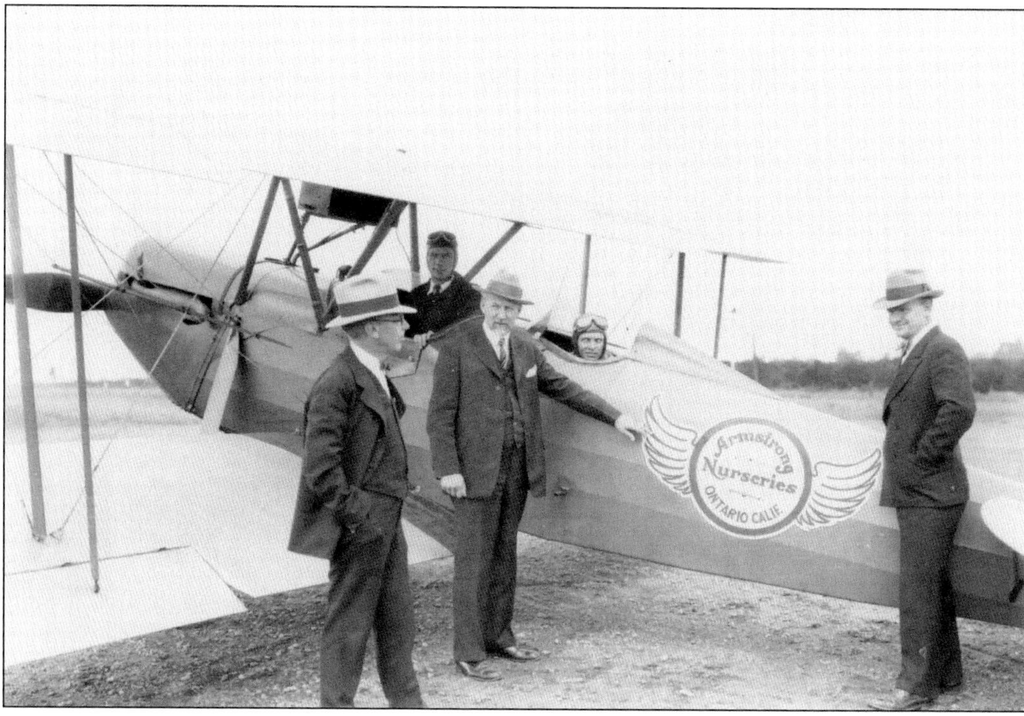

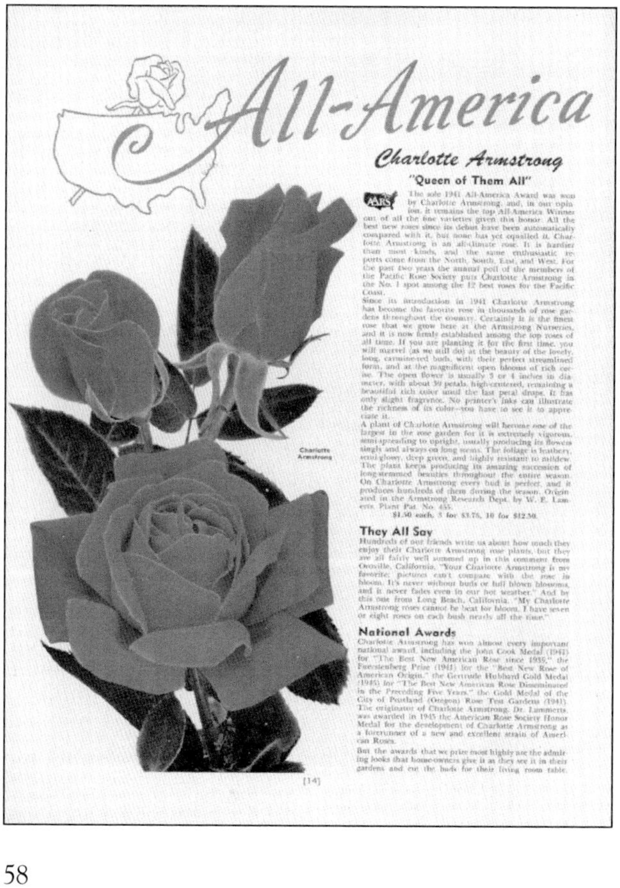

All-America

Charlotte Armstrong

"Queen of Them All"

AARS

The sole 1941 All-America Award was won by Charlotte Armstrong, and, in our opinion, it remains the top All-America Winner out of all the fine varieties given this honor. All the best new roses since its debut have been automatically compared with it, but none has yet equalled it. Charlotte Armstrong is an all-climate rose. It is hardier than most kinds, and the same enthusiastic reports come from the North, South, East, and West. For the past two years the annual poll of the members of the Pacific Rose Society puts Charlotte Armstrong in the No. 1 spot among the 12 best roses for the Pacific Coast.

Since its introduction in 1941 Charlotte Armstrong has become the favorite rose in thousands of rose gardens throughout the country. Certainly it is the finest rose that we grow here at the Armstrong Nurseries, and it is now firmly established among the top roses of all time. If you are planting it for the first time, you will marvel (as we still do) at the beauty of the lovely, long, carmine-red buds, with their perfect streamlined form, and at the magnificent open blooms of rich cerise. The open flower is usually 3 or 4 inches in diameter, with about 30 petals, high-centered, remaining a beautiful rich color until the last petal drops. It has only slight fragrance. No printer's inks can illustrate the richness of its color—you have to see it to appreciate it.

A plant of Charlotte Armstrong will become one of the largest in the rose garden for it is extremely vigorous, semi-spreading to upright, usually producing its flowers singly and always on long stems. The foliage is leathery, semi-glossy, deep green, and highly resistant to mildew. The plant keeps producing its amazing succession of long-stemmed beauties throughout the entire season. On Charlotte Armstrong every bud is perfect, and it produces hundreds of them during the season. Originated in the Armstrong Research Dept. by W. E. Lammerts. Plant Pat. No. 455.

$1.50 each, 3 for $3.75, 10 for $12.50.

Charlotte Armstrong

They All Say

Hundreds of our friends write us about how much they enjoy their Charlotte Armstrong rose plants, but they are all fairly well summed up in this comment from Oroville, California, "Your Charlotte Armstrong is my favorite; pictures can't compare with the rose in bloom. It's never without buds or full blown blossoms, and it never fades even in our hot weather." And by this one from Long Beach, California, "My Charlotte Armstrong roses cannot be beat for bloom. I have seven or eight roses on each bush nearly all the time."

National Awards

Charlotte Armstrong has won almost every important national award, including the John Cook Medal (1941) for "The Best New American Rose since 1939," the Foerstenberg Prize (1941) for the "Best New Rose of American Origin," the Gertrude Hubbard Gold Medal (1945) for "The Best New American Rose Disseminated in the Preceding Five Years," the Gold Medal of the City of Portland (Oregon) Rose Test Gardens (1941). The originator of Charlotte Armstrong, Dr. Lammerts, was awarded in 1945 the American Rose Society Honor Medal for the development of Charlotte Armstrong as a forerunner of a new and excellent strain of American Roses.

But the awards that we prize most highly are the admiring looks that home-owners give it as they see it in their gardens and cut the buds for their living room table.

[14]

In 1928, Armstrong plunged into the world of aviation, commencing air service for faster contact with his customers. Murray McNeil, his "contact man," trained to be a pilot in order to use this plane for his business journeys, allowing him to save travel time and provide prompt service to large clients such as contractors and landscape architects. McNeil's first business flight was to the Hearst ranch in San Simeon.

Over time, Armstrong Nursery became world-famous for its roses. They employed professional hybridists who developed award-winning roses and other plants, including the Charlotte Armstrong Rose, created by Walter Lammerts. This was the All-America Rose Selections winner for 1941 and is also Ontario's official flower.

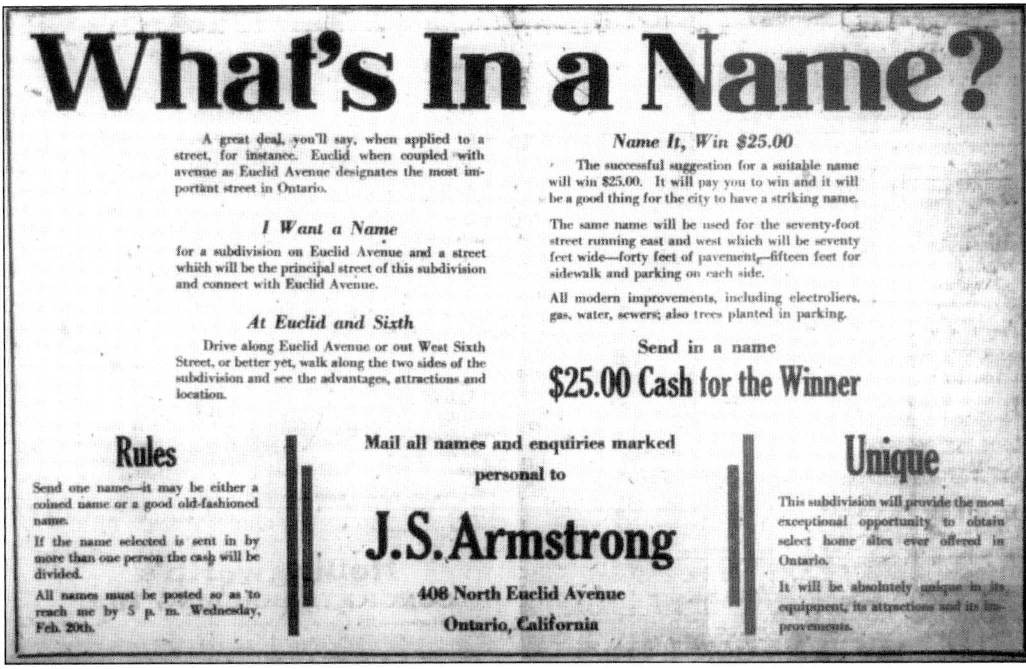

What's In a Name?

A great deal, you'll say, when applied to a street, for instance. Euclid when coupled with avenue as Euclid Avenue designates the most important street in Ontario.

I Want a Name

for a subdivision on Euclid Avenue and a street which will be the principal street of this subdivision and connect with Euclid Avenue.

At Euclid and Sixth

Drive along Euclid Avenue or out West Sixth Street, or better yet, walk along the two sides of the subdivision and see the advantages, attractions and location.

Name It, Win $25.00

The successful suggestion for a suitable name will win $25.00. It will pay you to win and it will be a good thing for the city to have a striking name.

The same name will be used for the seventy-foot street running east and west which will be seventy feet wide—forty feet of pavement,—fifteen feet for sidewalk and parking on each side.

All modern improvements, including electroliers, gas, water, sewers; also trees planted in parking.

Send in a name

$25.00 Cash for the Winner

Rules

Send one name—it may be either a coined name or a good old-fashioned name.

If the name selected is sent in by more than one person the cash will be divided.

All names must be posted so as to reach me by 5 p. m. Wednesday, Feb. 20th.

Mail all names and enquiries marked personal to

J.S. Armstrong

408 North Euclid Avenue

Ontario, California

Unique

This subdivision will provide the most exceptional opportunity to obtain select home sites ever offered in Ontario.

It will be absolutely unique in its equipment, its attractions and its improvements.

In the early 1920s, Armstrong purchased 20 acres just off the west side of Euclid Avenue, near Sixth Street, and developed what he called an "elite" subdivision. He promoted his new subdivision by devising a naming contest he advertised in the *Daily Report* in February 1924. "What's in a name?" he asks in one of his newspaper ads. The winner of the naming contest won a $25 cash prize.

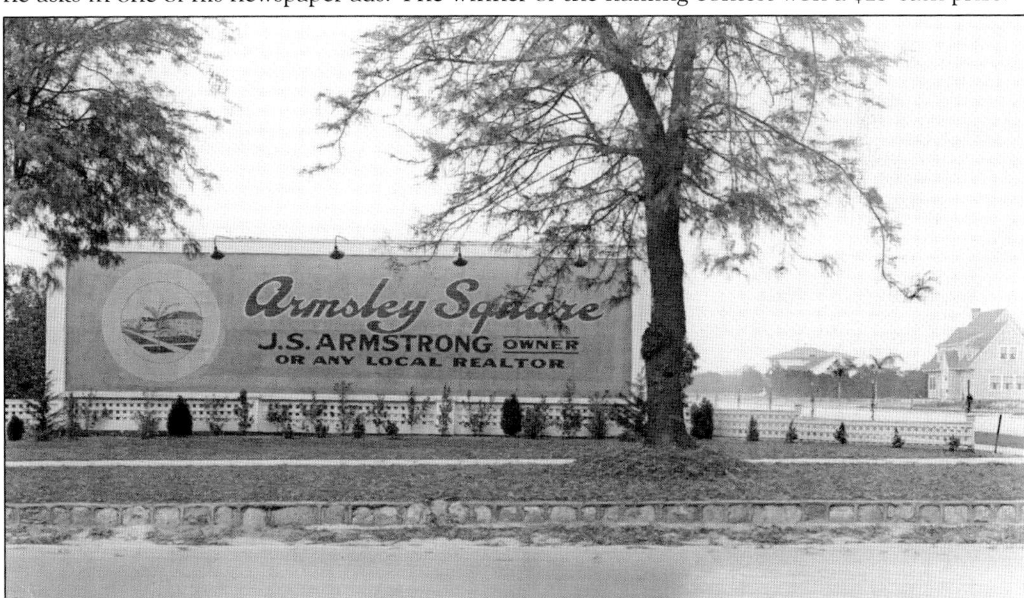

Out of 440 name suggestions, Armstrong chose Armsley Square, suggested by Mrs. Helen Hughes, who also wrote a poem called "A Toast to 'Armsley Square' ": "Here's to Armsley Square, the gem of the city, where our happy homes will be. / The pride of our fond aspirations, Mr. Armstrong we pay homage to thee. / For while we have been casually thinking of the wonderful things that were to be, / You have given to our fair city this beautiful square – Armsley."

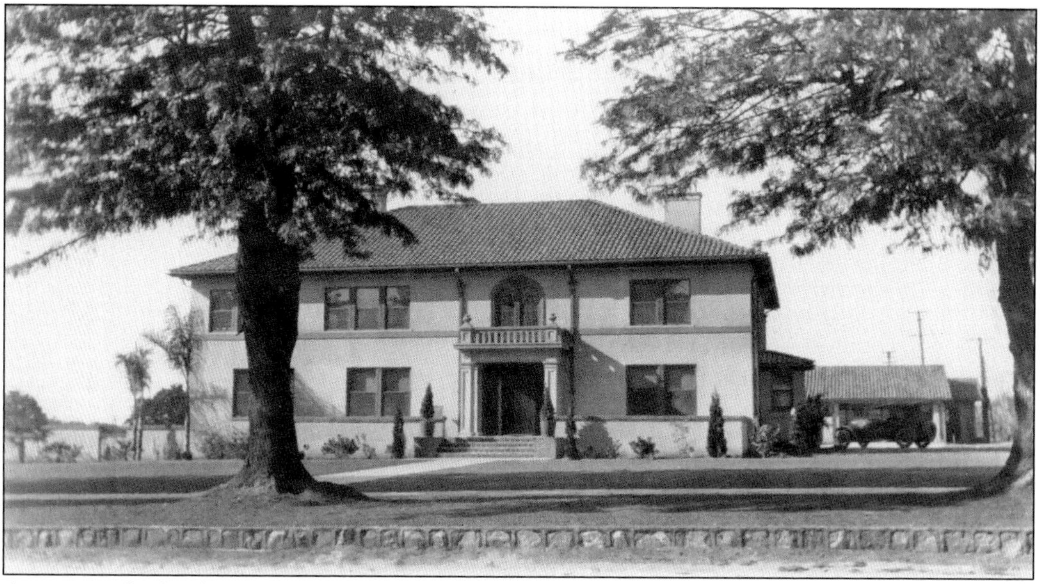

Armstrong built a home for his family in Armsley Square. The couple had six children, although, tragically, four of them died young. His son J. Awdry Armstrong and daughter Olive Freeman became well-known members of the community. Charlotte died in 1948 after complications resulting from an automobile accident. This home was later replaced by the Christian Science Church's Sunday school.

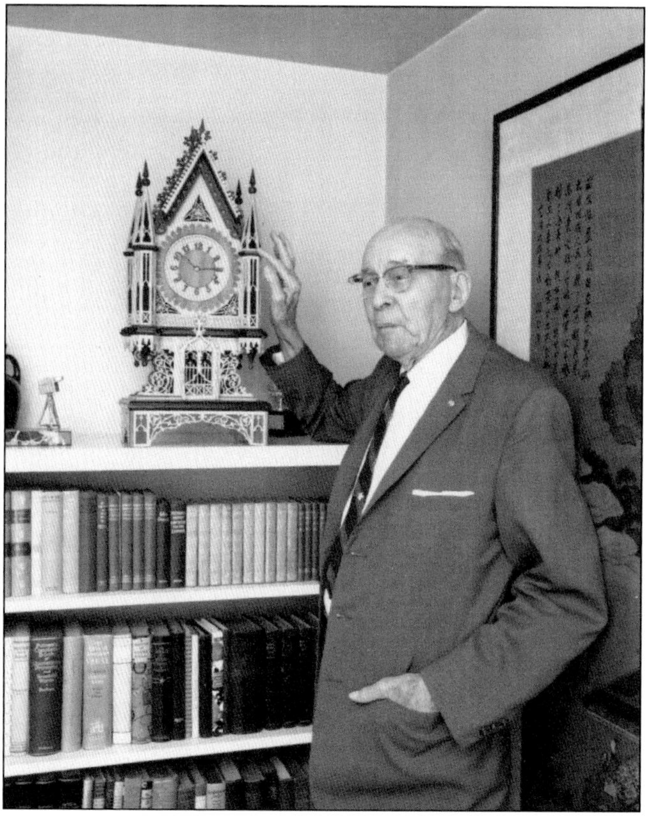

Armstrong poses with the ornate clock he sold to purchase his future as an Ontario nurseryman. About 15 years after he sold the clock, he returned to Clinton and found it in a bar. Apparently, the man who purchased it later traded it in exchange for liquor. After Charlotte's death, Armstrong married Willa Bradley and built a new home just north of Armsley Square. He died in 1965, just four months before his 100th birthday.

Five

Graber Olives, Ontario's Oldest Business

In 1892, brothers Clifford and Charles Graber came to Ontario seeking a healthier climate for Clifford, who suffered from a chronic lung illness. While they first grew oranges and lemons on the colony acreage they bought, Clifford, or "C.C.," as he was known, soon began experimenting with curing olives that grew in an abandoned grove nearby. The olives became so popular that, in 1894, he founded Graber Olive House, Ontario's oldest business, which is still family-owned and in business today.

As the business grew, Graber Olives expanded its olive groves, first to Hemet and then to the San Joaquin Valley. Processing the olives continues today at the Ontario homestead, on East Fourth Street between Euclid and Sultana Avenues. C.C. Graber invented a grading machine for his olives, becoming the first in the industry to standardize olive sizes. Graber's olives are cured using a recipe developed by C.C. Graber that is still a family secret. The olives are then canned, labeled, and sold worldwide.

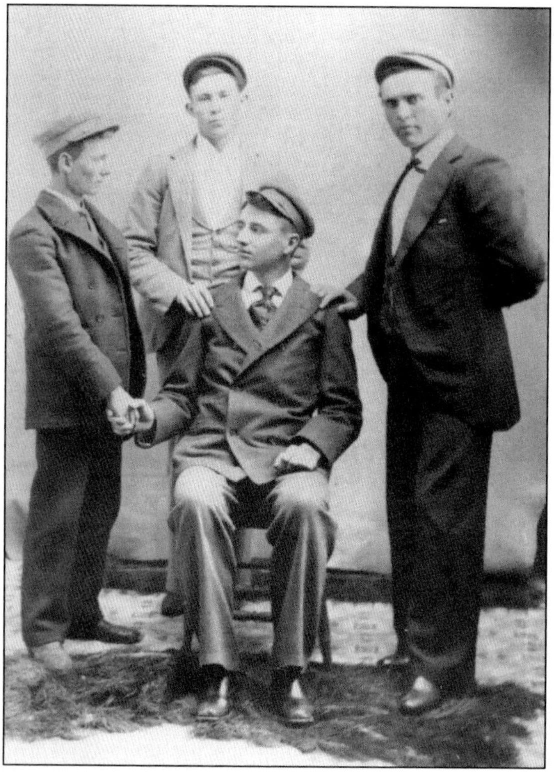

Clifford C. Graber (seated) was born in 1873 in Clay City, Indiana. His father ran a brickyard, and after leaving school in the eighth grade, Clifford went to work in the family business. Like many Ontario pioneers, Graber came to California seeking a healthy climate due to a chronic lung illness. He arrived in 1892, soon after this photograph was taken. He and his brother Charles invested in prime Ontario ranch land and began growing citrus.

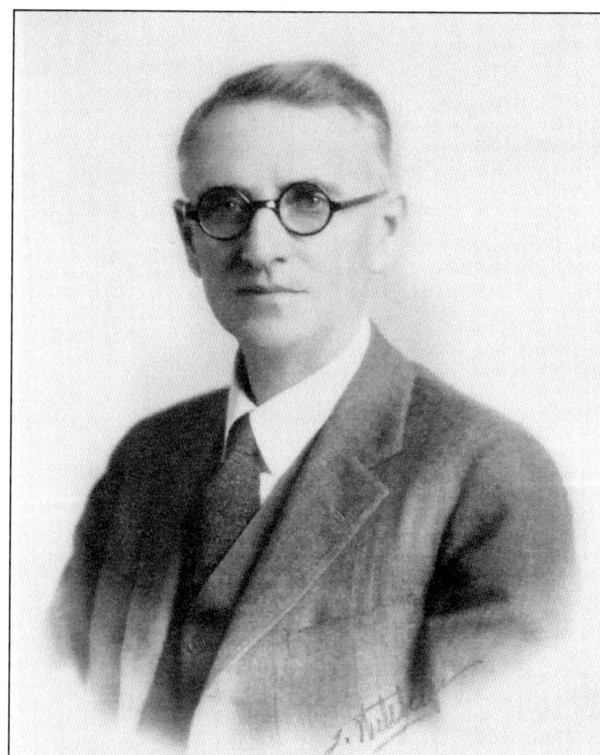

While waiting for the citrus trees to produce, Clifford Graber started harvesting olives from an abandoned grove a few blocks east of the Fourth Street ranch. His partnership with his brother eventually dissolved, but Clifford continued to harvest olives with his new wife and partner, Georgia Belle Noe, whom he married in 1906 at her parents' home. In the early years, the couple lived on H Street.

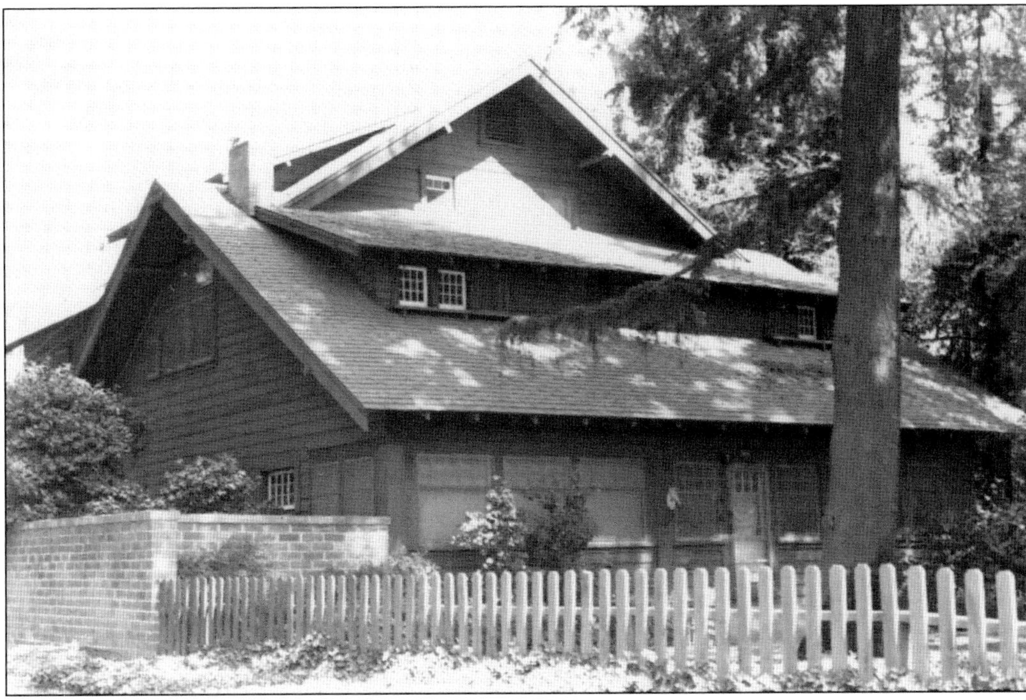

In 1907, Clifford and Georgia Belle (right) built their Fourth Street home to be closer to the barn and the olive sheds they had already constructed. All four Graber children, Mary, William, Robert, and Georgianna, were born at the house. The home was often busy and bustling late into the night. Georgia Belle Graber worked in the fields during the day, took care of the children in the evenings, and was available into the night should customers ring the bell to buy olives. All four children attended Chaffey High School, and Clifford Graber served on the school's board of trustees. Graber also served on the Ontario City Council from 1918 to 1925. Their son William went on to become a star athlete, competing twice on the Olympic pole vaulting team, in 1932 and 1936.

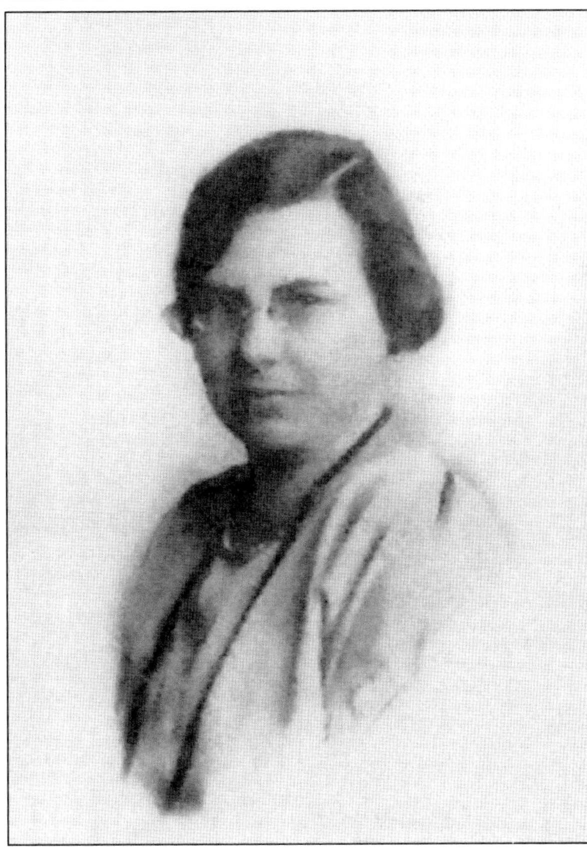

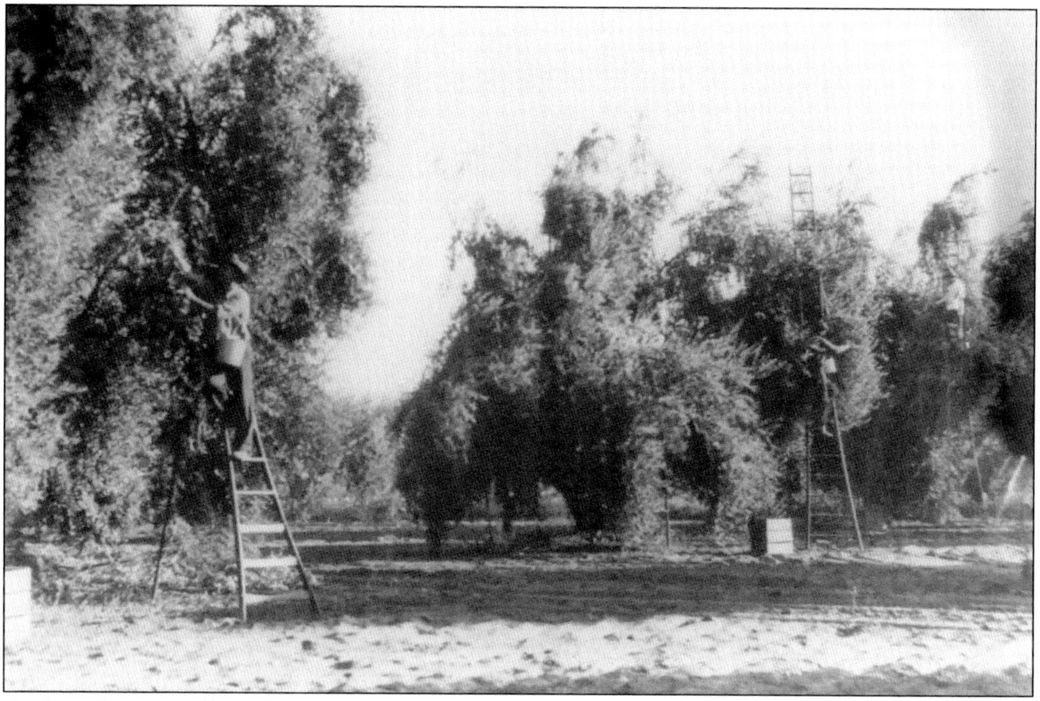

Graber olives are allowed to ripen on the tree and are cured without oxidation. This allows them to retain their original green color, speckled with red and brown. They are carefully picked, and only the mature olives are taken from the tree. Harvests are repeated several times each season in order to allow all the olives to ripen naturally.

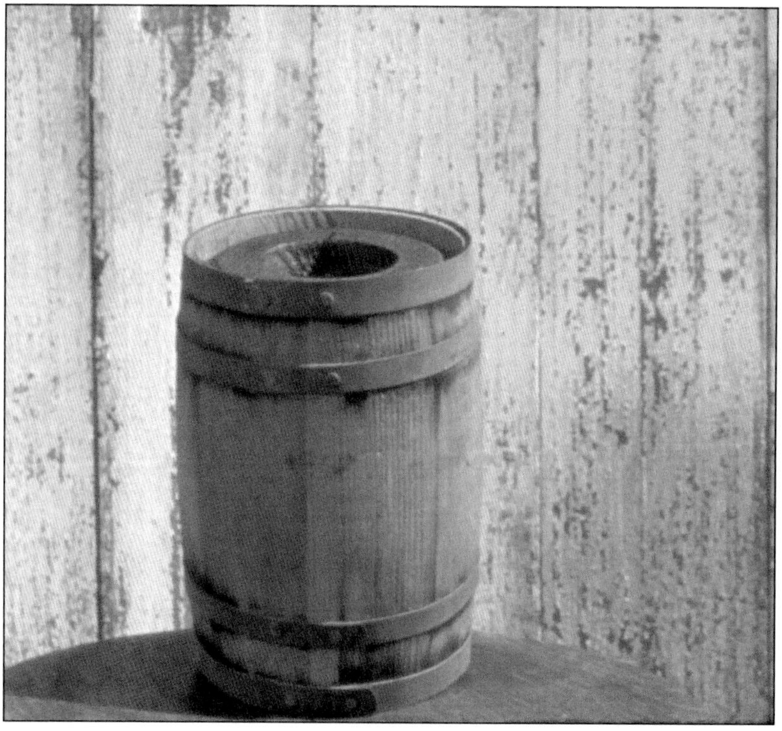

In the early years, Graber supplied olives to shops throughout town in wooden kegs like this. Customers scooped out what they wanted and took home olives in their own buckets. Before the Graber shop was open on weekends, customers would drive through, scooping their own olives and leaving money in a slot on the door using an honor system.

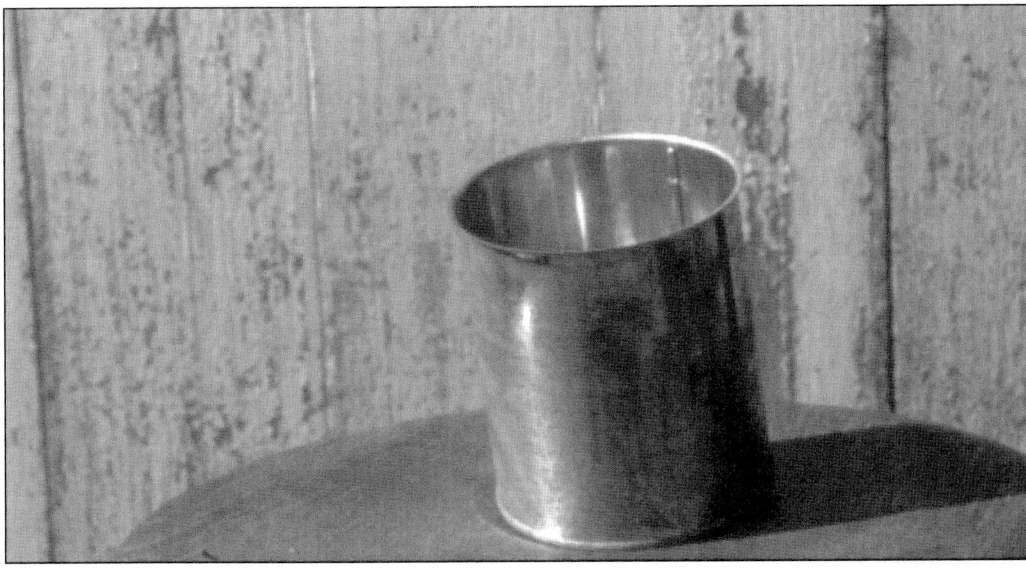

Canning laws had an unintended consequence for Graber Olives. Since canned olives are preserved, they were able to expand their territory and no longer had to rely on local markets. From 1910 to 1925, olives were sold in plain tin cans, so customers would ask shopkeepers for the olives with no label. Gallon-cans sold at local markets were purchased by Graber with two-inch holes in the top, and the olives were added by hand. A group of 20 cans were then placed on a wooden rack inside a crate of water. An open fire burned for 90 minutes underneath the cans, which were then soldered shut. In 1930, a California state law required that all cans had to have labels. Graber added a label with a silver background, which looked similar to the original unlabeled cans and was used for 15 years.

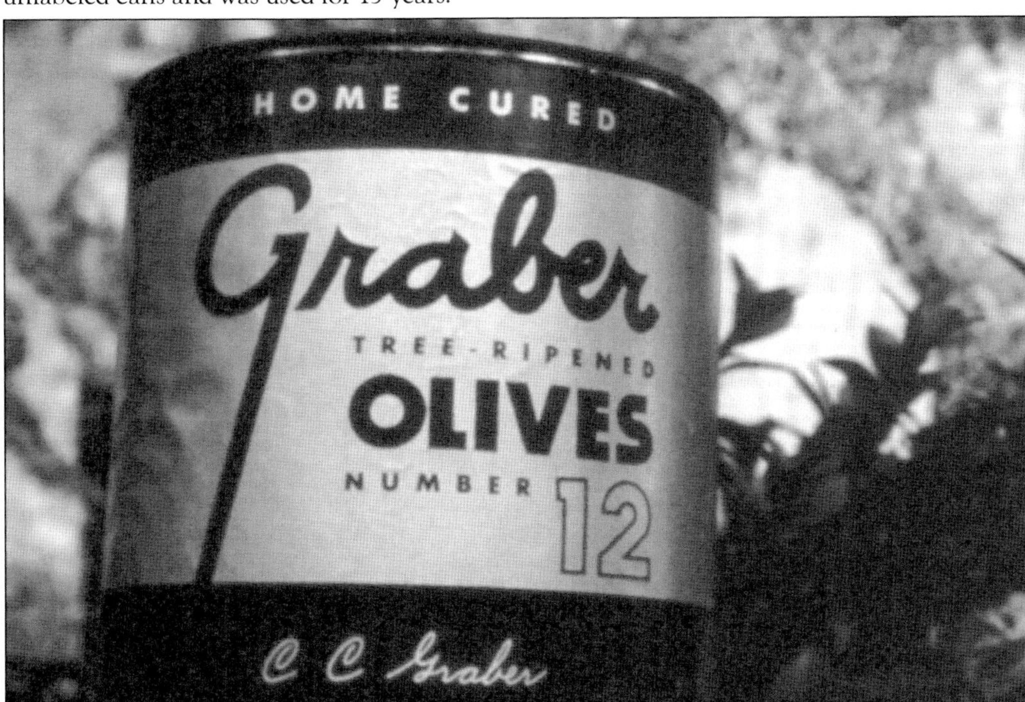

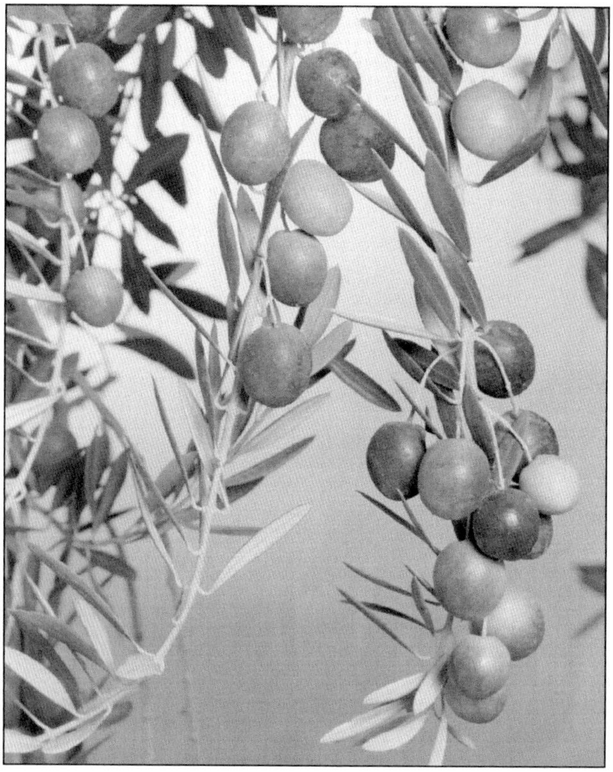

Manzanillo means "little apple" in Spanish and is the name of the most common type of olive. First planted in California by Franciscan missionaries at the Mission San Diego de Alcalá in 1769, they were perfected by Graber in 1894. The olives turn a cherry-red color when they are allowed to ripen naturally on the trees, but after curing and canning, the shades vary. The trees have a soft, gray-green leaf and a gnarled trunk, making them look aged. Olive trees are hardy, with a significant root system that allows them to persevere through drought, disease, and fire. Olive trees can live for a long time, with an average life expectancy of 500 years.

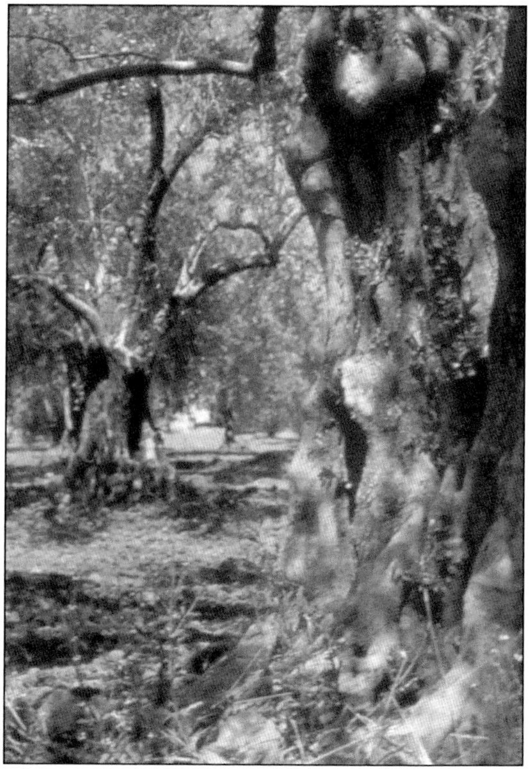

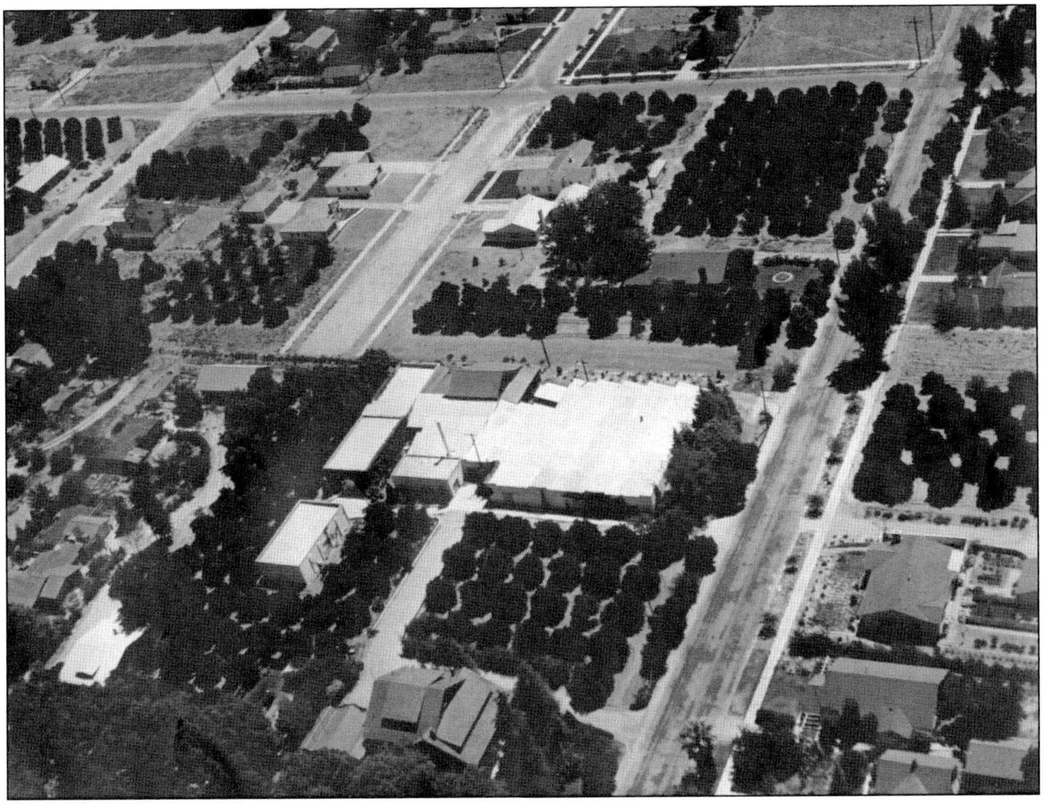

The Graber home and olive house is located in what would later become the College Park Tract, subdivided in 1914 by Lydia Belle Ford. It was one of the first subdivisions in Southern California to feature underground utilities and ornamental streetlights. Several early pioneers lived in College Park, including Benton Ballou, Judge Archie Mitchell, and Gardiner Spring. While the lots were put up for sale in 1914 by Parkford Realty Company, most of the homes in the tract were constructed in the 1920s, making the Graber homestead (above) one of the oldest in the subdivision, encompassing the greatest area. Graber continued to harvest olives from the abandoned grove nearby until the land came up for sale in the early 1920s. Graber could not afford to purchase the land, so he moved the growing operations to Hemet.

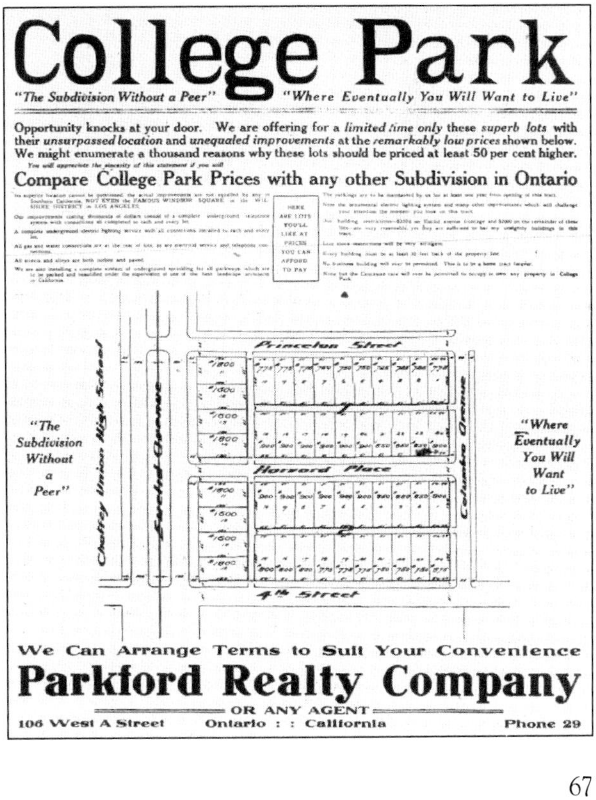

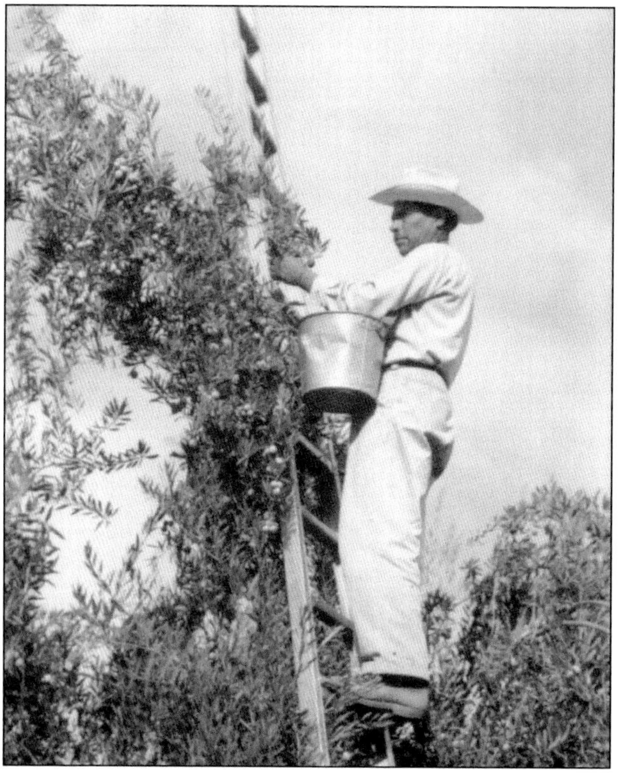

The olives are carefully picked in the fall, after most other fruit has been harvested. Pickers may go over each tree many times, picking only olives that have fully ripened. Picking has always been done by hand using a container with a felt bottom, keeping the fruit free of bruises. Pickers only take three or four olives in each hand at one time to avoid damaging the delicate fruit. In the early days, most pickers were Mexican migrant workers from a labor camp near Hemet, but the camp closed in 1963. Graber Olives then purchased land in the San Joaquin Valley. Called Round Valley Ranch (below), the growing site is located near the city of Lindsay, which has an ideal climate for growing olives. Olives are delivered by truck at night to avoid the fruit shrinking in the central California heat.

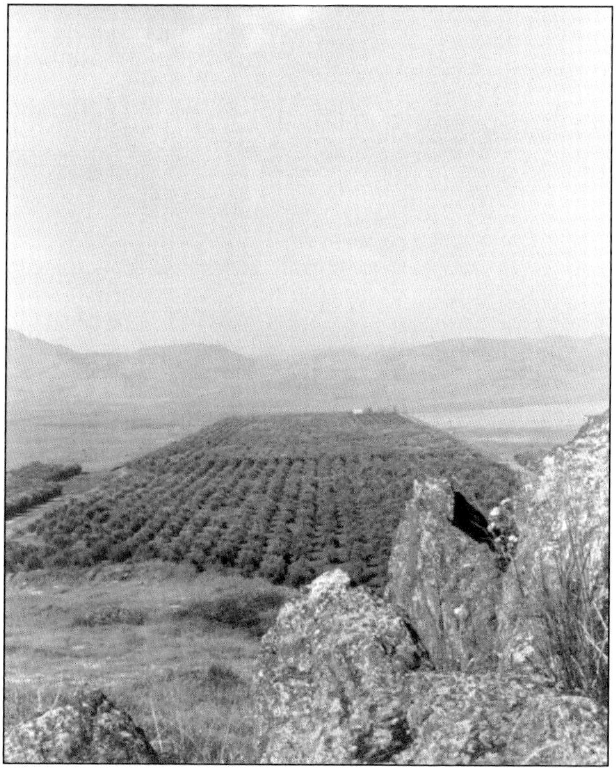

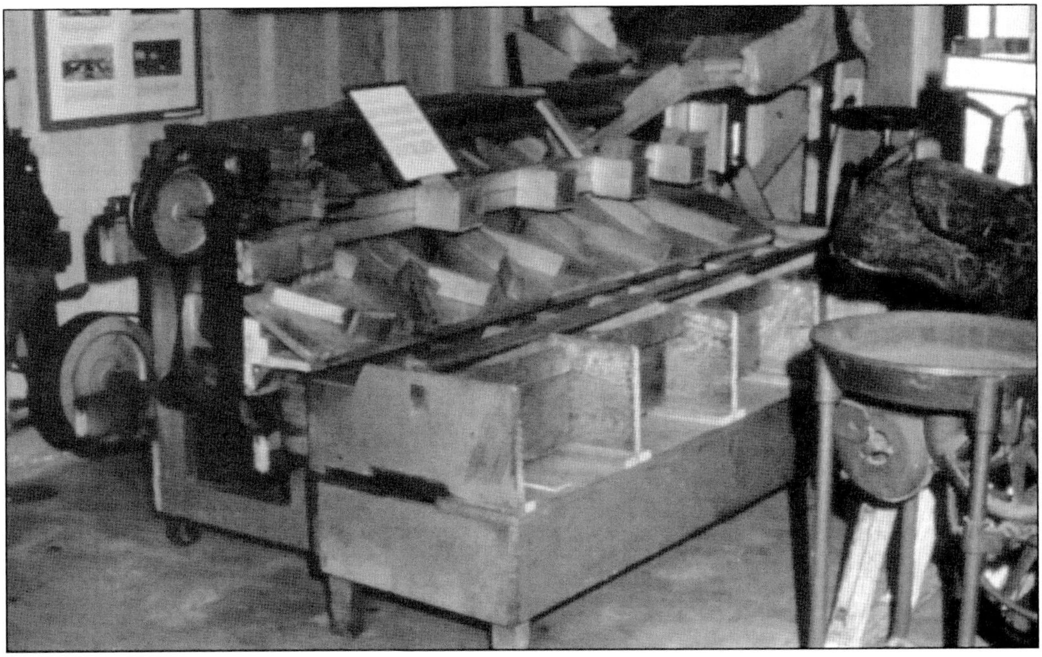

Olives are unpacked and then sorted by size using a grading machine developed and built by Clifford Graber many decades ago. Hearing from customers that they wanted olives to be a uniform size, Graber created an innovative machine to sort the fruit. Sorting the olives in this way was revolutionary in the industry, as there were no standard sizes at the time. He measured the diameter to a sixteenth of an inch and sorted like-sized olives together. Olives are poured in at one end, and workers remove imperfect olives from the line as the rest slide through. The rollers taper, allowing the grader to drop the correct-sized olives onto a soft, stretched canvas. The machine was designed to be powered by a Ford Model T motor, and is still in operation. Today, over one million olives can pass through the grader during one day.

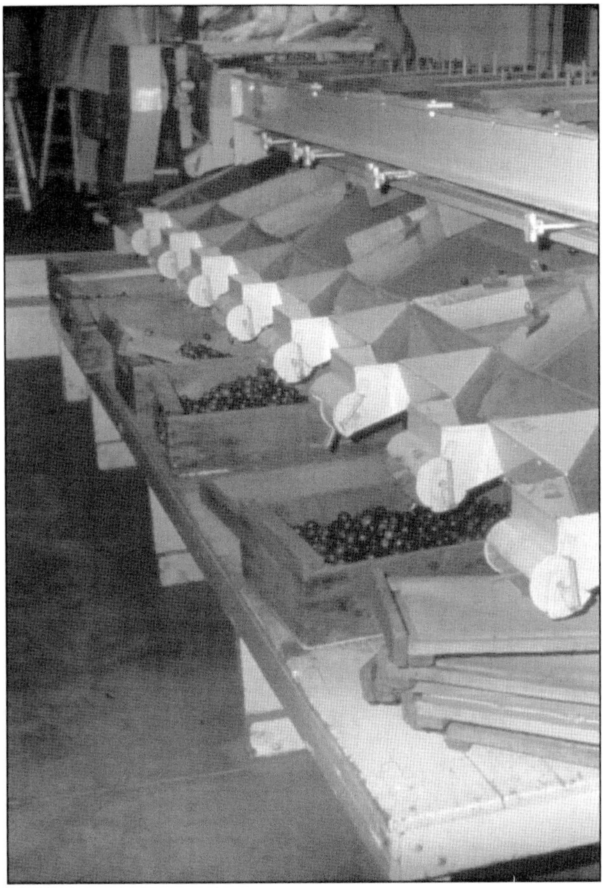

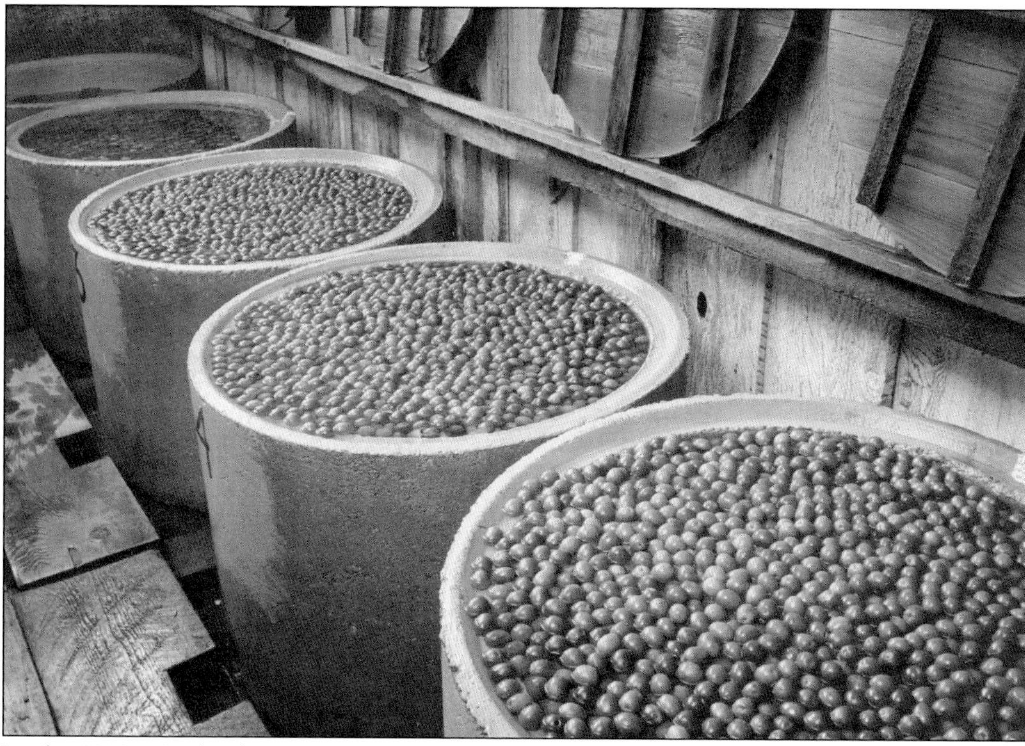

In the 1890s, Graber began to experiment with curing olives through borrowed recipes. The brining cure is a secret family recipe developed by Clifford Graber, based on a recipe he obtained in the 1890s from the University of California at Davis, which became the foundation for his secret olive cure, still used today. Olives must be cured before they are eaten to remove a bitter substance and make them edible. After being sorted, Graber olives are cured for two to three weeks in one of 500 vats filled with brine. The brine is changed daily, and the vats are carefully weighed and checked for quality aging.

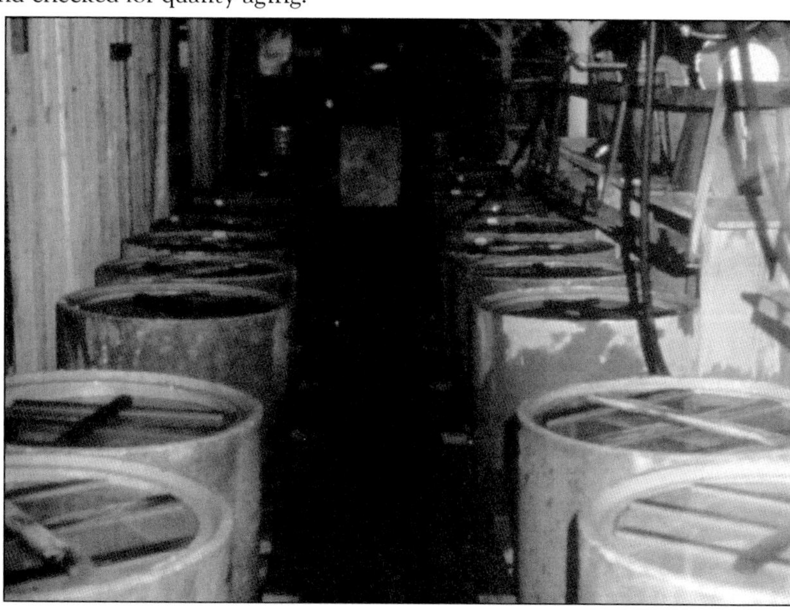

After being cured and placed into cans with other like-sized olives, 200-degree water is added to the cans. The lids are sealed by a machine that can seal approximately 750,000 cans per season. The cans are then packed 300 at a time into a pressure cooker for about one hour with 12 pounds of steam pressure applied at 242 degrees. An engineer monitors the machines for quality control, ensuring the best olives possible.

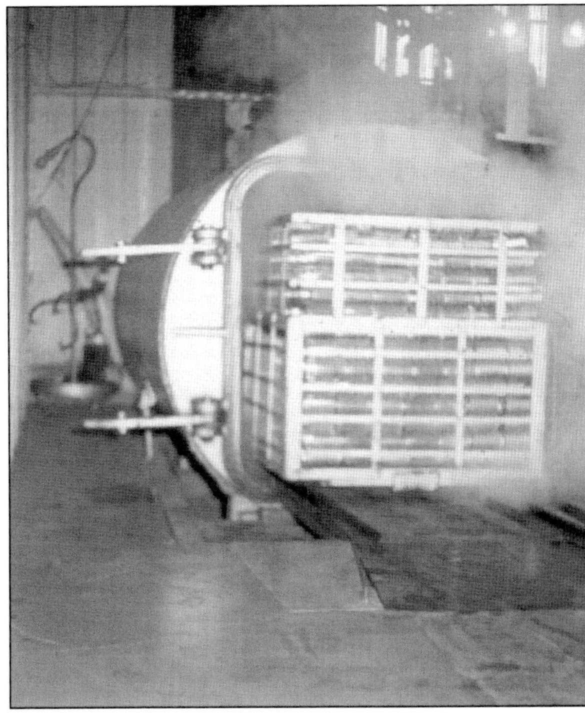

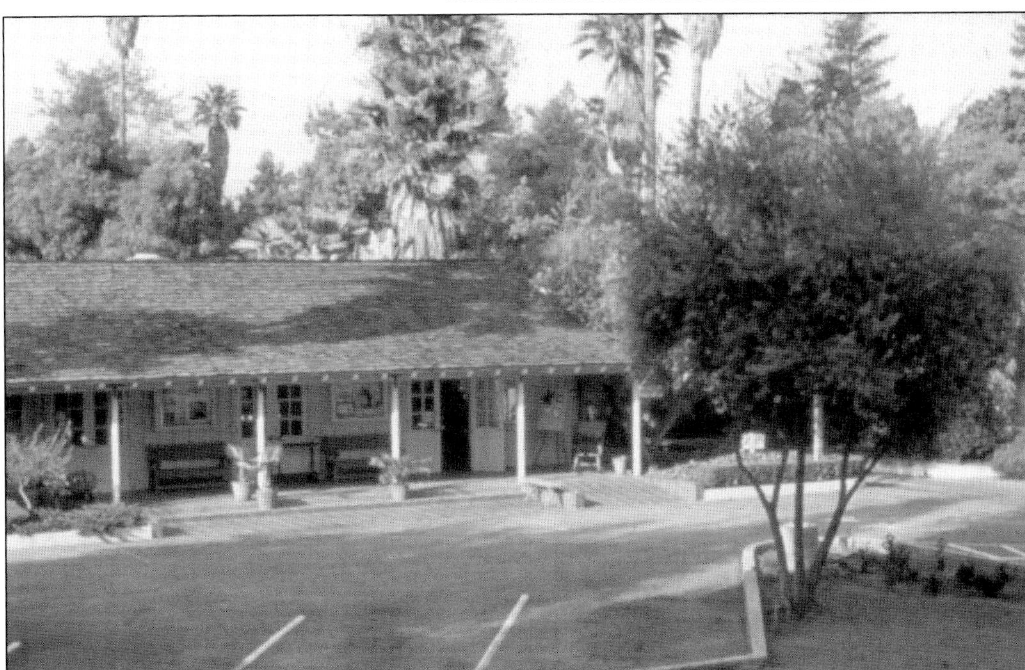

Clifford and Georgia Belle Graber ran the olive house until 1943, when their sons Robert and William, along with their son-in-law Donald Curry, purchased the business. Although he had sold the business to family, Graber continued to be involved in the day-to-day operations until his death in 1955. Many seasonal employees return every year to help harvest, cure, can, and sell olives, particularly at Christmastime.

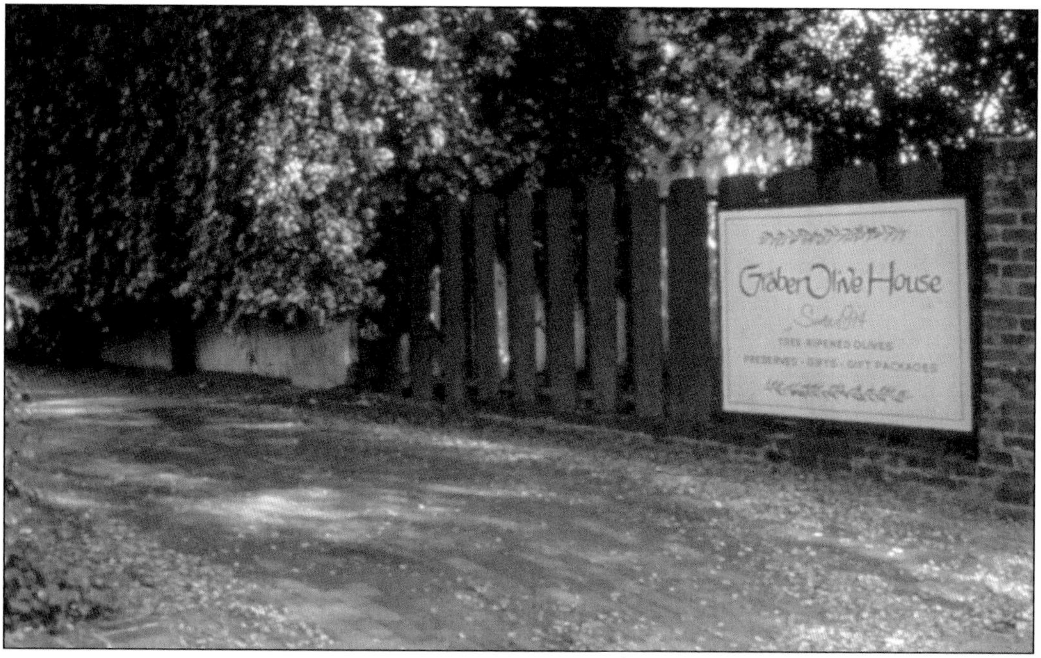

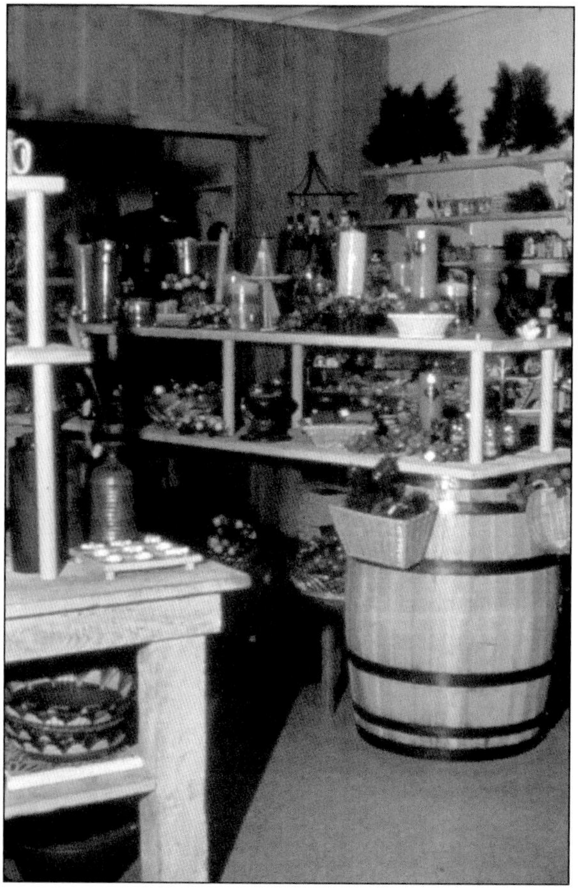

The grounds at Graber are inviting and a reminder of times past. The old olive mill sits in the yard, surrounded by the lawn and redwood, walnut, palm, citrus, and, of course, olive trees. A portion of the original packing shed has been turned into a small museum that houses memorabilia from days gone by.

In 1963, after an olive shortage, Betty Graber expanded the retail operations to include specialty products, and the shop became known as Casa del Olivo. The Graber site now features two shops that include specialty foods, unique gifts, and kitchen tools and are decorated with lovely paintings, ceramics, and art. Visitors are welcome to explore the grounds, bask in the serene setting, and tour the historic plant that is still used today.

Six

Secondo Guasti and the Italian Vineyard Company

One of Southern California's earliest vineyards was planted over 200 years ago by the Franciscans at Mission San Gabriel Arcángel. This and other mission vineyards flourished in Southern California's arid climate, and their success later led to the establishment of commercial wineries in California.

The first vineyard in the Cucamonga area was planted by Tiburcio Tapia around 1840 using local Native Americans for labor. His winery building, one of the oldest buildings in the area, would later become Thomas Brothers Winery and still stands today on the corner of Foothill Boulevard and Vineyard Avenue in Rancho Cucamonga.

The Italian Vineyard Company was established in 1900 by Italian native Secondo Guasti in an area between Ontario and Cucamonga just north of the present Ontario International Airport. This successful winery was built as a company town called Guasti, where Italian winemakers, coopers, and other skilled laborers lived and worked. Almost every step in winemaking was done on-site, from transporting the grapes from the fields by narrow-gauge rail to crushing them, building the wine casks, and storing and bottling the wine. The field work, like in the citrus industry, was initially done primarily by Asian workers before there was a large migration of Mexican and Mexican American workers in the late 1910s and 1920s as a result of exclusionary laws. These workers were not allowed to live in the company town and were housed in labor camps south of the property.

Secondo Guasti, who died in 1927, left the family business to his son Secondo Guasti II. In poor health, Secondo II died in 1934, and his mother, Louisa, died in 1937. The Italian Vineyard Company was purchased by Garrett & Company in 1945 and then by the Biane family in 1957, which ran Brookside Winery on the site until the 1980s.

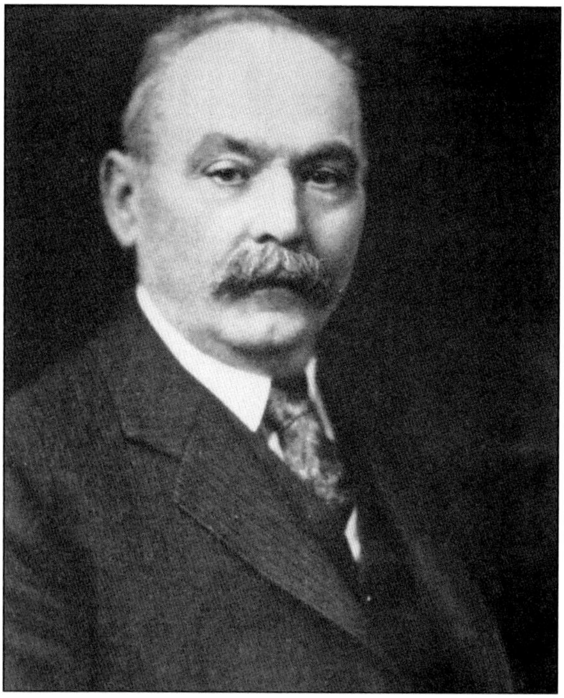

Secondo Guasti was born in the Piedmont region of Italy in 1859. He arrived in Los Angeles in 1883 and worked as a cook at an Italian restaurant, where he met Louisa Armillo, his future wife and the daughter of his employer. In 1887, Secondo, 28, married Louisa, 16, and went to work as a wine merchant.

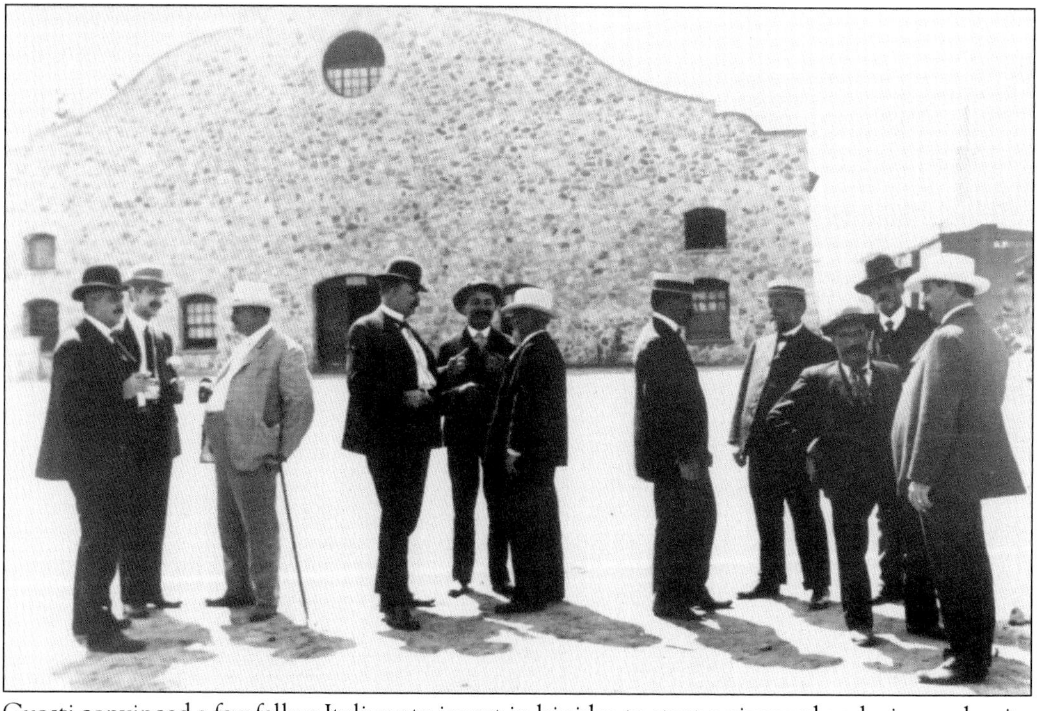

Guasti convinced a few fellow Italians to invest in his idea to start a vineyard and winery, despite the sandy, dry location just south of Cucamonga. He determined that there was enough moisture below the surface to sustain grape vines, as others had been growing non-irrigated grapes in the region for decades. In 1900, Guasti founded the Italian Vineyard Company, located just north of what is now Ontario International Airport.

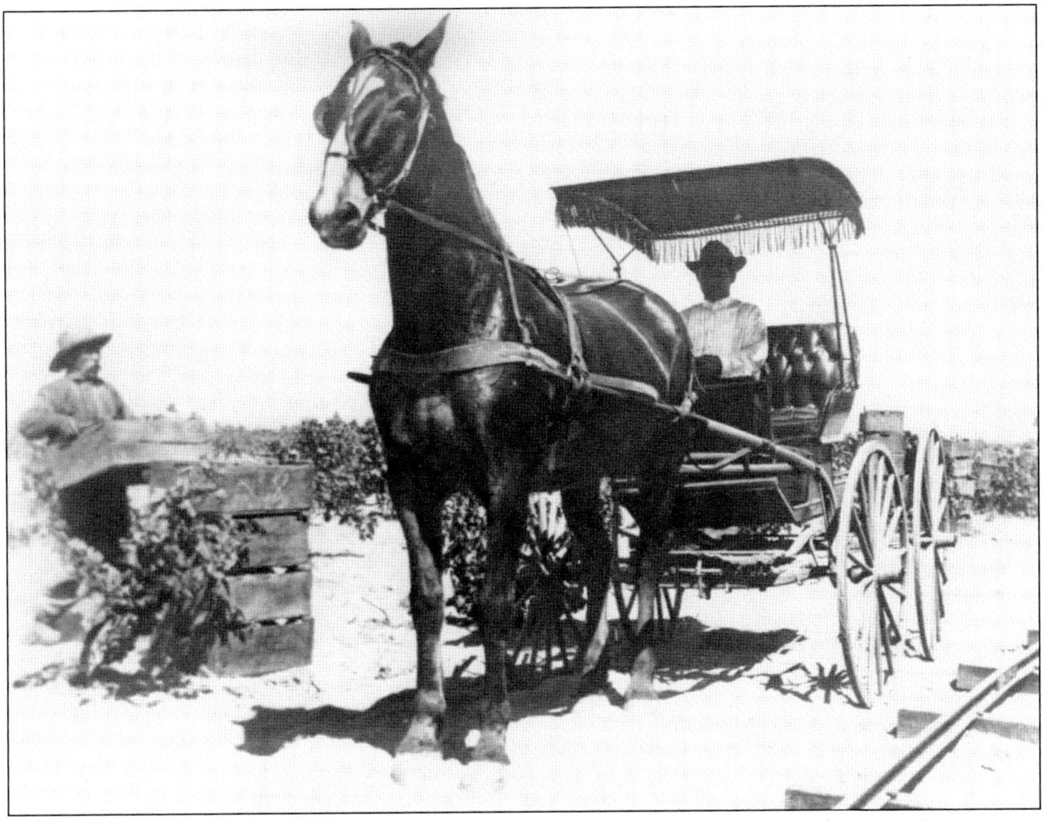

Antonio Signorio, sitting in the buggy, was the Italian Vineyard Company's foreman. He was one of the company's original stockholders, and as a vineyard expert, was asked by Guasti to examine the soil at the initial stockholder meeting before the land was purchased. Signorio had already attempted his own winery in the area a few years before, so he knew the soil was perfect for grape vines. After the land was purchased, Signorio oversaw the planting of the vines.

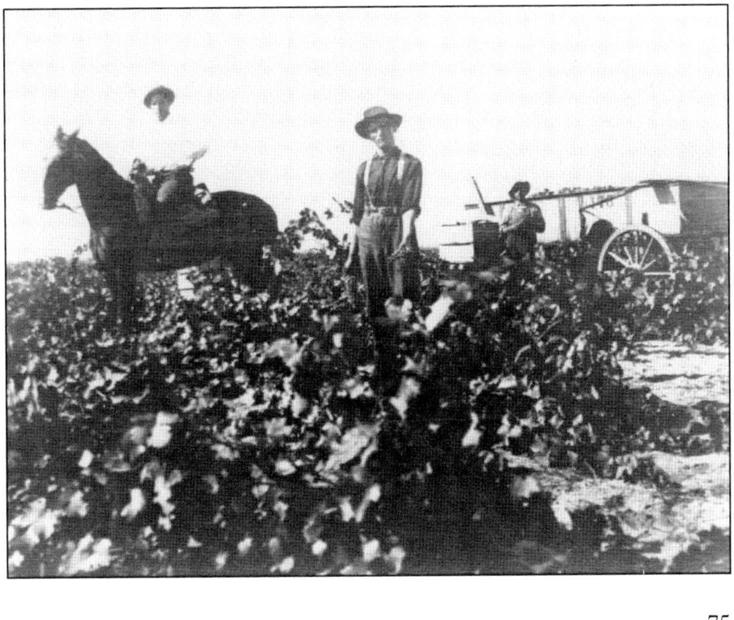

After a long drought the vines finally flourished, and in 1908, the first wines were produced. Guasti recruited other Italians to work at the Italian Vineyard Company, and other workers, including Hispanics, Asians, and African Americans, were hired as migrant workers. The Italian workers lived within Guasti, but all other workers were segregated, living in various labor camps south of the compound.

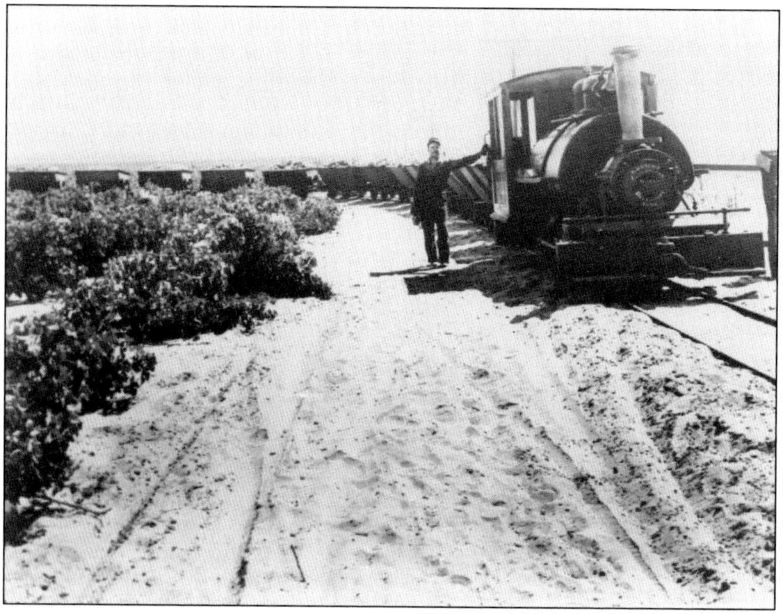

Instead of relying solely on livestock to transport the grapes, the Italian Vineyard Company installed a unique narrow-gauge railroad system in 1910. The tracks were mobile and could be moved throughout the fields depending on the need, greatly increasing the efficiency of the harvest. The steam-powered train could pull 40 carloads of grapes along 20 miles of track.

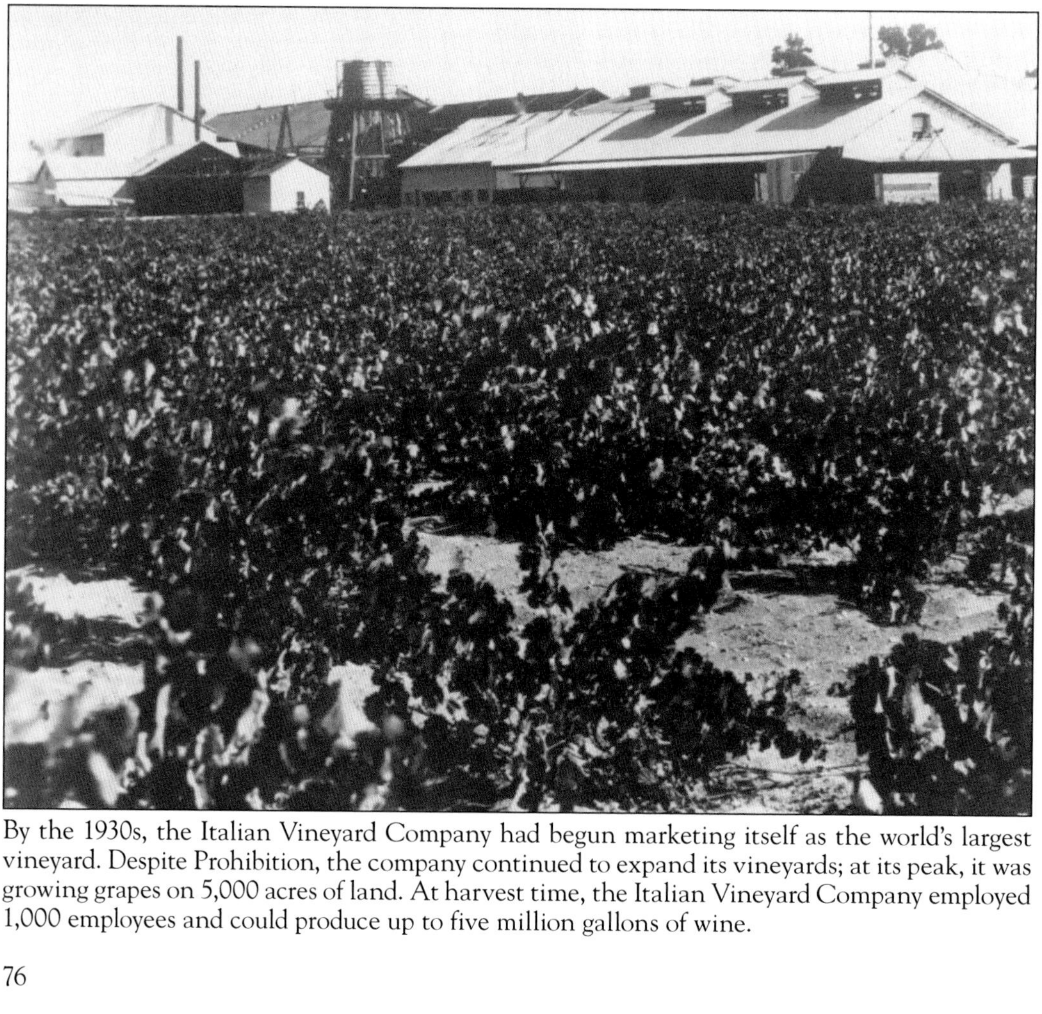

By the 1930s, the Italian Vineyard Company had begun marketing itself as the world's largest vineyard. Despite Prohibition, the company continued to expand its vineyards; at its peak, it was growing grapes on 5,000 acres of land. At harvest time, the Italian Vineyard Company employed 1,000 employees and could produce up to five million gallons of wine.

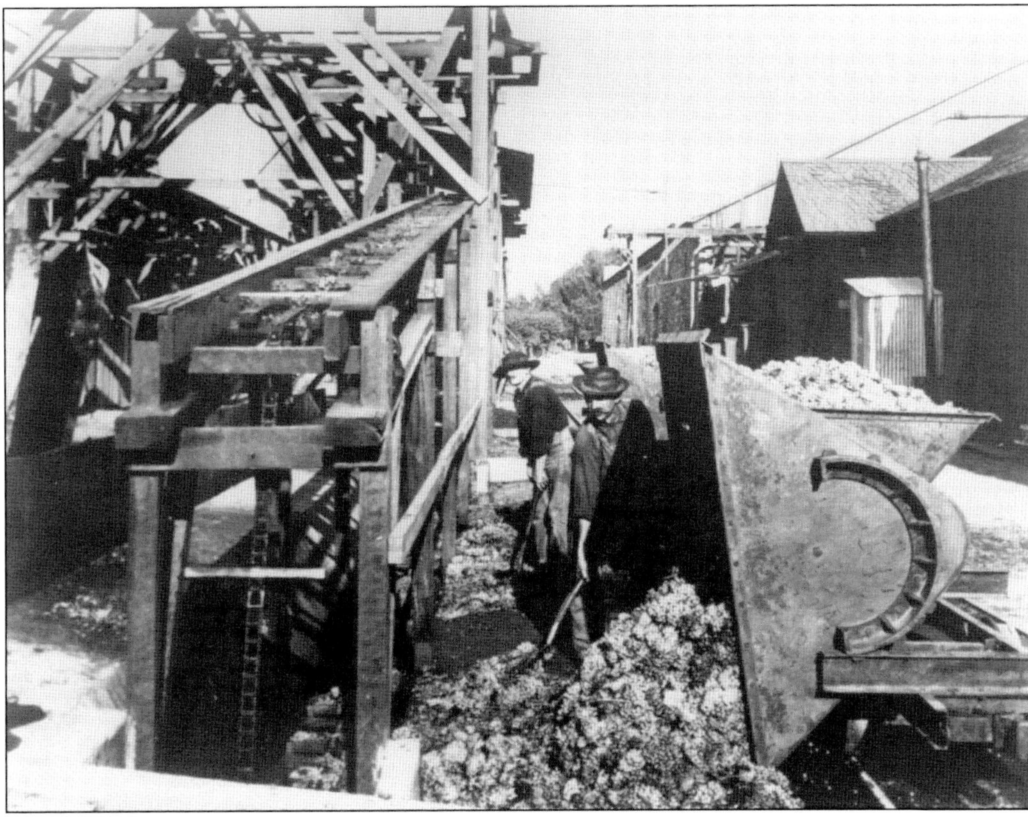

Despite popular belief, grapes have not been crushed under foot for a very long time. In fact, grapes were never trampled underfoot at the Italian Vineyard Company, as the winery was built as a modern factory. In the early days, the vineyard train would deliver the grapes to the crusher, where they were dumped as workers shoveled them toward the crusher.

Later, the grapes were delivered from the field by truck and dumped onto the crusher. Crushing the grapes is necessary for fermentation, and speed is necessary in order to discourage bacterial infestation. Modern crushers, as opposed to traditional foot crushing, get the job done much faster, allowing the juice to reach the fermentation vats more efficiently.

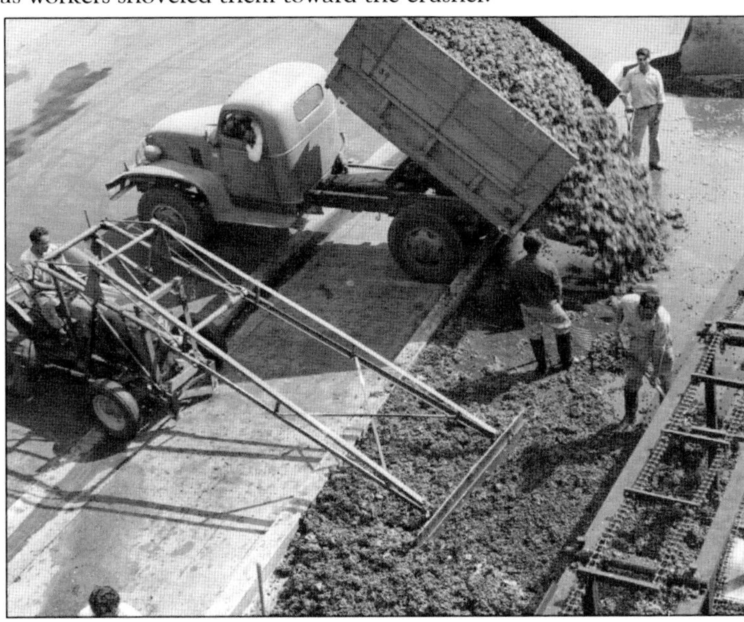

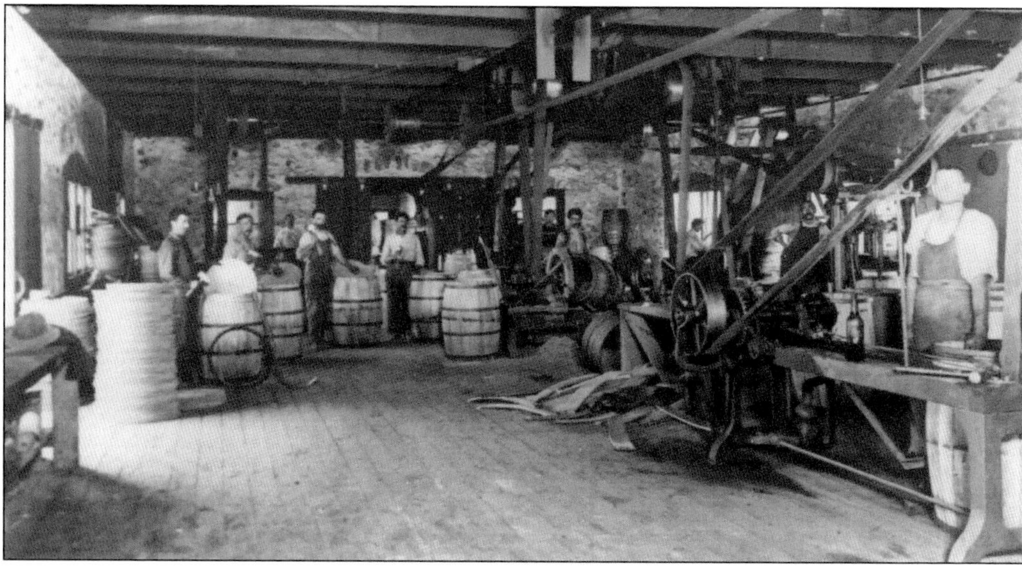

Because Guasti was developed as the Italian Vineyard Company's "company town," nearly every aspect of winemaking was done on-site. This included the manufacture, maintenance, and repair of wooden wine barrels, vats, and tanks managed by the Italian Vineyard Company's cooperage. A cooper is someone who is specially trained in the manufacture of wooden vessels, and the profession dates to ancient times.

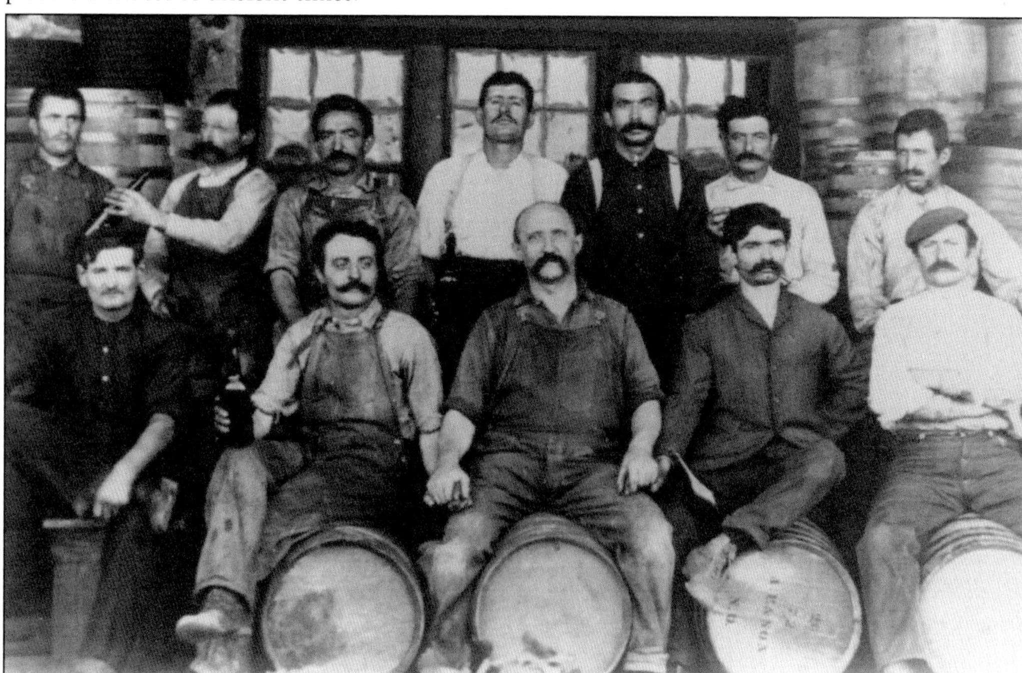

These coopers were master craftsmen who were recruited by Secondo Guasti to bring their expertise from Europe to California. Those wishing to enter the profession worked as apprentices and trained to become master coopers. Most coopers in Europe were members of local cooperage guilds, which helped to ensure the integrity of their craft. In the wine industry, wooden storage vessels are made primarily of oak imported from Europe.

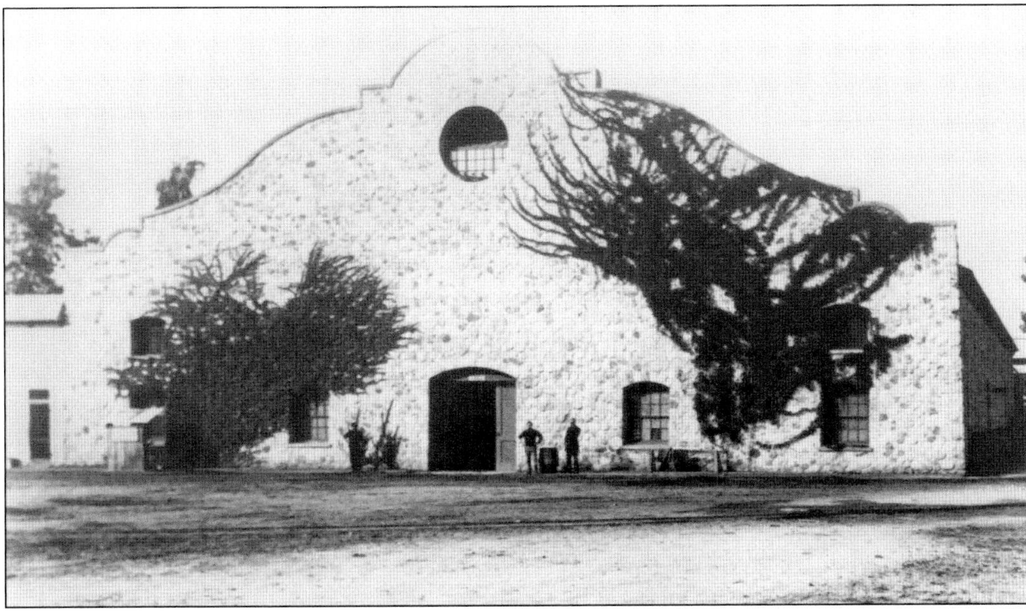

Stone chateau buildings such as this one at the Italian Vineyard Company provided a naturally cool environment for fermenting, aging, and storing wine before the luxury of electronic climate control was available. The stone chateau building was built from stones hauled down from the foothills in Alta Loma at the turn of the 20th century.

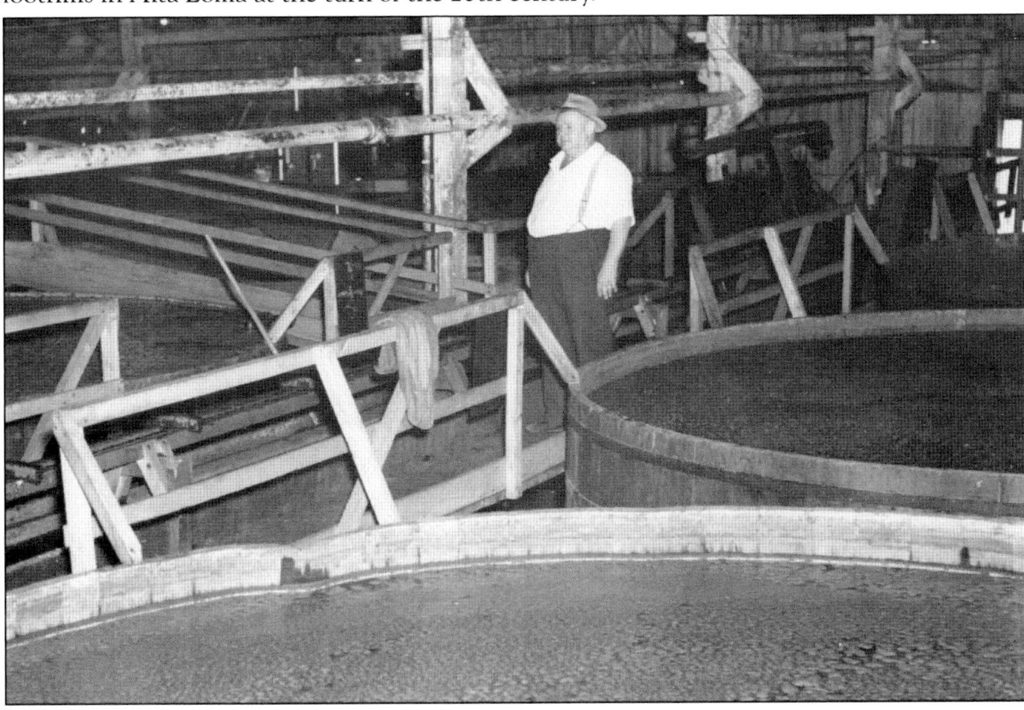

The production of wine at the Italian Vineyard Company was so immense that the fermenting vats were enormous and required that scaffolding be built in order for workers to access the wine for testing and monitoring. The cooperage crafted the wooden vats, which continue to be widely used for the fermentation of red wine.

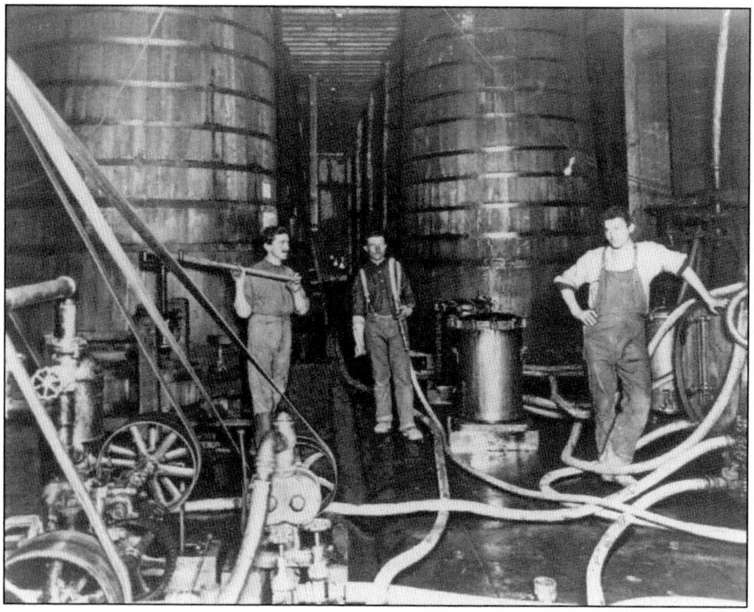

This photograph reveals the chai room and workers at the Italian Vineyard Company around 1910. Chai, pronounced "shay," is a French term for an over-ground storage building or barrel hall. Wine would be pumped into large wooden barrels and stored during the aging process prior to bottling, as seen here. Most chai rooms are built to stay cool like an underground wine cellar.

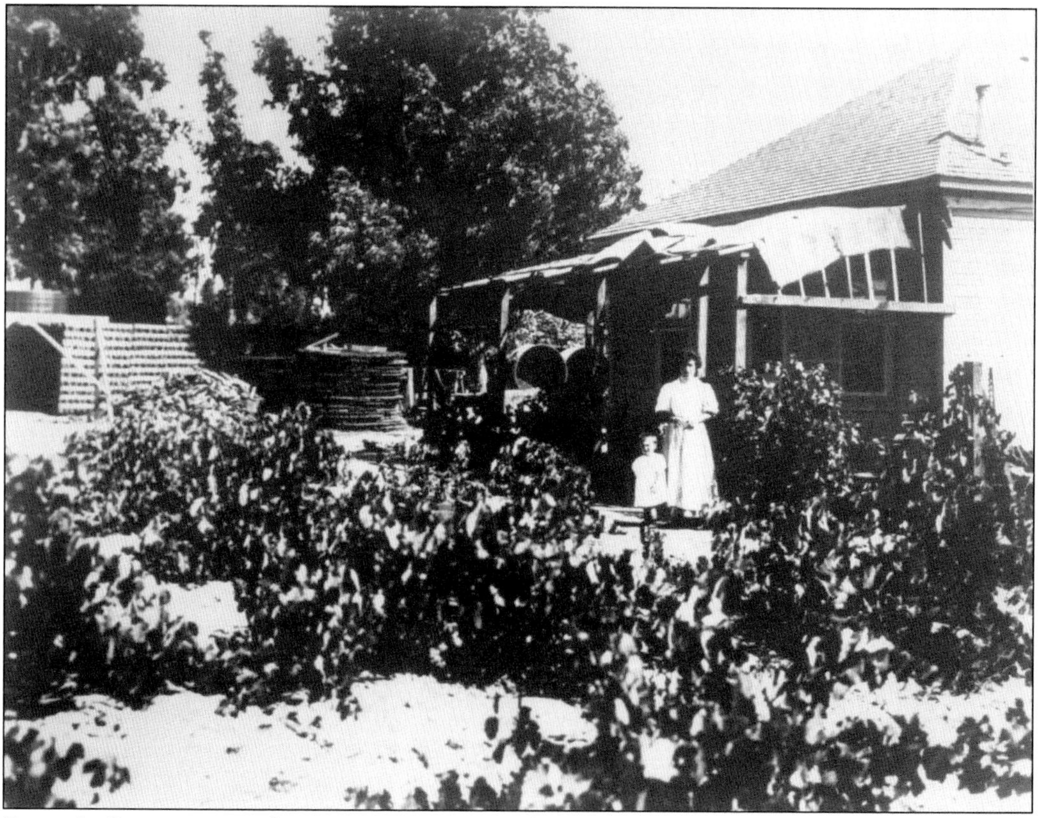

Secondo Guasti recruited permanent winery workers from his native Italy and set up an entire town within the winery itself. The town of Guasti was complete with small clapboard cottages such as this one for workers with families. The children attended a school on-site, and the married women prepared food for the unmarried workers. Everyone in Guasti had their responsibilities.

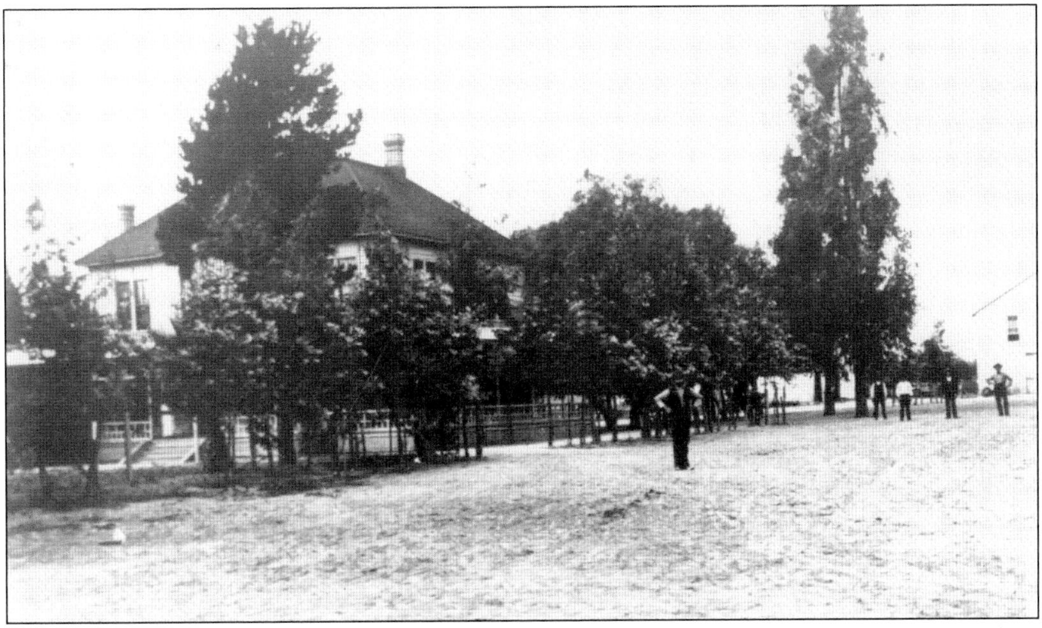

The "big house," as it was called, was originally built to house the Guasti family and Italian Vineyard Company shareholders when they visited from Los Angeles. Later, Secondo Guasti had a Mediterranean-style mansion built for his son and daughter-in-law as their permanent residence, and this house was moved to another location on the property. Secondo and Louisa Guasti resided in a large mansion in the West Adams district in Los Angeles.

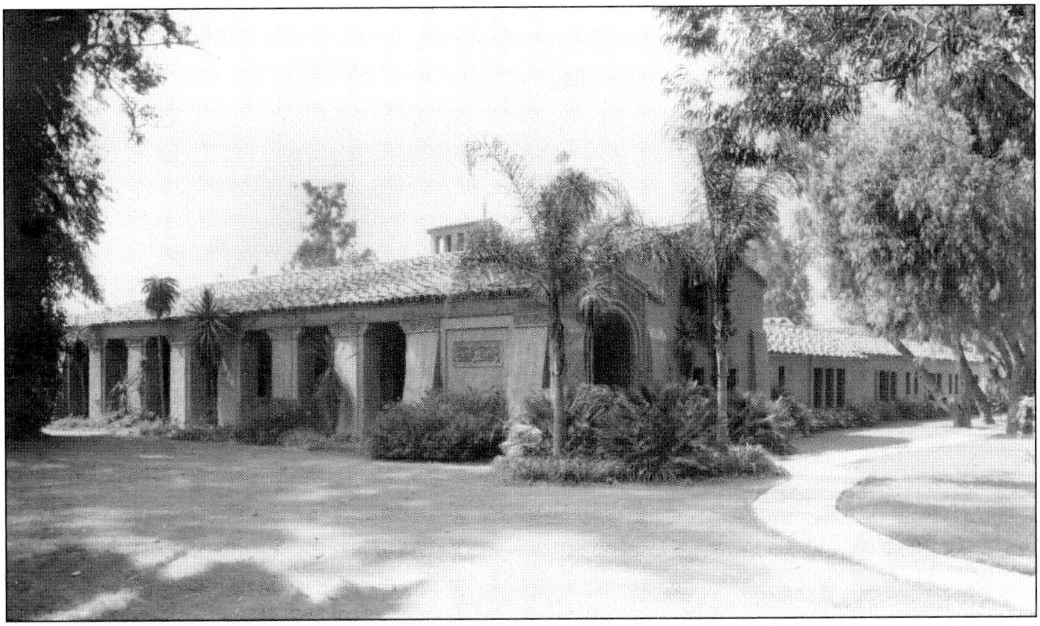

Begun in 1923, the Guasti mansion was built by Secondo Guasti for his only son, Secondo Guasti II, and his new bride. Costing $108,000 to build, the equivalent of several million dollars today, the extravagant Spanish-style residence boasted 20 rooms, six bathrooms, and three fireplaces. The mansion was designed by Los Angeles–based Morgan, Walls, & Clements, well-known for designing such buildings as the El Capitan and Pantages Theaters in Hollywood.

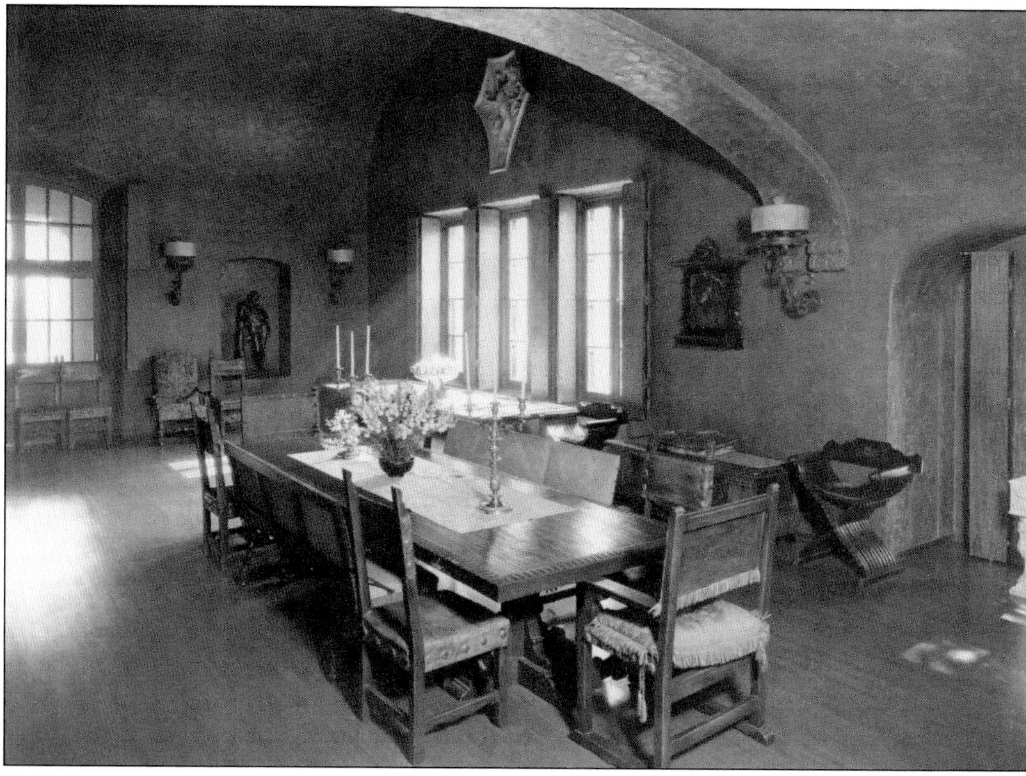

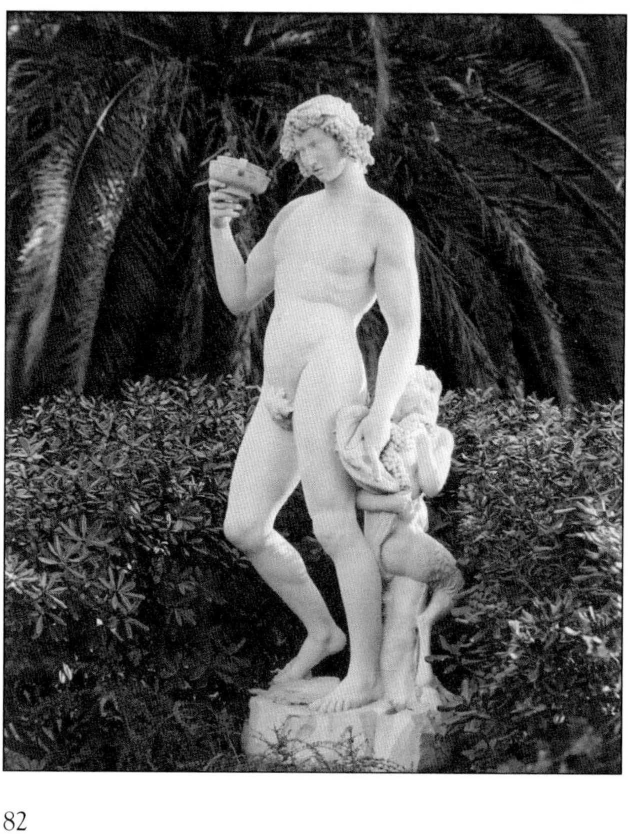

The interior of the mansion featured dome ceilings, which can be seen here in the dining room, and was decorated by Mrs. Guasti and her new daughter-in-law. The ladies traveled to Italy to shop for furnishings, and Hollywood set designer Norman Kennedy was commissioned to paint murals inside the mansion.

The mansion's exterior was spared no expense either, and included an aviary, a tennis court, luscious gardens, a central courtyard with a marble fountain, 15th-century della Robbia terra-cotta sculptures, and marble sculptures such as this piece depicting Bacchus, the Roman god of wine. A swimming pool was added by a later owner.

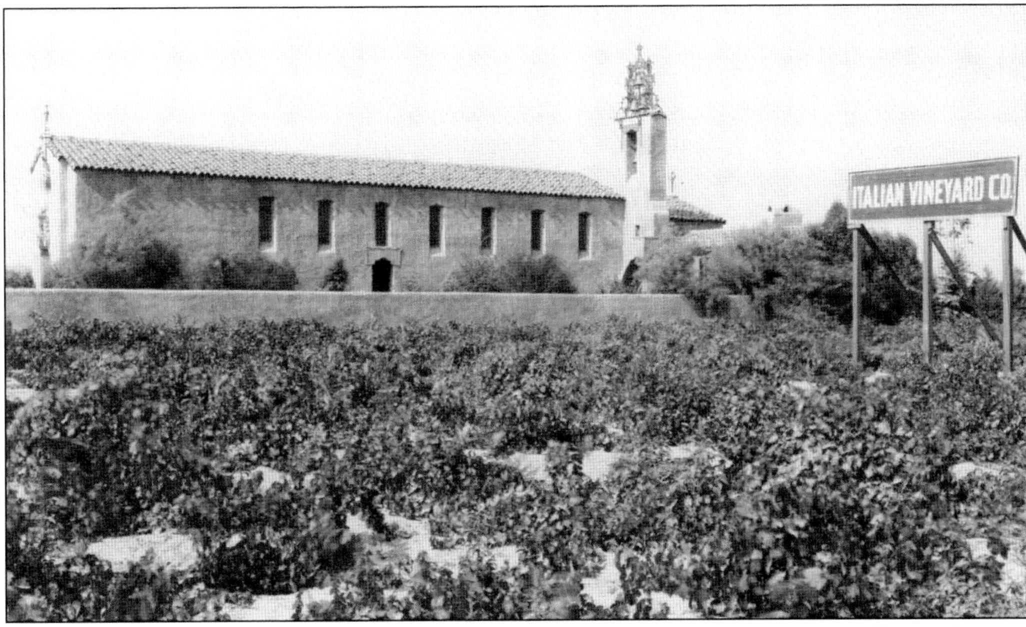

The Church of San Secondo d'Asti was built between 1924 and 1926 for the residents of Guasti. While not an exact replica, the church was designed to resemble the 17th-century San Secondo d'Asti church in Guasti's birthplace of Asti, in Italy's Piedmont region. The Hispanic workers and their families who lived in the labor camp outside Guasti were welcomed but segregated, attending separate services from the Italian residents.

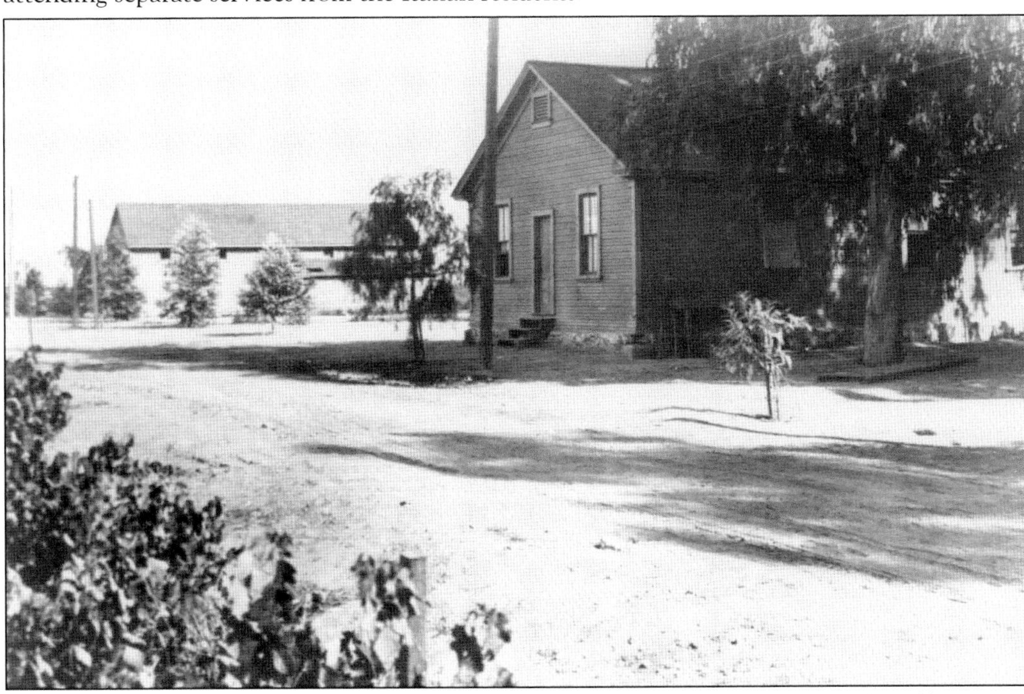

Many of the unmarried workers lived in shared residential quarters, but some rented small one-room cottages. The cottages did not have kitchen facilities, so the men living in these quarters would go to the boardinghouse for their meals, prepared by some of the married women in the town.

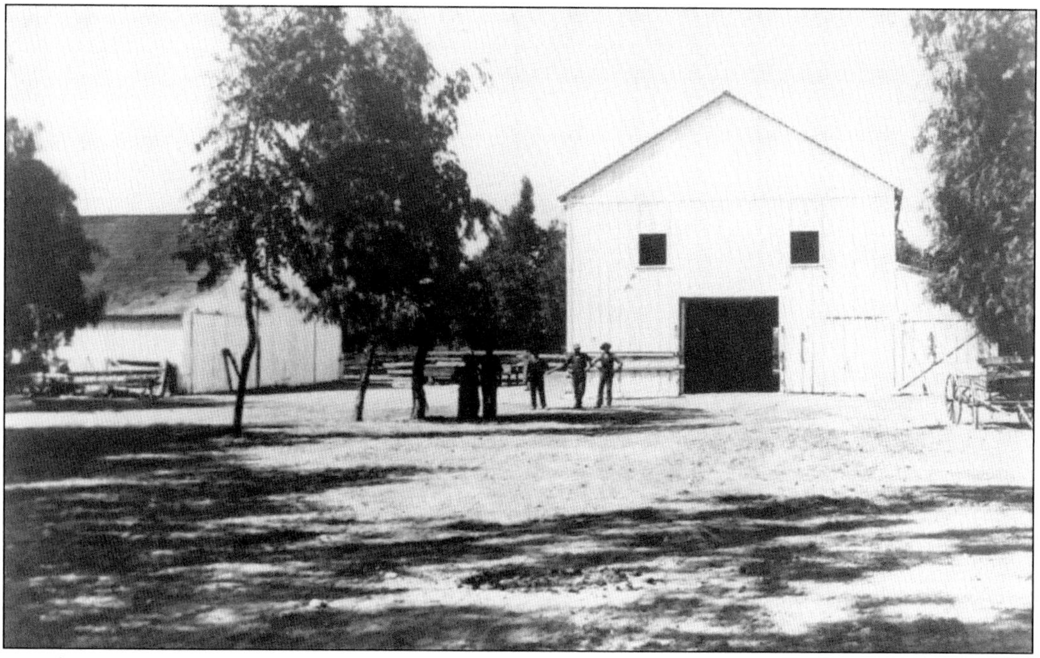

Families lived and grew in Guasti for generations, and its residents were close-knit. In addition to housing, a grocery, a bakery, a post office, and a fire station were also established in the town. However, the non-Italian workers in labor camps south of Guasti often lived in harsh conditions with little comforts and conveniences. Disease and high infant mortality rates were commonplace in the camps in the early 1920s.

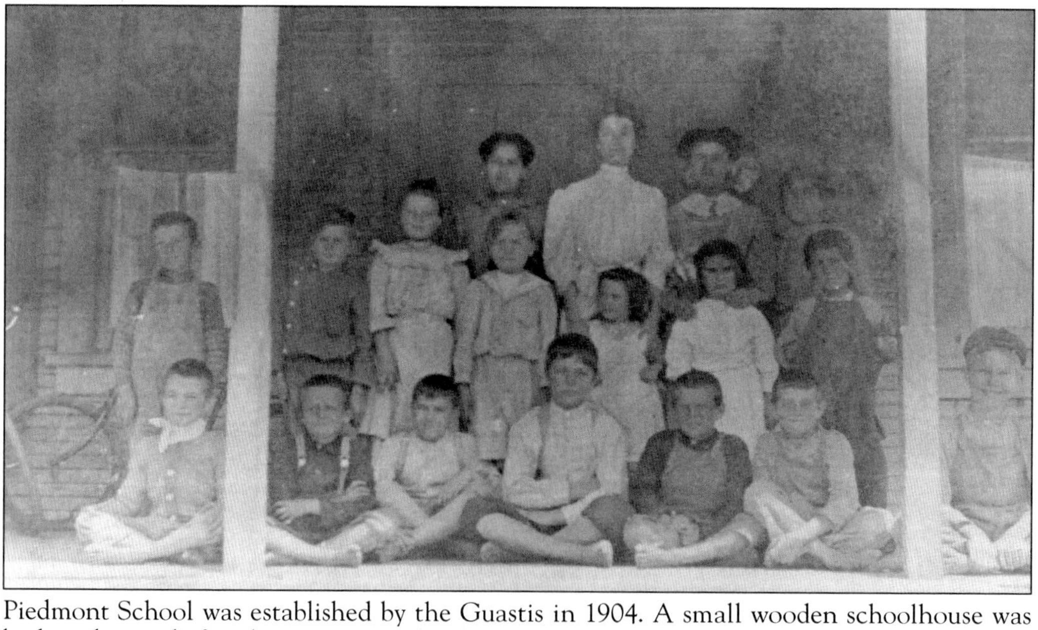

Piedmont School was established by the Guastis in 1904. A small wooden schoolhouse was built and named after the region in Italy where Guasti was from, and he deeded the land to the Piedmont School District for $5. This photograph, taken in 1908, shows children from the school's first class. This building burned down in 1935, and Louisa Guasti School was erected in its place using funds from the Work Projects Administration.

Seven

The Development of Hotpoint

Earl Holmes "E.H." Richardson was born in Wisconsin in 1871. Energetic as a child, he took to electricity after sitting in on some high school lectures, which led to a job with an electric company in Illinois. His wife was told to move to a drier climate for her health, so they came to Southern California, where he was hired by Charles Frankish and worked for the Ontario Electric Company, managing the "Stone Castle" powerhouse in San Antonio canyon.

Noticing that customers only used power at night to light their electric bulbs, he and friend Harry Strunk built several small electric appliances that they gave away to power customers to encourage an increase in daytime electric usage. In May 1904, he incorporated the Pacific Electric Heating Company, renamed the Hotpoint Electric Heating Company in 1912. It became the largest electrical appliance manufacturer in the world. Besides irons, the company made electric hot plates, coffee pots, chafing dishes, and teapots, among other household appliances. During World War I, they made electric aviator suits to keep pilots warm in unheated cockpits.

The company attracted the notice of General Electric, and it merged with the large conglomerate in 1918 and was renamed the Edison Electric Appliance Company. Later, it would be known as the General Electric Ontario Works. Richardson continued as the general manager of the Ontario plant but died in 1934 due to poor health after a failed real estate endeavor in Adelanto. His Hotpoint legacy lived on until 1982, when General Electric closed the Ontario plant.

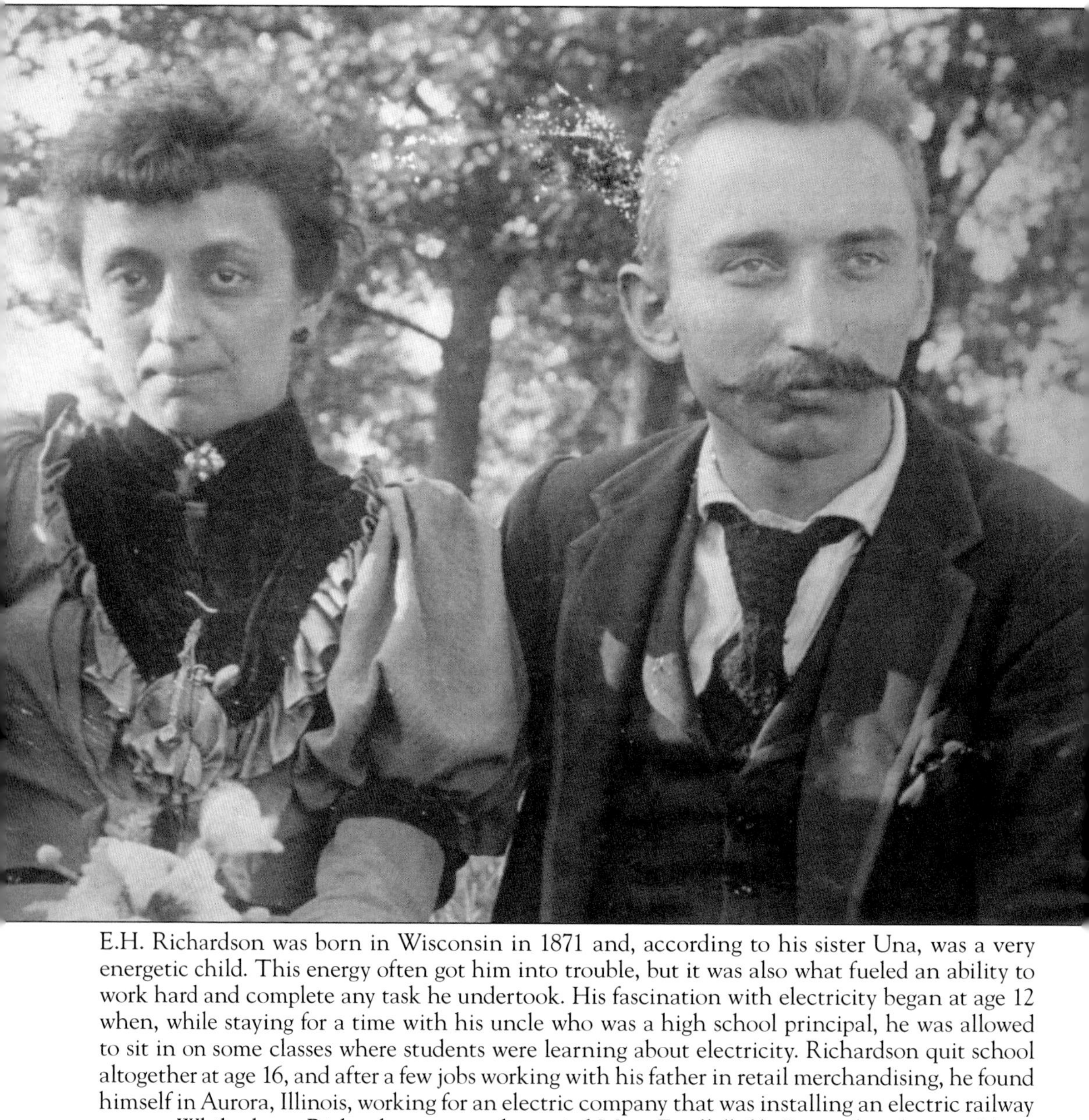

E.H. Richardson was born in Wisconsin in 1871 and, according to his sister Una, was a very energetic child. This energy often got him into trouble, but it was also what fueled an ability to work hard and complete any task he undertook. His fascination with electricity began at age 12 when, while staying for a time with his uncle who was a high school principal, he was allowed to sit in on some classes where students were learning about electricity. Richardson quit school altogether at age 16, and after a few jobs working with his father in retail merchandising, he found himself in Aurora, Illinois, working for an electric company that was installing an electric railway system. While there, Richardson met and married Mary Essell (left). Soon after their wedding, Mary was diagnosed with tuberculosis and was advised to move to a dry climate for her health. The Richardsons decided to come to California, and they arrived in Pomona in 1895.

After some time looking for work, Richardson, pictured here in his later years, was hired by Charles Frankish to fix a generator at the Stone Castle powerhouse in the San Antonio Canyon. He succeeded in fixing this generator, and this success landed him a two-year job as superintendent of a streetcar company in San Diego. He returned to Ontario and was hired again by Charles Frankish to manage the Stone Castle powerhouse.

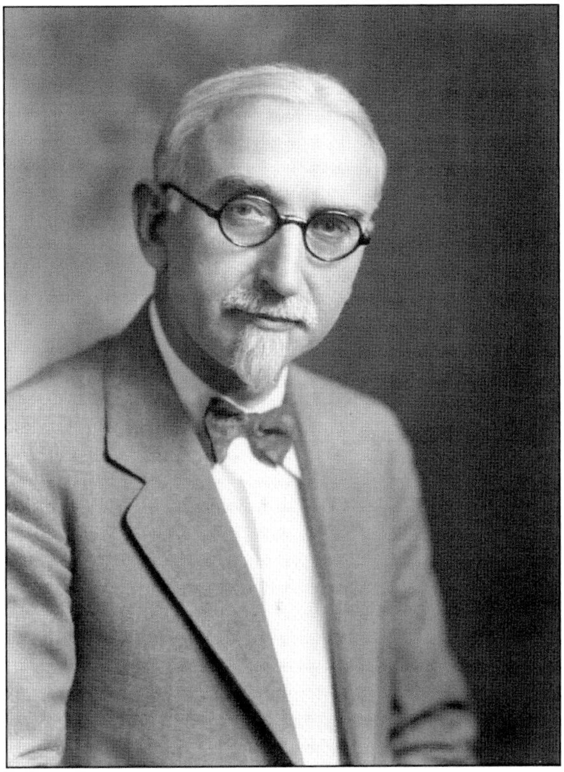

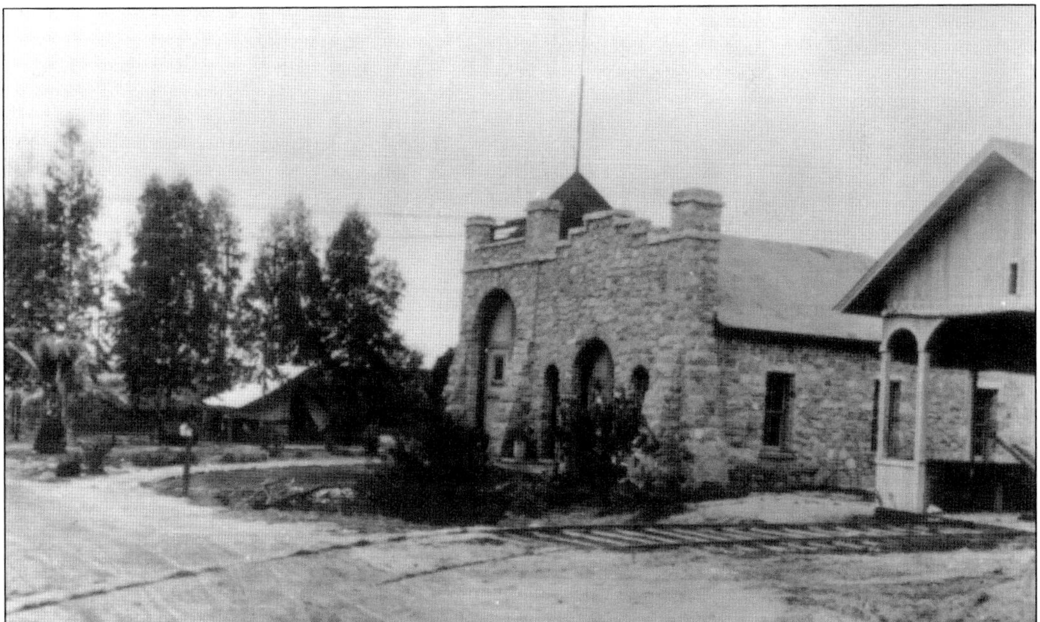

For the next few years, the Richardsons lived in a small tent home in the San Antonio Canyon next to the Stone Castle (pictured). Their daughter Ardis was born in 1899. Richardson spent his free time building small household appliances to help make their lives warmer and more comfortable. This included a room heater, a hotplate, and a flatiron.

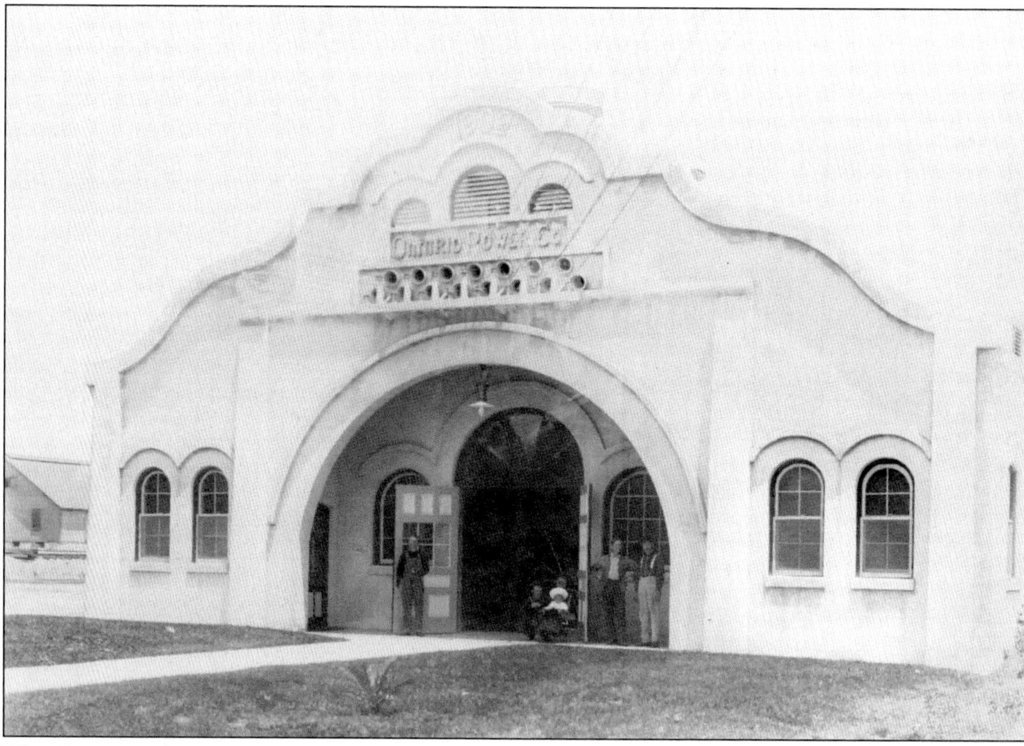

The Ontario Electric Company was taken over by the Ontario Power Company in 1902, and a new substation (pictured) was built on Euclid Avenue near the Santa Fe tracks in what is now Upland. Richardson was made electrical engineer, and the family moved into an apartment at the new substation. The power company saw that the plant was only generating electricity at night, as residents were only using power for lighting after dark.

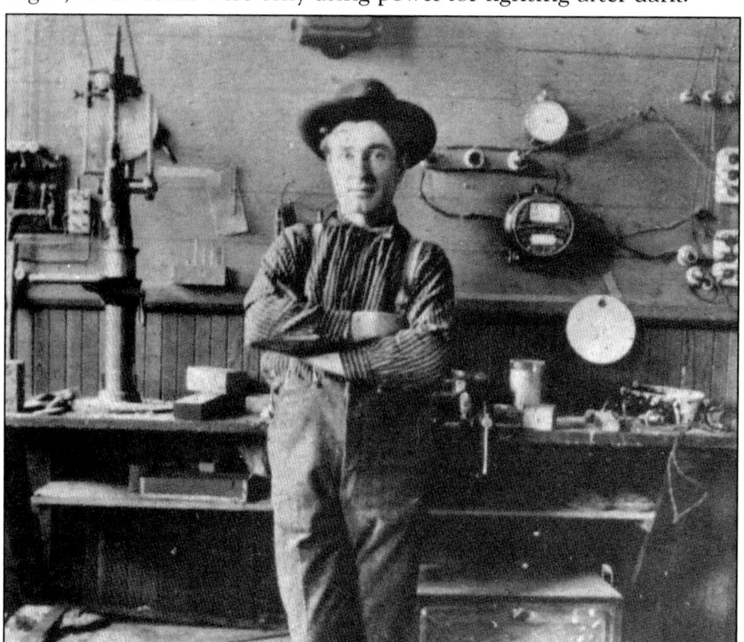

Richardson determined that he could increase daytime electricity consumption by providing residents with some of the appliances he had invented, so he and his friend Harry Strunk, pictured here, started building ovens, hotplates, and of course, flatirons. Richardson handed his small appliances out, and soon, daytime electricity use increased. The appliances received so much praise that Richardson decided to start his own business.

In May 1904, the Pacific Electric Heating Company incorporated. Richardson rented a small suite in the Bank Block, located on the west side of Euclid Avenue at Main Street. This building might be better remembered as the Grand Palace. Richardson hired his friend Harry Strunk and three other young men, and together, the crew began manufacturing flatirons and other small appliances.

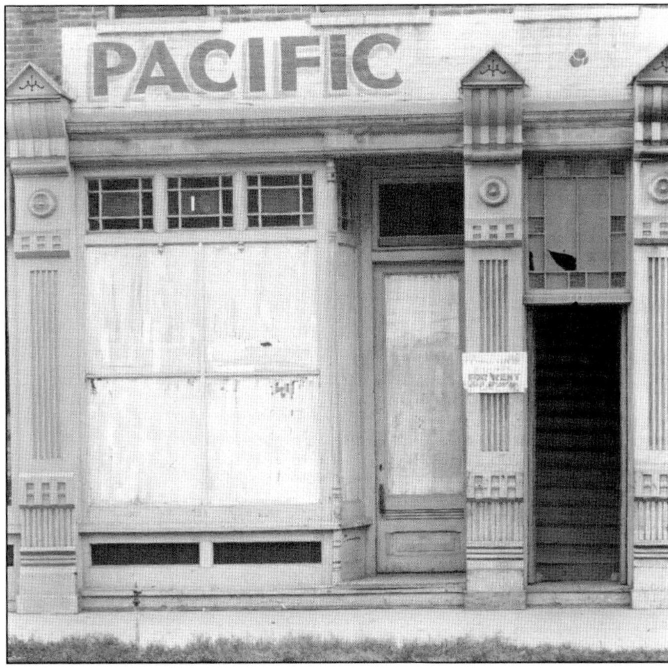

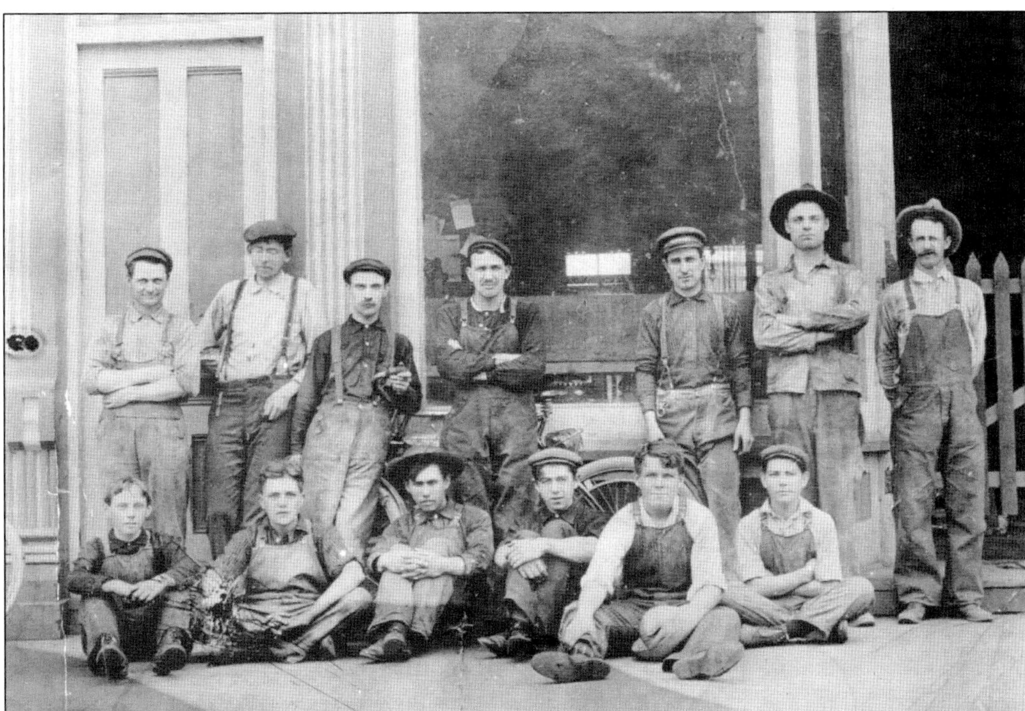

Business was so successful that Richardson hired some of the local boys to work at the plant during their summer vacation from school. This photograph was taken in the summer of 1904 at the Bank Block building and shows a very young Archie Mitchell on the lower right, sitting on the ground. About 20 years later, Mitchell became instrumental in the development of Ontario's airport, and was later a successful local attorney and judge.

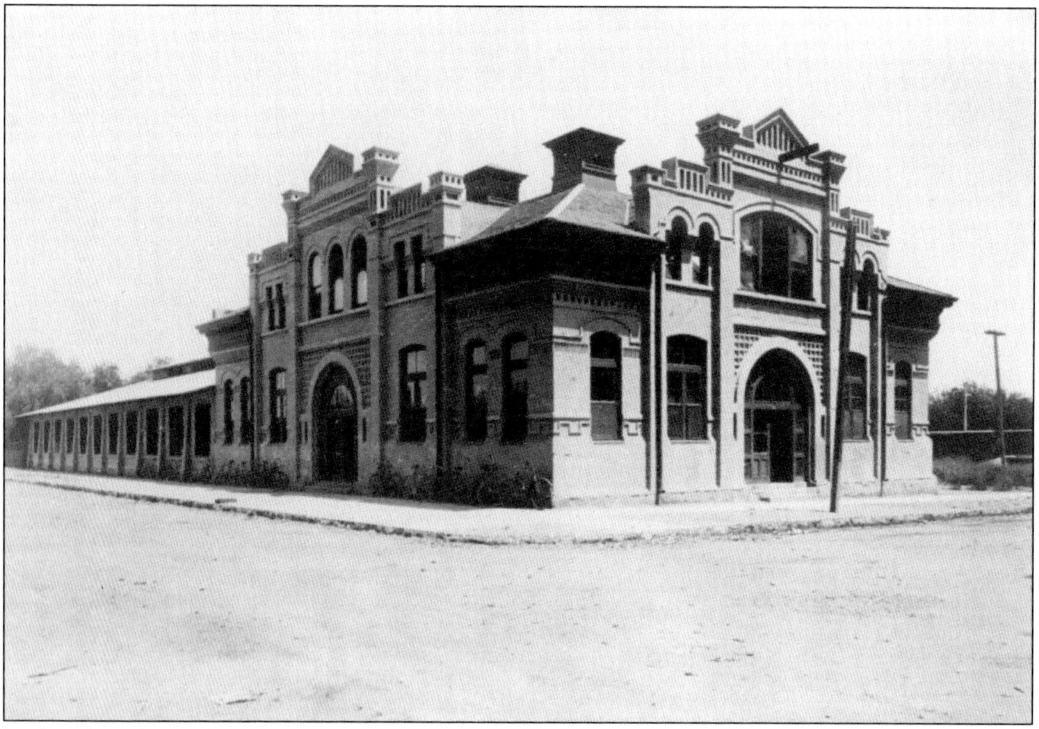

Richardson formed a partnership with the Booth brothers of Pomona, owners of the Western Laundry Machinery Company, to obtain financial backing. Soon, Richardson needed more space, so the Booth brothers pressured him to relocate to Pomona, but Ontario did not want to lose this successful company. The Ontario Chamber of Commerce raised $6,000 to purchase a vacant building, giving it to Richardson on the condition that the factory remain in Ontario. The company moved to this building, on East Main Street, in 1907.

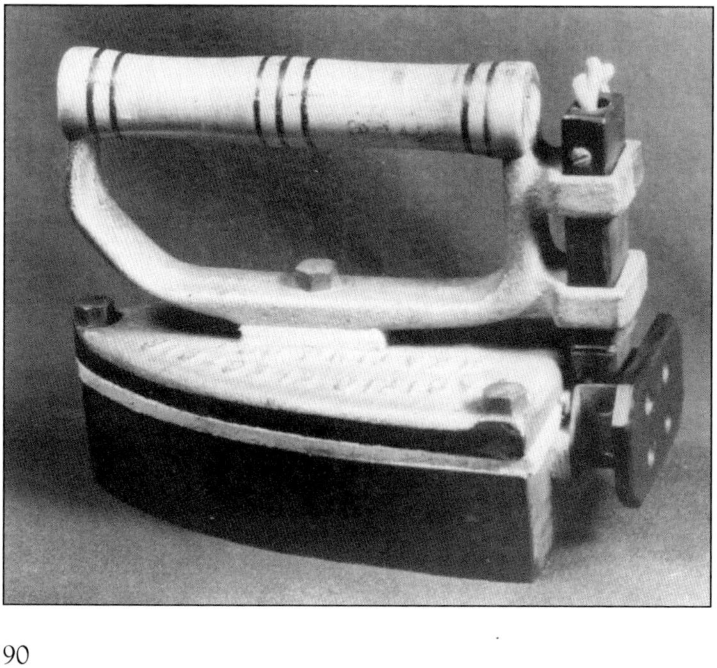

The first flatirons manufactured by the company used local mud as insulation, which radiated heat along the sole plate of the iron. Over time, the mud would crack, ruining the heating elements, and the heat generated through this process was uneven along the sole plate. Richardson developed an iron using nickel chromium alloy for the heating element, which provided even heating extending into the iron's point. The Hotpoint iron was born.

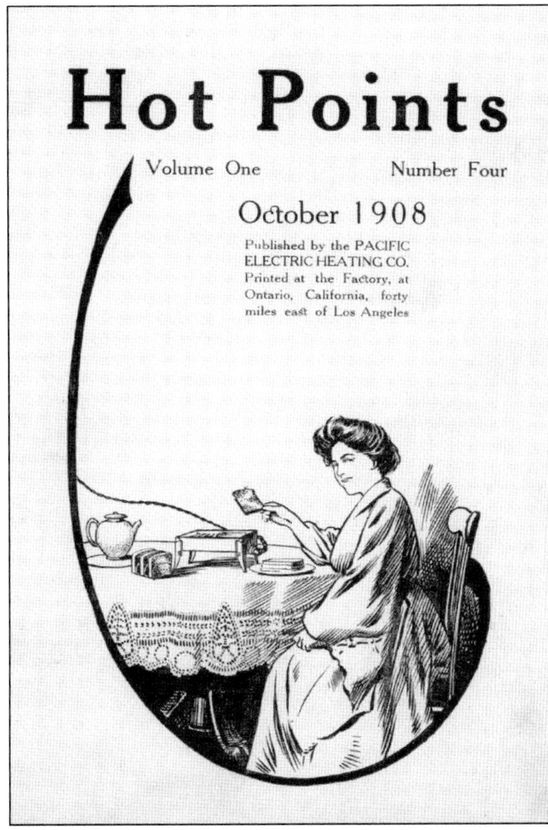

Hot Points

Volume One Number Four

October 1908

Published by the PACIFIC ELECTRIC HEATING CO. Printed at the Factory, at Ontario, California, forty miles east of Los Angeles

The business continued to grow, and in 1907, the Booth brothers hired a full time salesman and opened a branch office and small factory in Chicago. That same year, the Ontario factory added a printing plant to produce product brochures and advertisements. From his early work experience in retail merchandising, Richardson understood that advertising was key to a company's success. In 1908, the company introduced *Hot Points*, a newsletter created for retailers designed to help them market Pacific Electric Heating Company products. Later that year, the company introduced the "El" line of products, starting with El Tosto, an electric toaster.

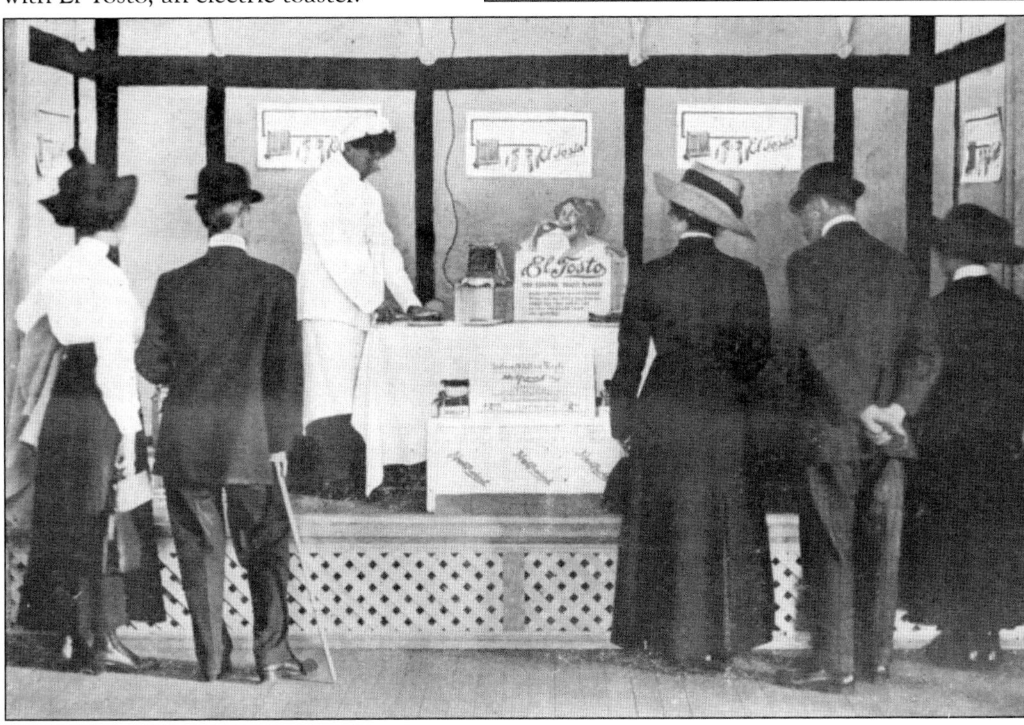

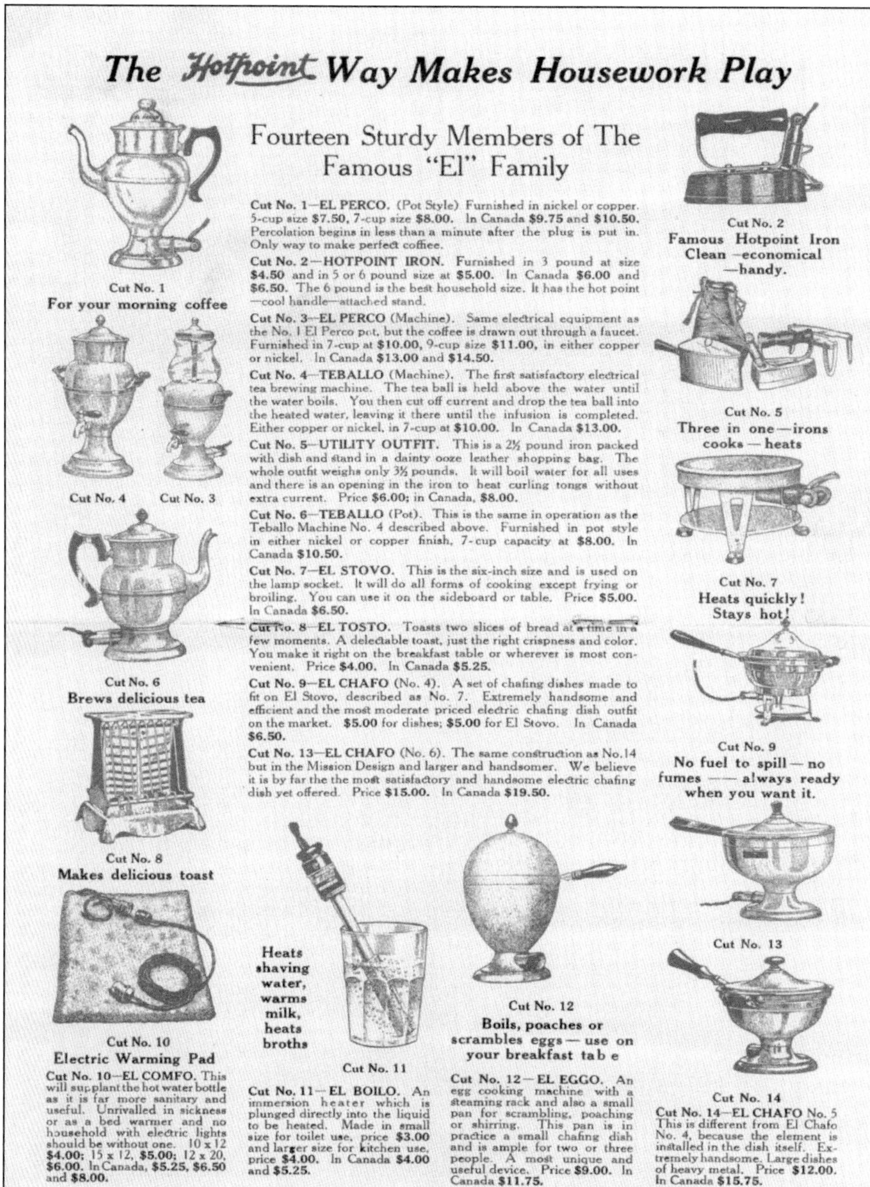

The "El" brand was described in the October 1908 issue of *Hot Points*: "El Tosto is a coined word. It sounds rather Spanish, which is appropriate, since it is made in sunny Southern California where the early Spanish padres have left their influence on language, architecture, customs, and even on business methods. But El Tosto is not Spanish, for the deceptive 'El' is simply an abbreviation for electric while 'Tosto' is a coined word to suggest toast." Some of the other members of the "El" family included the El Perco, for coffee, a hotplate called El Stovo, an egg-cooking machine called El Eggo, two different styles of El Chafo chafing dishes, and an electric teapot called Teballo. Hotpoint employees also adopted the terminology, creating the *El Amigo* newsletter in 1916 and organizing clubs such as the El Comfo Club, a club that discussed current topics and events. While the coined names were easy to remember, the "El" line was discontinued in 1916 after repeated criticism by the company's Spanish-speaking customers.

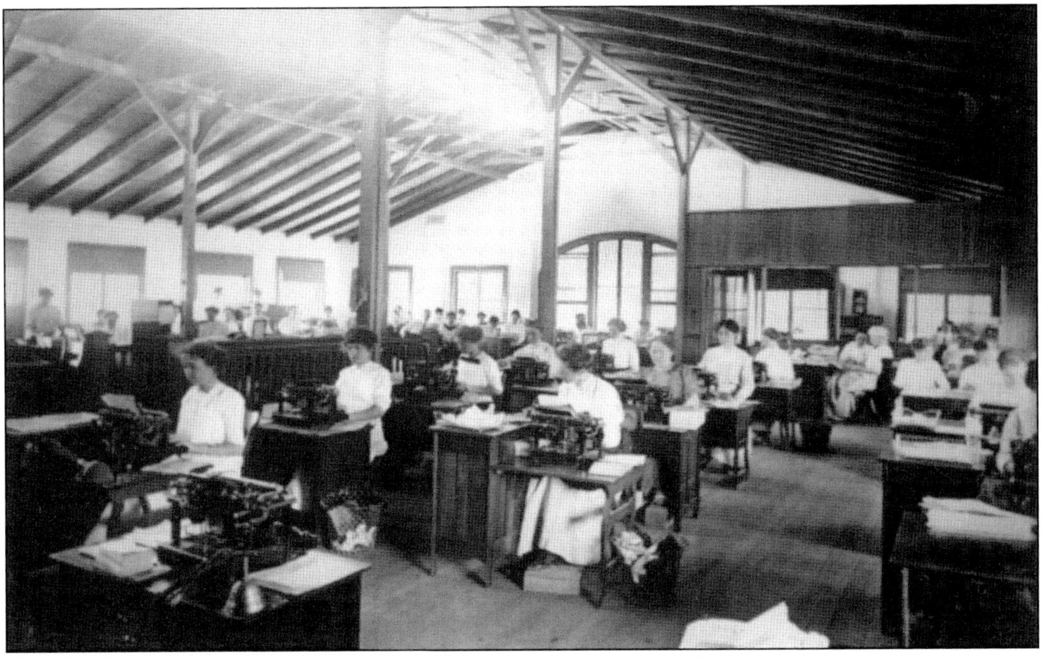

As the company grew, so did its workforce. In 1907, it employed 125 people and was producing 500 irons a day to keep up with demand, and new products continued to be developed and added to the line. That year also saw the first female employees working in the company's business offices, including Ida Snyder, Richardson's secretary.

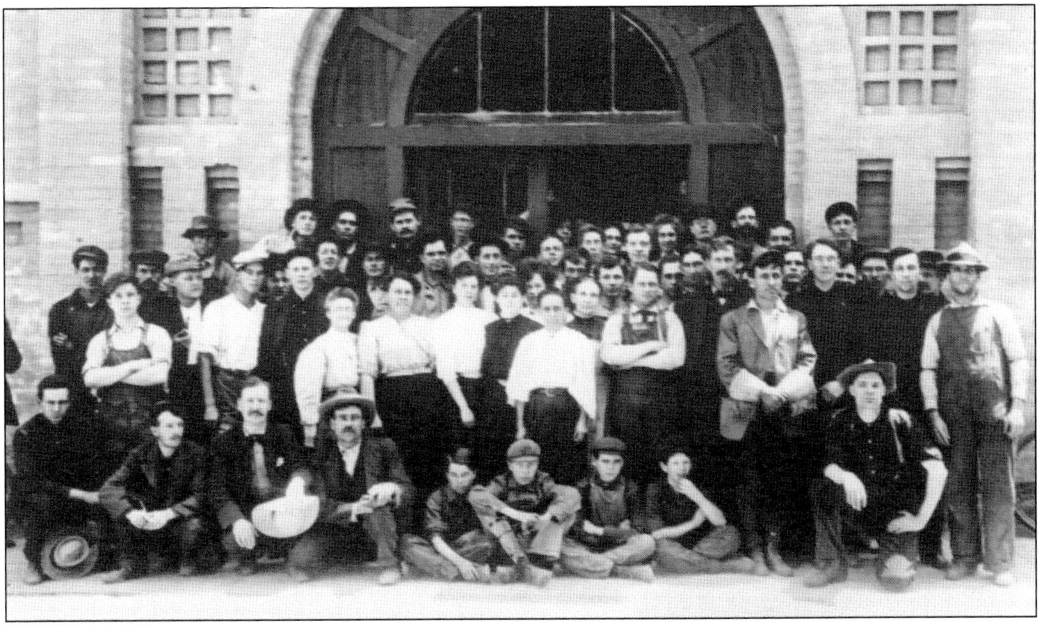

Here, Pacific Electric Heating Company employees pose for a photograph in 1908. While successful, the company did have its setbacks. The company would receive huge orders, including one single order for 5,000 irons. But it had trouble keeping up with the demand. In addition to the large orders being placed, cancellations would also ensue, causing major disruptions in production and financial uncertainty.

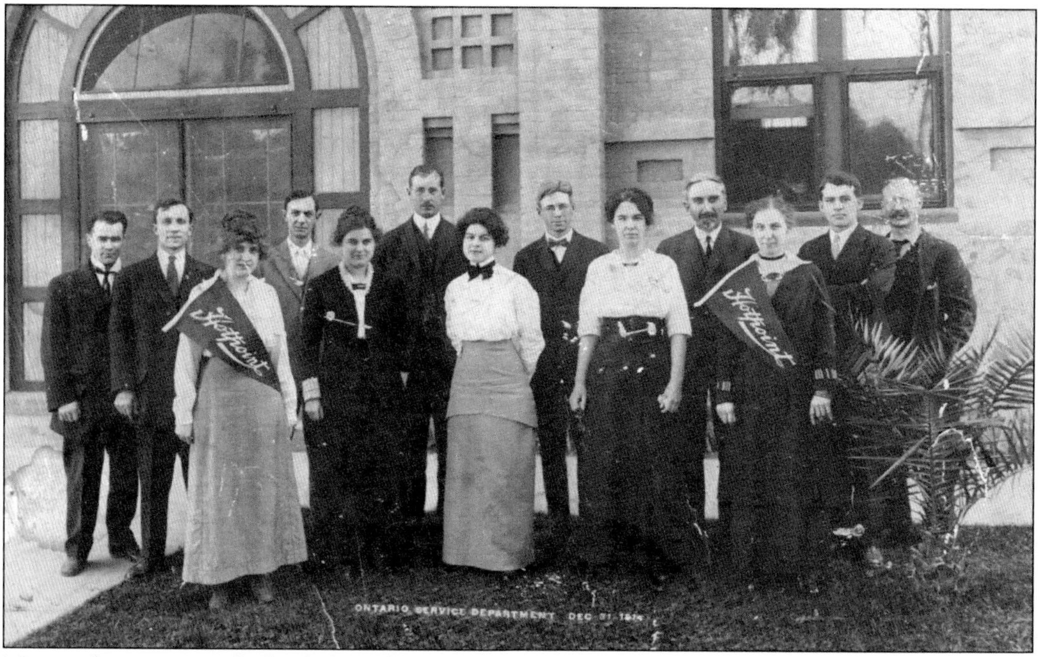

Men and women worked side by side at the Pacific Electric Heating Company. The company created several departments, including the Ontario Service Department, pictured here in 1914. Each department was responsible for handling specific inquiries and transactions. The Hotpoint trademark logo, seen here on the pennants the women are wearing, was developed in 1909.

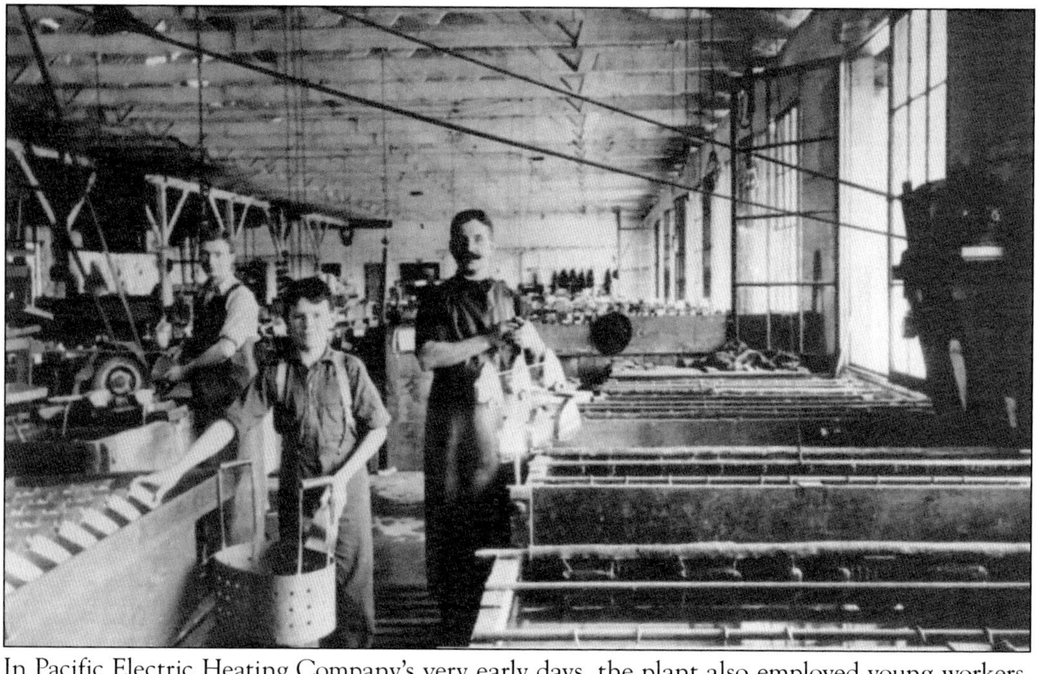

In Pacific Electric Heating Company's very early days, the plant also employed young workers. This undated photograph shows a very young boy working in the factory. Boys were often hired by the company to work during the summer school break before federal laws were enacted in the 1930s banning the employment of young children.

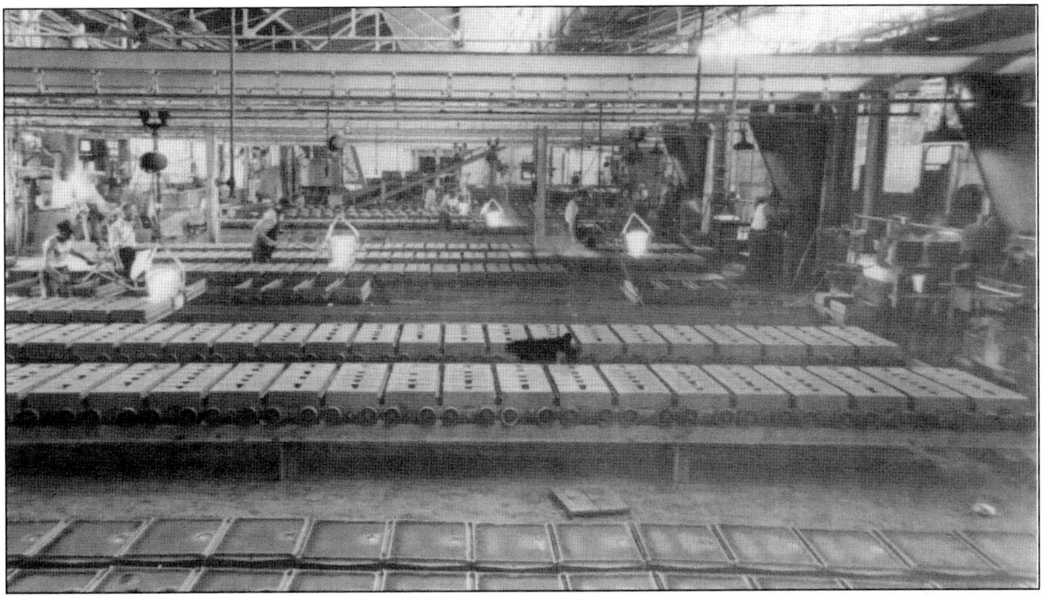

The Pacific Electric Heating Company added new buildings to the factory as it continued to grow. In 1908, the company built its own foundry, where the iron sole plates were poured. Men would pour molten iron into molds to produce castings of the sole plates. This was done using manpower until the early 1930s, when the process was mechanized.

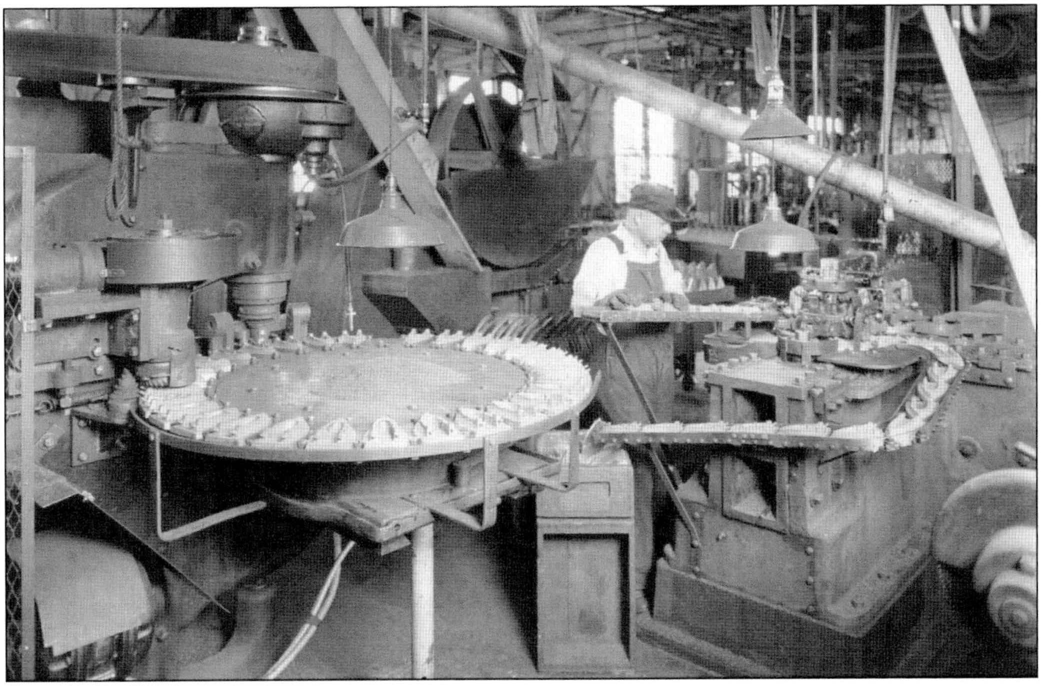

While manpower was dominant in the production of the Pacific Electric Heating Company's products, the company also developed assembly line production units after they were made popular by Henry Ford. Iron sole plates are seen here on a wheeled conveyor. Each worker along the line would add a part in succession until the iron completed the assembly line as a finished product. This efficient form of manufacture continues today.

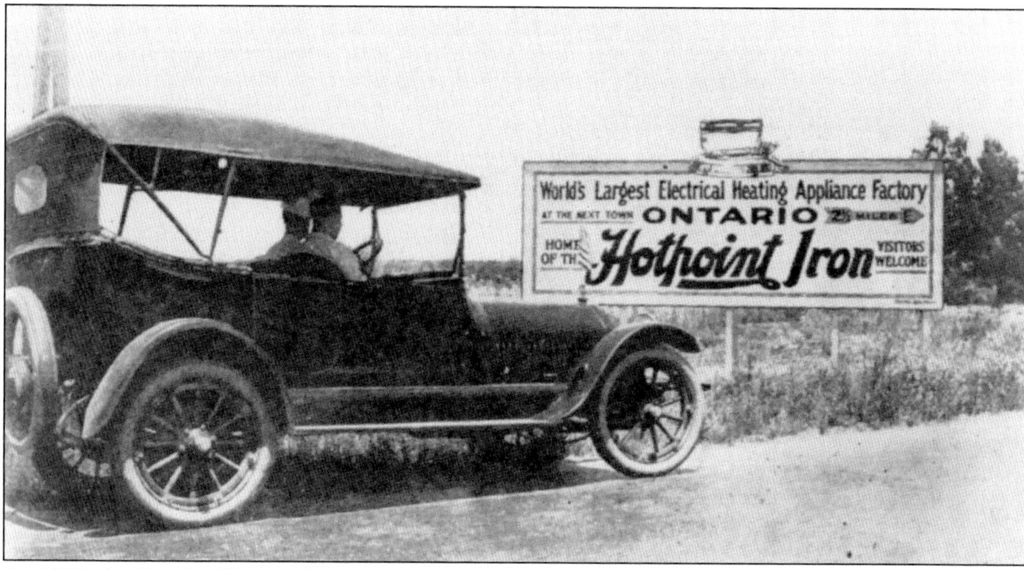

In 1909, the Pacific Electric Heating Company began marketing its products with the Hotpoint trademark. The Ontario and Chicago factories expanded in 1912, and due to the popularity of the Hotpoint brand, the company changed its name to Hotpoint Electric Heating Company. Within a few years, the plant was Southern California's largest manufacturing company and was known as the world's largest electrical appliance manufacturer.

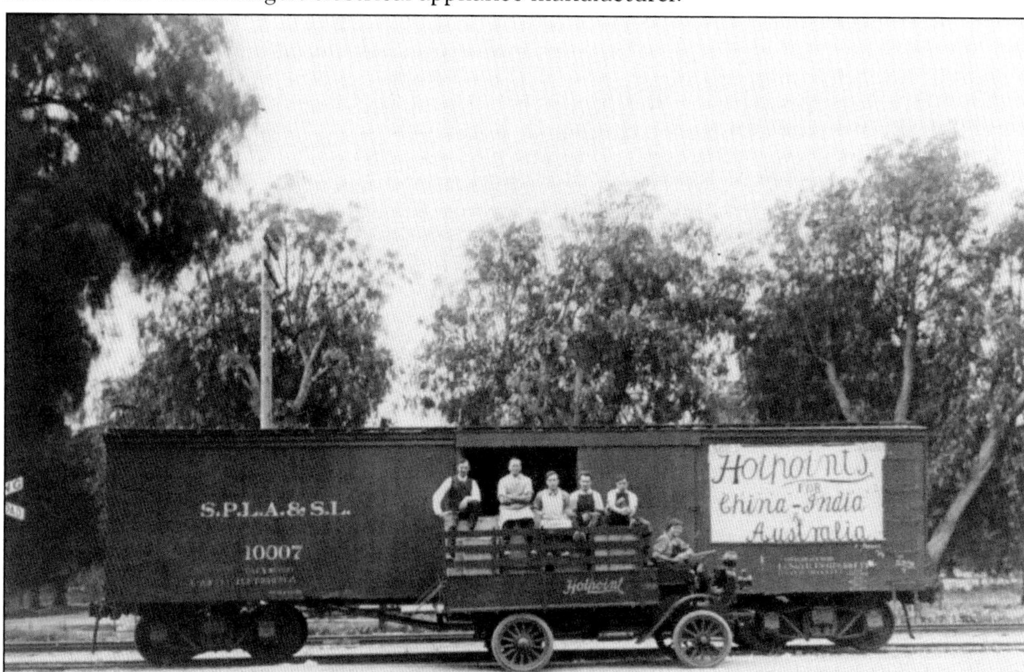

This photograph taken in 1916 shows Hotpoint employees standing outside a train car loaded with 5,000 Hotpoint irons being exported overseas to China, India, and Australia. According to the June 1916 edition of *El Amigo*, the Hotpoint employee newsletter, the employees pictured here are, from left to right, William Davis, Alexander "Scotty" Clarke, Andrew Millard, Charles Warner, Lester Danks, and Theodore Barrett.

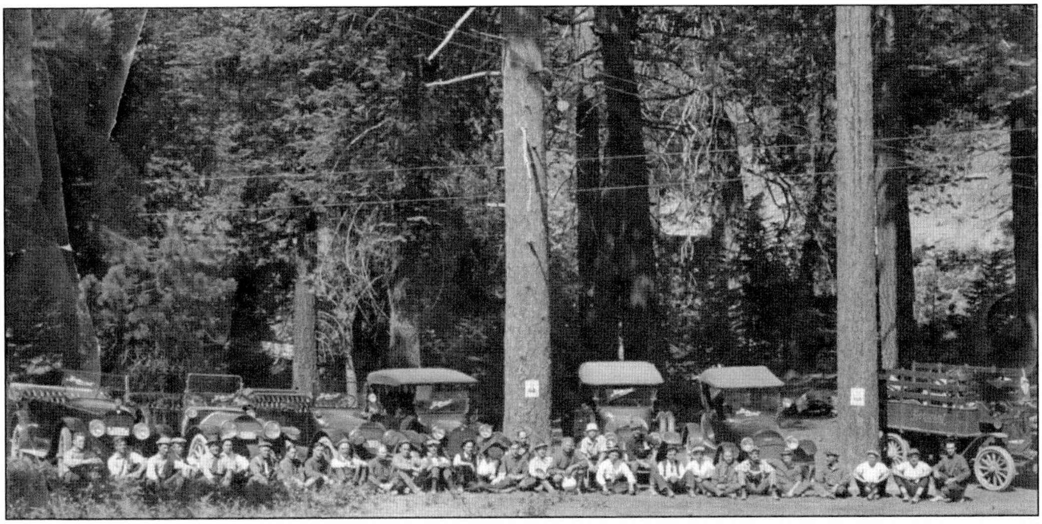

Richardson loved the great California outdoors and took outings with his coworkers. Groups would drive up to the local mountains on a Saturday afternoon and camp outside overnight. Sunday mornings were spent hiking after a camp breakfast. Peter Vanden Berg, a longtime Hotpoint employee, stated that the outings provided Hotpoint employees an opportunity to relax with each other and regain a sense of camaraderie during stressful times at the factory.

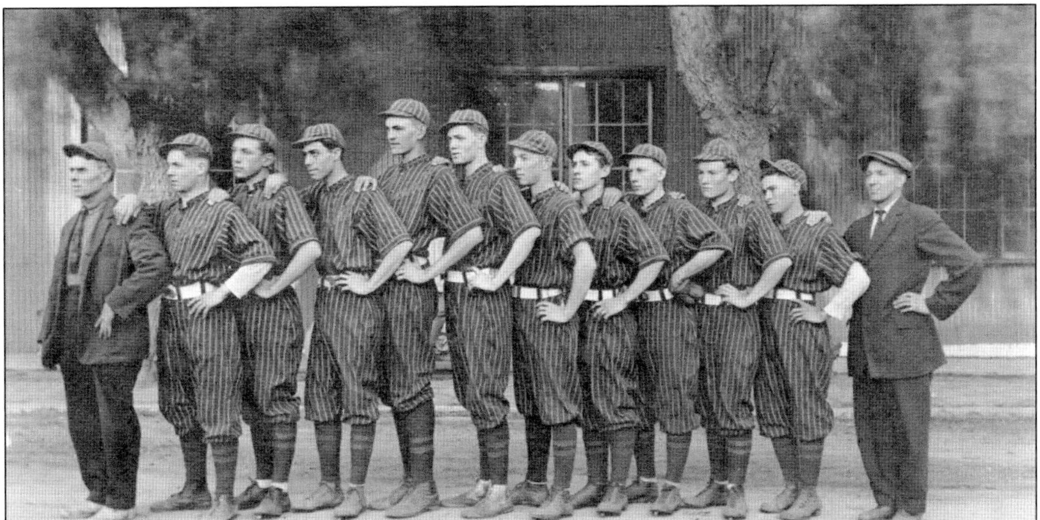

In March 1916, the inaugural edition of *El Amigo* announced that the Ontario plant wanted to develop a baseball team "for a series to be played during the coming Spring and Summer months." The team wore blue and white uniforms, and Alexander "Scotty" Clarke, pictured at far right, was their manager.

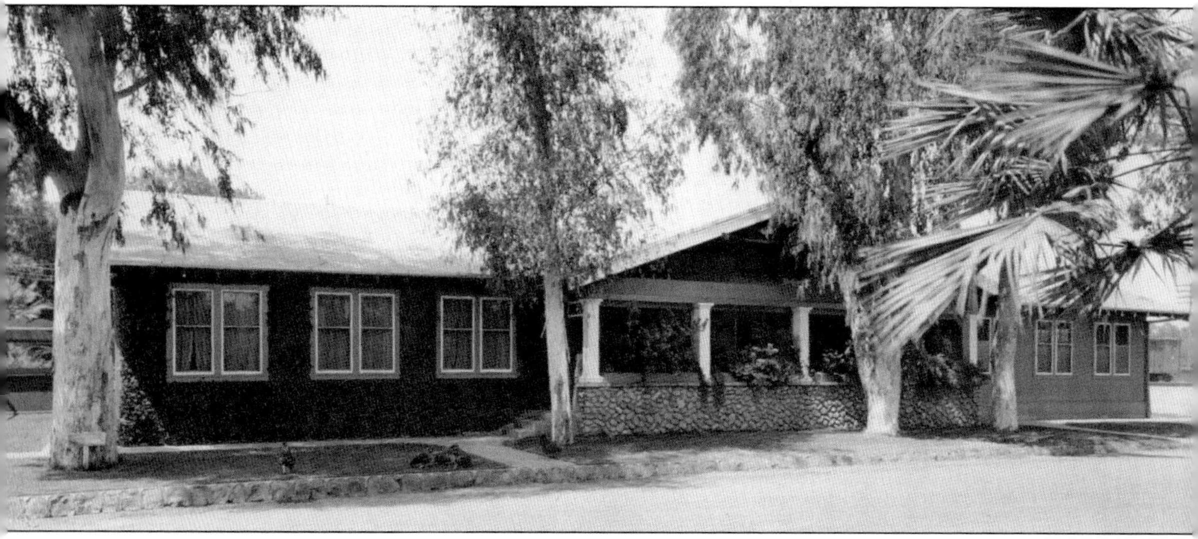

Employees of Hotpoint organized the Hotpoint Club in 1913 as a way to promote good fellowship among employees. Initially, the club was open only to foremen and department heads, but by 1916, it was open to all employees. The company was very supportive of the club and provided space within the plant for both a cafeteria and a store run by the club. The club also worked with the company to develop tennis courts, croquet grounds, and later, a baseball diamond. A library was started in 1913, and in 1915, many female employees organized the Triangle Club to promote physical health and social improvement. In 1916, the company determined that the space provided for these clubs within the plant was needed to expand production, so the construction of a dedicated clubhouse building was proposed.

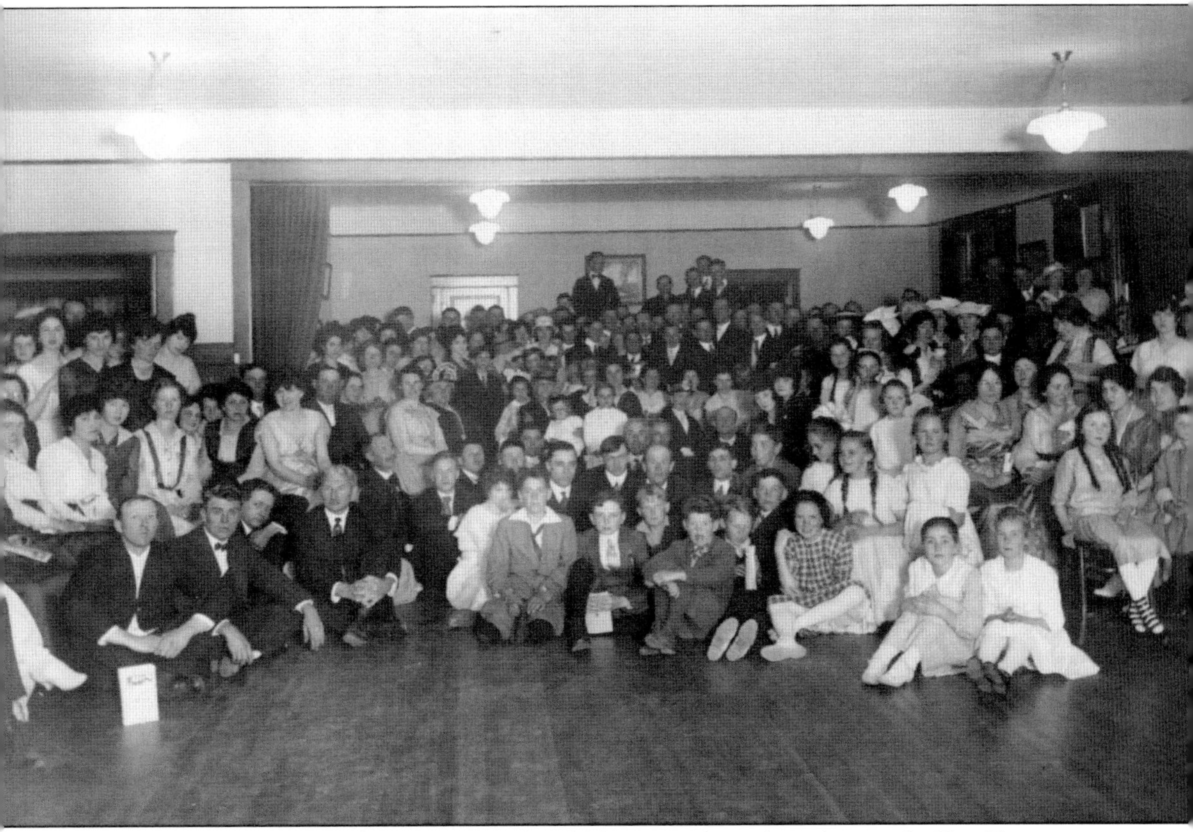

The company gave the club $1,000 toward the clubhouse and purchased a parcel of land between the Southern Pacific tracks and Main Street for the building. The Hotpoint Club obtained a loan for an additional $4,000. The loan would be paid off using profits from the cafeteria and club store. The store sold groceries and men's clothing at a discount and was open each weekday. The cafeteria had a large cobblestone fireplace and was used as a meeting room for the clubs. The building was given a rustic design, with wood flooring and a long, enclosed porch, and also had a large assembly room for dances, parties, and club meetings. Outside organizations were allowed to use the building for various events as well. In this photograph, the Hotpoint Club House celebrates its housewarming on May 26, 1917.

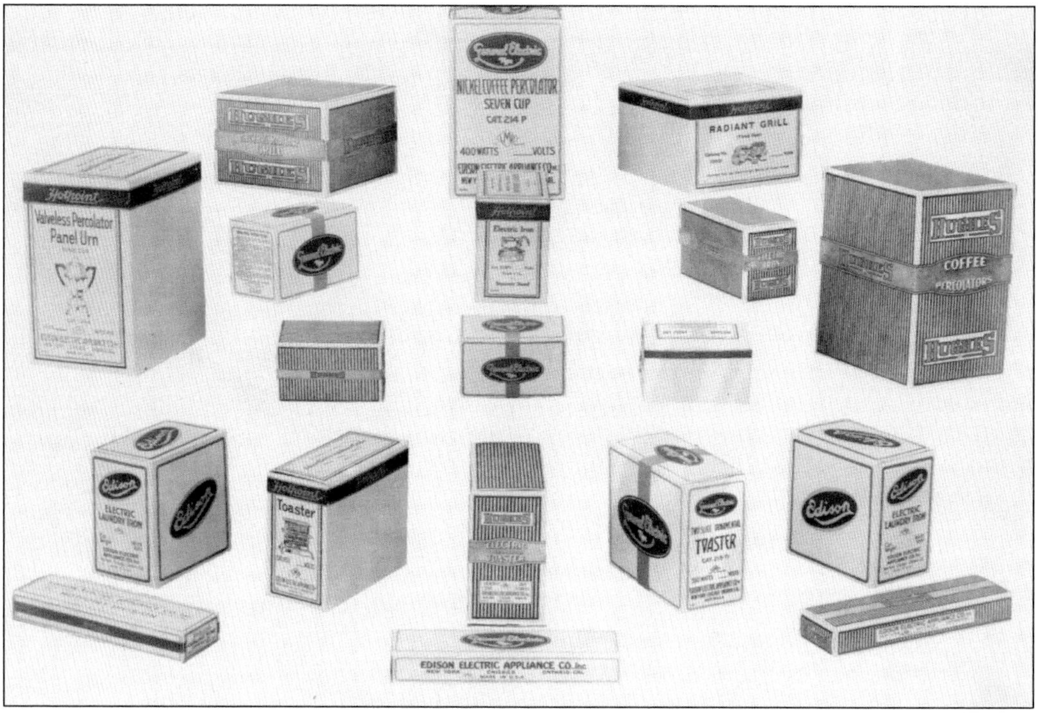

In the late 1910s, Hotpoint had been so successful that General Electric, which was looking to expand its small appliance division, began to take notice. Hotpoint merged with General Electric and Hughes, an electric range manufacturer based in Chicago. On January 1, 1918, the company became known as the Edison Electric Appliance Company Inc. The manufacture of the popular Hotpoint flatiron was concentrated in Ontario and Chicago.

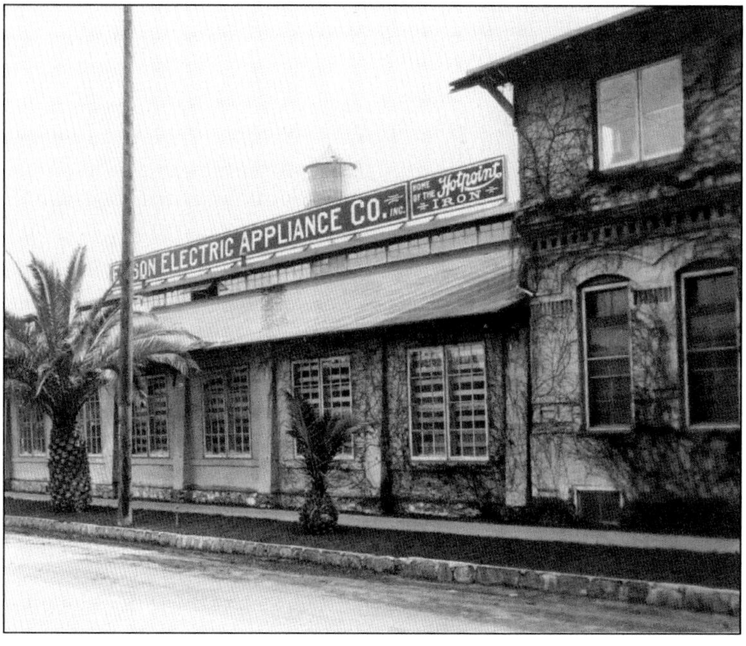

The Ontario factory changed its name again in 1927 to the General Electric Ontario Works, and remained a major employer in Ontario until its closing in 1982, at which time it had produced 158,718,298 flatirons. Richardson served as the Ontario plant manager and also unsuccessfully attempted to develop the town of Adelanto. The stress of the project had serious effects on his health, and he died in Ontario in 1934 at age 62.

Eight

Early Education in Ontario

When the Chaffey brothers laid out their model colony, they had four principles guiding them. The third principle was that they would provide general education for the colonists' children. In 1883, they built the first Chaffey College, attracting students from as far away as Hemet. Two rooms in the college building were set aside to teach younger students. In the same year, the Ontario School District was formed. In 1887, a separate grammar school was built called Central School, which held 250 students. Other grammar schools followed as the colony was built, including Southside School, San Antonio School, Lincoln School, and Edison School.

Grove School was one of the first segregated schools in America that educated only "foreign" children. It operated until the 1940s, when the school board decided that any child could go to any school in the district. Elementary schools went through eighth grade until 1921, when Ontario's first junior high school was built. Called Ontario Junior High School, it was later renamed in honor of its first principal, Vina Danks. Ontario High School took over the Chaffey College building in 1901 and was later named Chaffey High School. The current Chaffey College restarted in 1916, and until 1959, shared the campus with Chaffey High School. This chapter, while not exhaustive of all of Ontario's schools, offers some early history of Ontario's education system.

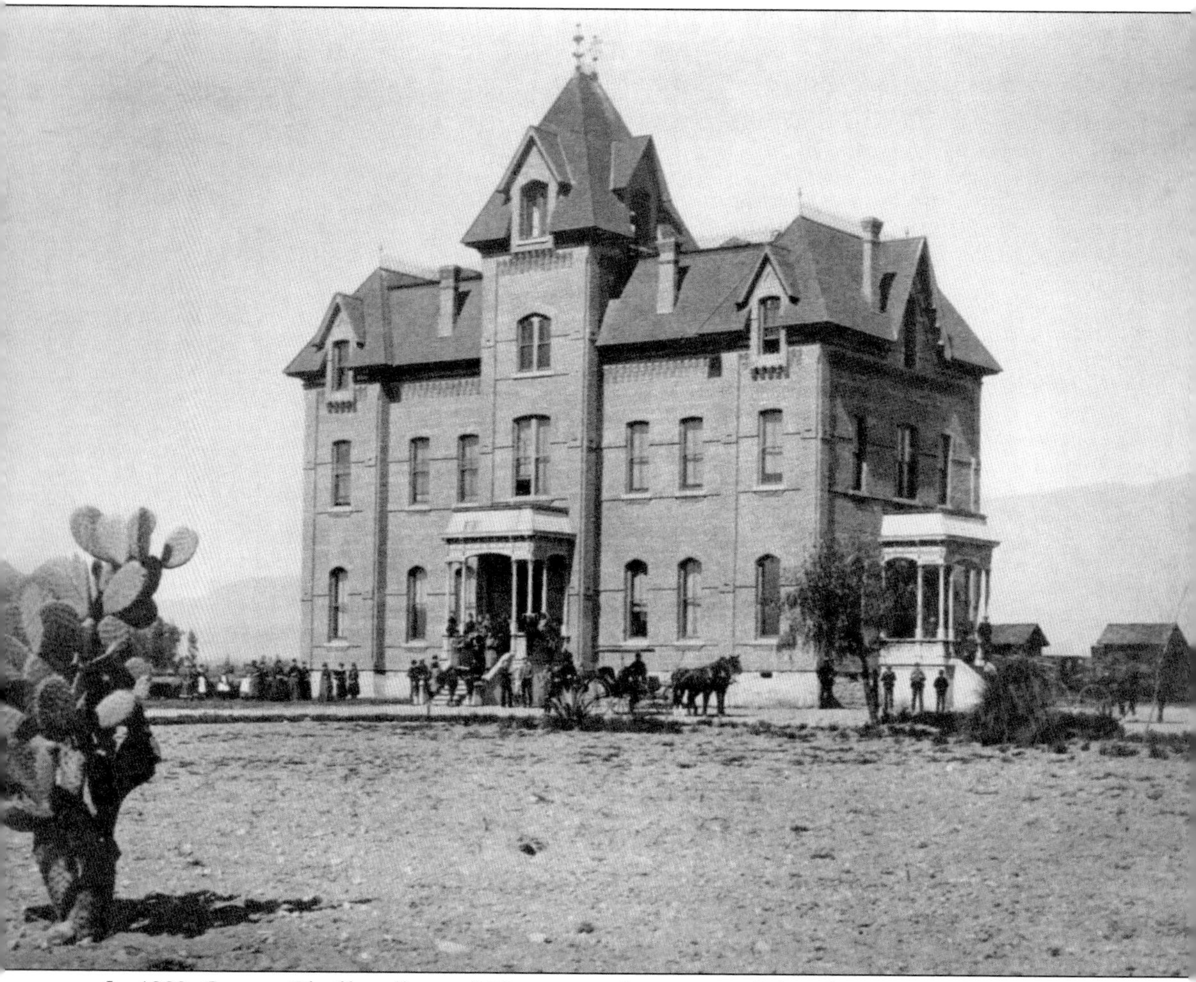

In 1882, George Chaffey allocated 20 acres at the corner of Fourth Street and Euclid Avenue for a college of agriculture. He entered into a trust agreement with the University of Southern California to develop future buildings. The cornerstone of Chaffey College was laid on March 17, 1883, with much fanfare, although construction did not actually commence until January 1884. The building was constructed using more than 300,000 bricks and was complete with a chapel, four large lecture rooms, 11 offices, a library, and a museum. The college was completed and opened in October 1885 with 10 students. By 1890, the courses emphasized classical studies instead of agriculture. Upon its completion, the *Ontario Fruit Grower* newspaper stated, "From every window views of the colony of Ontario, the valley, and the mountains are delightful."

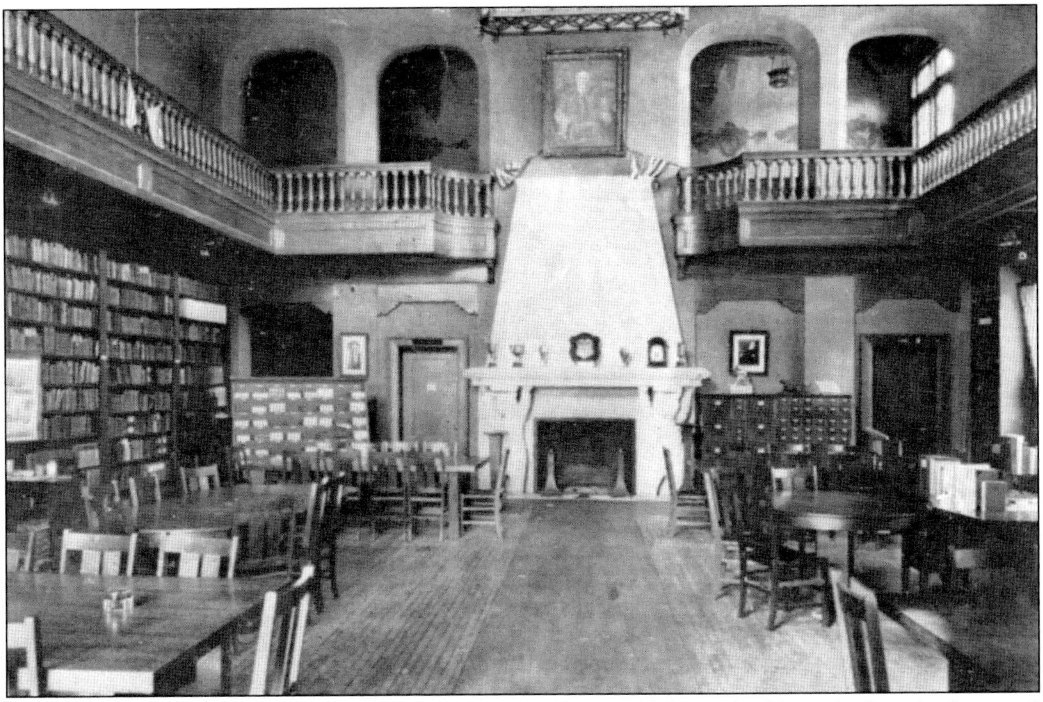

By 1901, the college's ties with the University of Southern California had been broken for financial reasons, and the school had become Ontario High School. After several years, the trust agreement was settled, and income from the trust went toward the library (pictured) and book fund. The Chaffey Union High School District was created in 1911. George Chaffey provided the district with an $8,000 endowment, and Ontario High School became Chaffey High School.

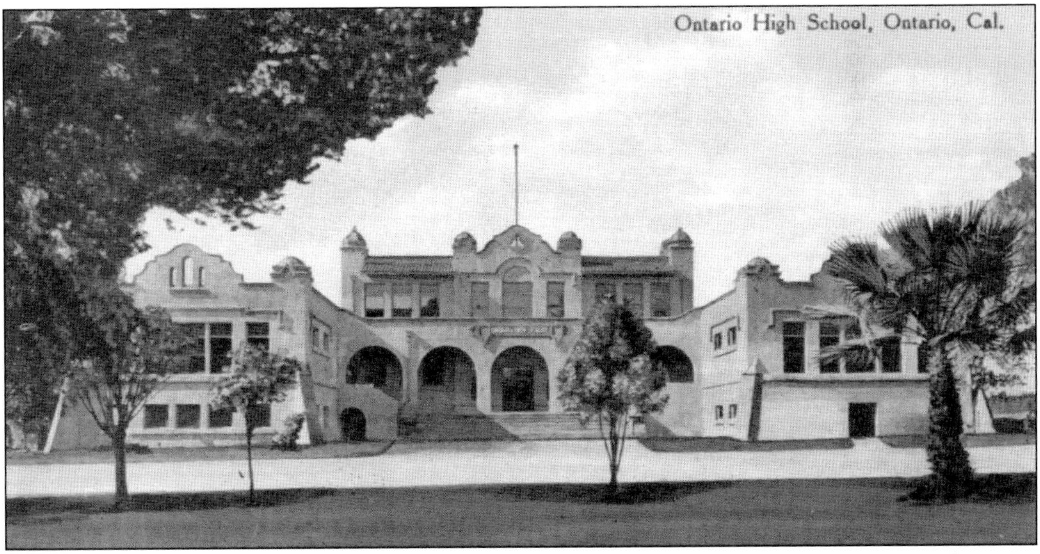

Between 1909 and 1916, the original three-story building was remodeled, creating an auditorium and library. New construction included the science, administration, and mechanic arts buildings. In 1916, the Chaffey board approved funding for a junior college department to be co-located on the high school campus, and Chaffey Junior College opened with 100 students. Chaffey Junior College expanded and eventually moved its campus to Alta Loma in 1959.

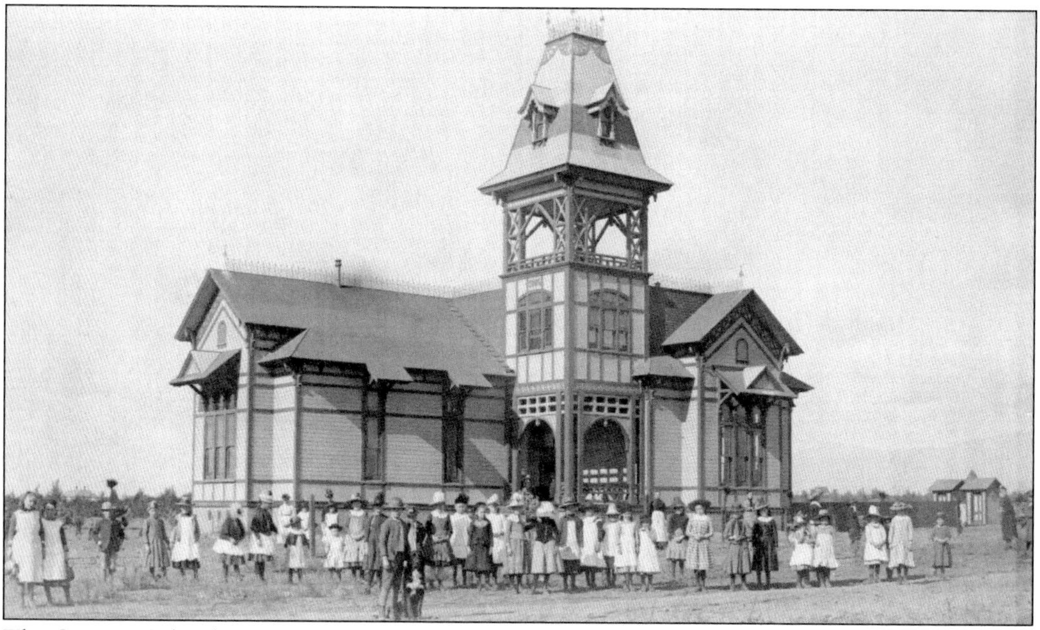

The Ontario School District was created in 1884 to provide a general education for the colonists' children. Two rooms at the new Chaffey College were used for teaching elementary children. Jamie Nellie Case of Riverside was the first teacher and earned a salary of $50 a month. A new school building was constructed at the corner of G Street and Sultana Avenue and called Central School. It opened in 1887 and accommodated 250 pupils. Central School's first building (above) was a two-story, wooden, five-room structure that cost $6,000 to build and was in use between 1887 and 1912. Due to complaints of overcrowding, poor lighting and ventilation, and fire danger, Central School was rebuilt in 1913 (below). The Long Beach earthquake of March 1933 damaged the building, so the school board closed it, sending students to Edison, San Antonio, and Lincoln Schools.

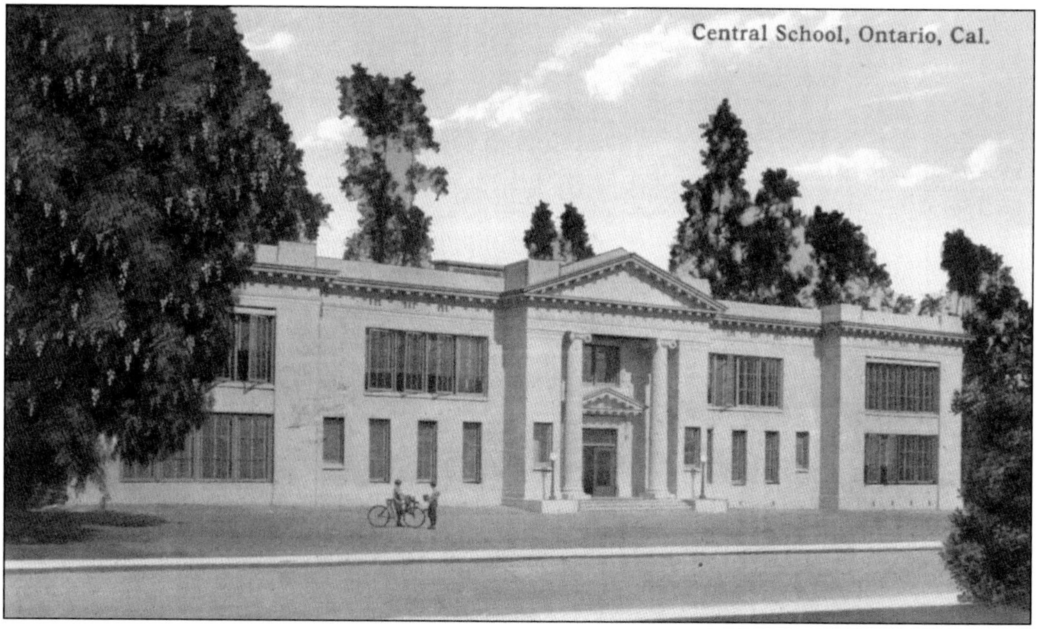

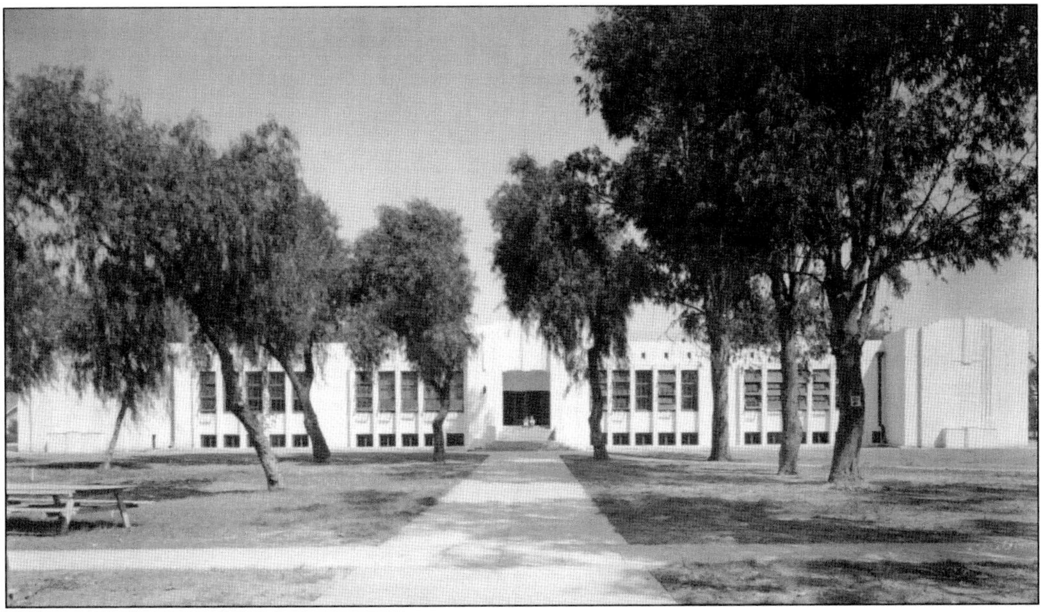

Central School's third building was constructed at G Street and Sultana Avenue in 1935 at a cost of $87,360. Half of this came from Works Progress Administration funds as an unemployment relief measure. The new building included a full-size auditorium and a basement cafeteria. It was built to the Field Act earthquake codes that were enacted in 1935.

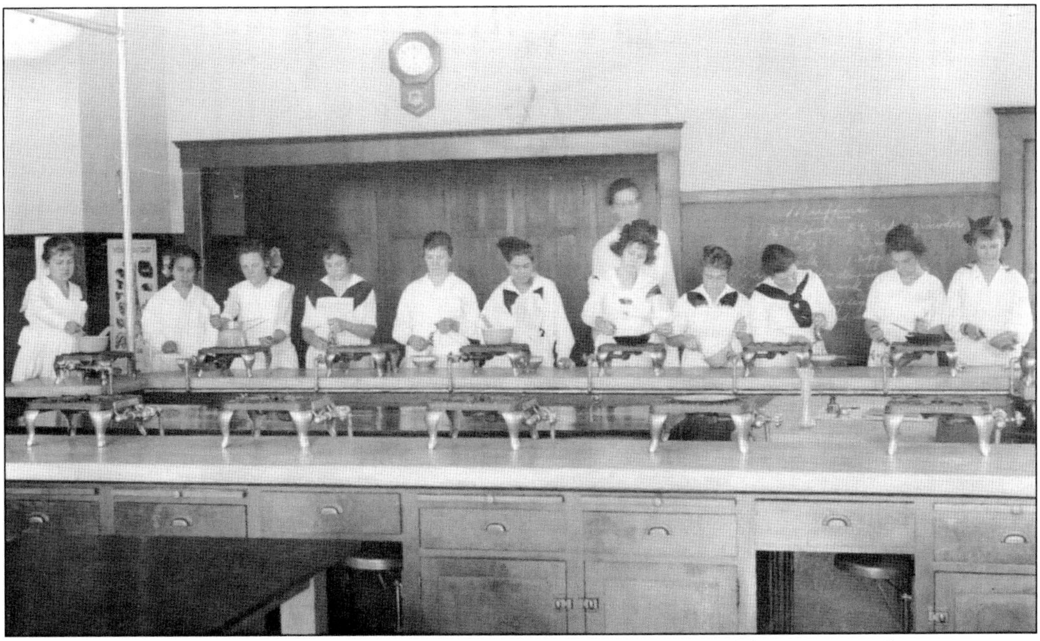

Until 1921, Central School taught through the eighth grade. In addition to academic courses, older students also took courses in practical subjects such as domestic science, seen here, where cooking was taught. Central School closed to students in 1978 due to declining enrollment, but after three decades as a district schoolbook repository, it reopened in 2008 as a new magnet school, the Central Language Academy.

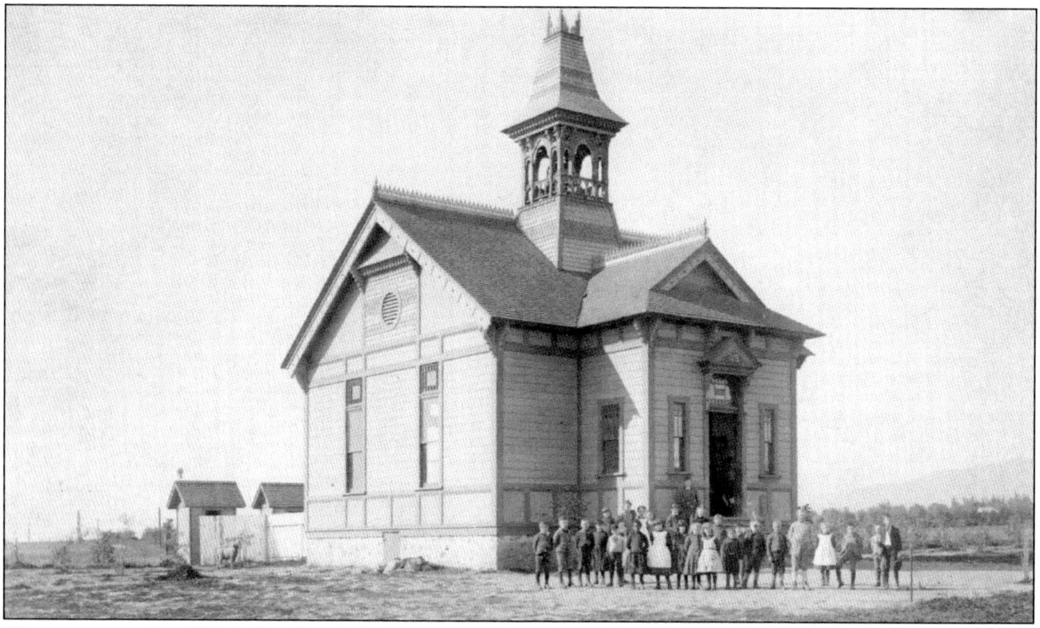

The area south of Holt Boulevard was known as the south side of Ontario. In 1889, South Side School (above) was built at the northeast corner of State and San Antonio Streets. In 1912, a new Southside School was built at the southwest corner of Euclid Avenue and Ralston Street at a cost of $31,525. Since it was a brick building, it sustained considerable damage in the Long Beach earthquake. In 1936, it was replaced by the current building, which was built with Works Progress Administration funds and is now called Euclid School (below). Homer Briggs began his career as a sixth-grade teacher at Euclid School in 1935. He was the first male elementary school teacher hired in the Ontario School District. He became superintendent of the Ontario-Montclair School District in 1951 and retired in 1972.

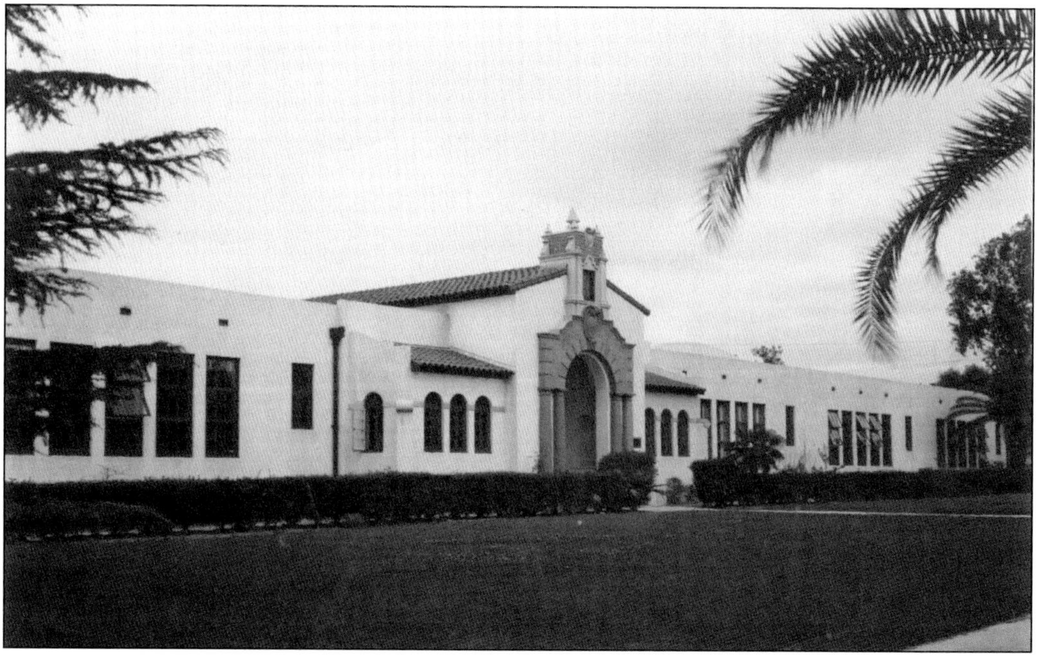

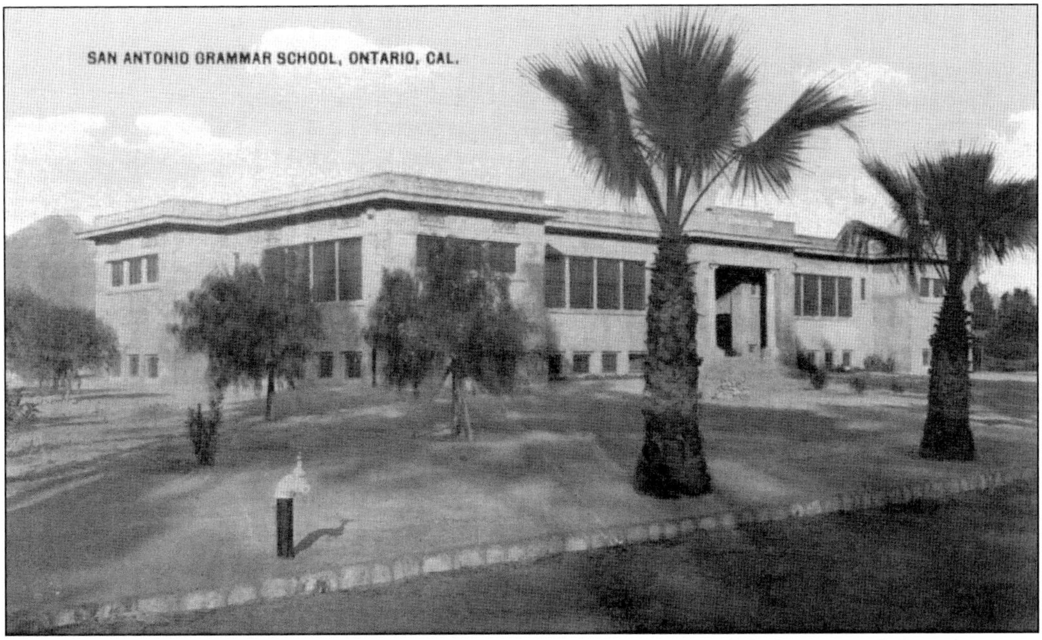

San Antonio Grammar School (above) was built at the corner of D Street and San Antonio Avenue in 1908 at a cost of $3,000. It burned down in 1931 after two fires within 48 hours. Arson was suspected as the cause. It was rebuilt in 1933 (below) at a cost of $46,680. It survived the Long Beach earthquake but closed in 1973 because it did not meet modern earthquake standards. It was demolished in 1976, and the property became San Antonio Park. Its name was changed to James R. Bryant Park in May 2002, and the land is still owned by the Ontario-Montclair School District.

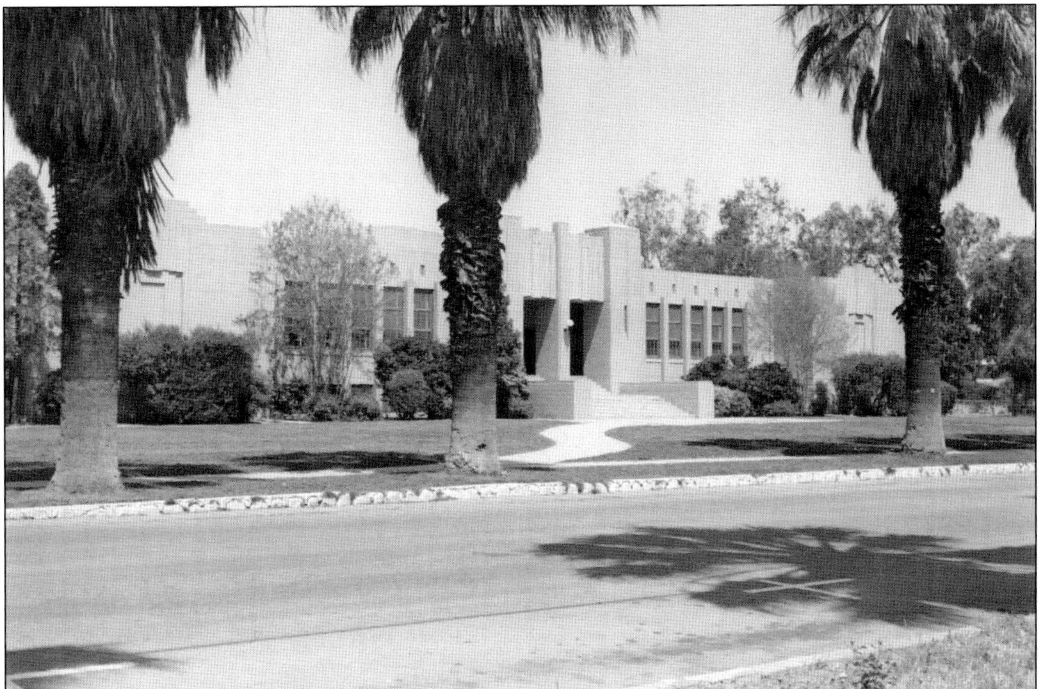

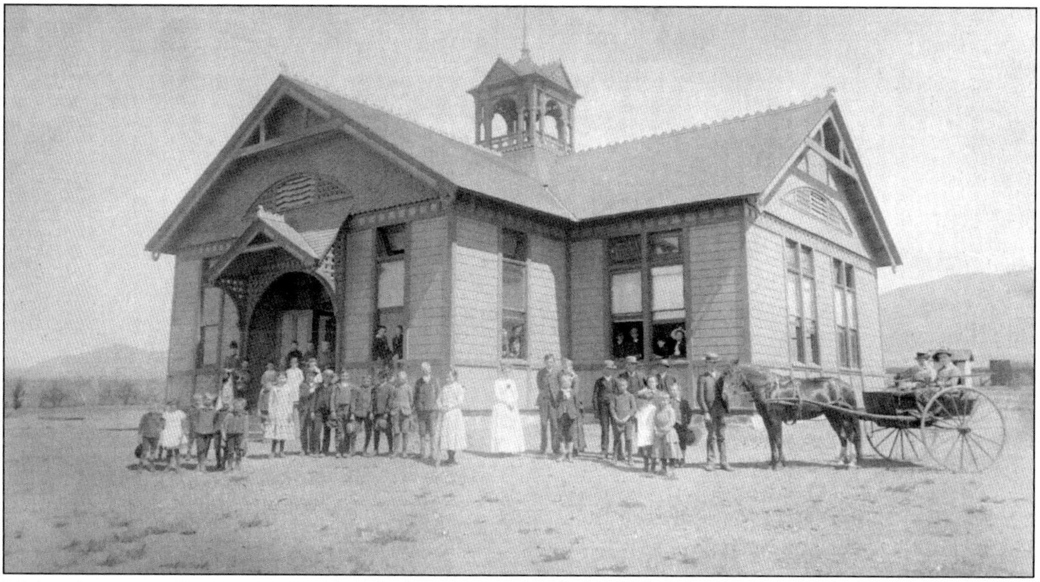

Upland, originally known as North Ontario, established the San Antonio School District in 1886, building this wood-framed structure on Eighteenth Street for 10 children who either lived north of E Street or were residents of San Antonio canyon. This building was moved in 1919 to the corner of Campus Avenue and Thirteenth Street and renamed Sierra Vista School.

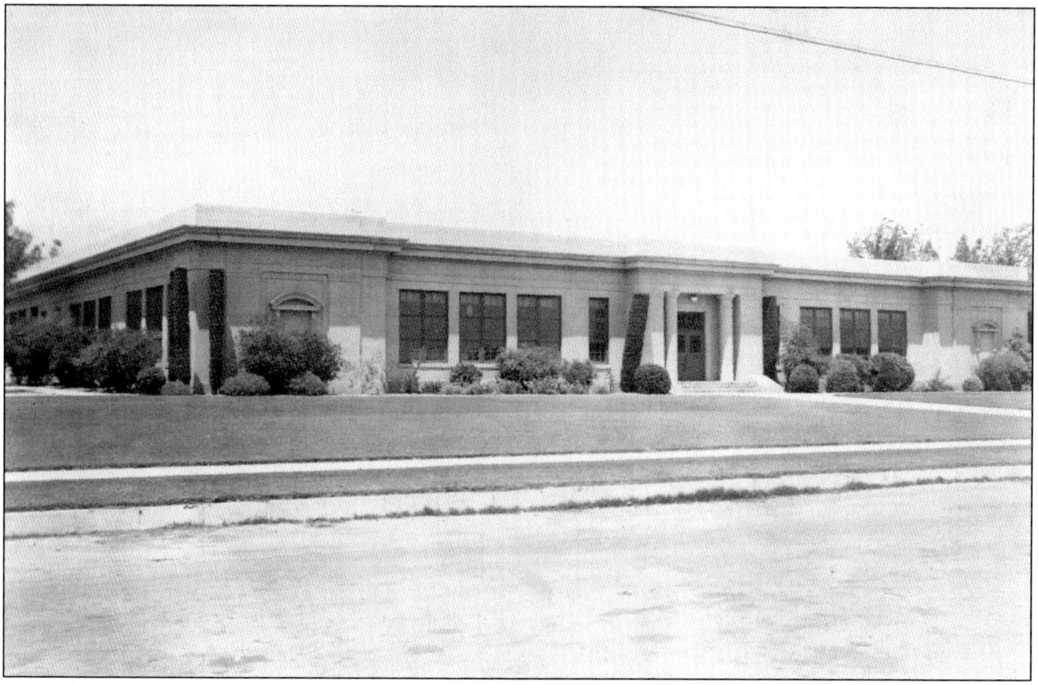

Lincoln School (pictured) was built on the northeast corner of D Street and Allyn Avenue in 1926. It closed in 1971 because it did not meet current earthquake standards. The Lincoln Development Center was built on the site in 1976 for children and young adults with developmental disabilities. Today, Lincoln School provides general instruction in addition to serving students with special needs.

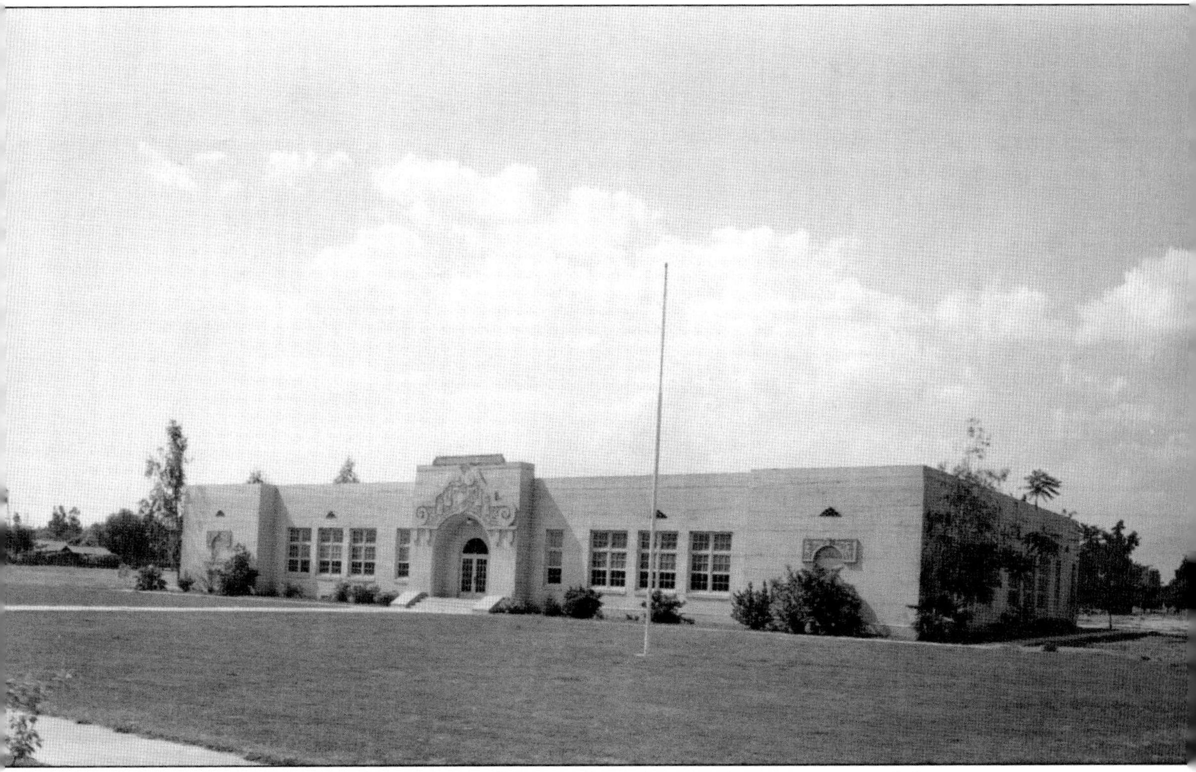

Grove School was completed in 1928 and located on the northwest corner of Campus Avenue and Grove Street, which later became Sunkist Street. Grove School, also known as the "Mexican School," was a segregated school touted by the local newspaper as "one of the finest schools in the nation, devoted solely to the education of foreigners." All Hispanic children in the colony, regardless of where they lived, were assigned to attend Grove School, even if they lived closer to another school. In 1946, after a US district court judge in California ruled that "separate but equal" was unconstitutional, the school board announced that the school would no longer be segregated. There was much debate throughout the community after this decision, and arguments about the drawing of school boundaries continued all summer. Nevertheless, all Ontario schools were open to any student starting in the 1946–1947 school year. By 1968, this school was no longer in use because it did not meet structural standards, and in 1970, the nearby Sunkist plant acquired the property.

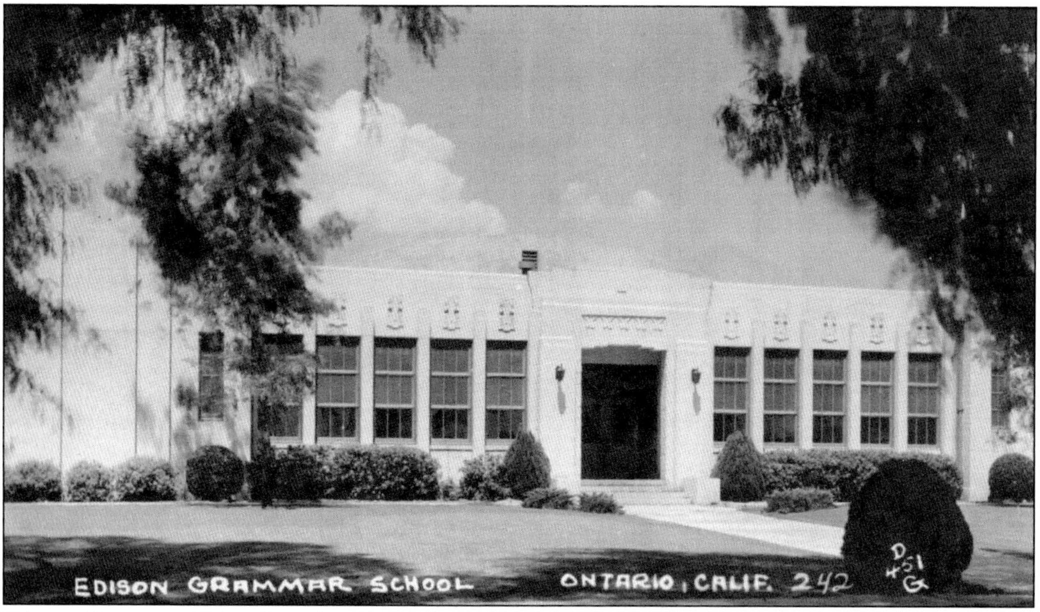

Edison Grammar School was built in 1931 at Sixth Street and Sultana Avenue for $26,500. The original building (pictured) was demolished in 1969 in order to meet new state laws related to wind and earthquake damage standards, and a new building was constructed in 1970. Because the site only encompassed five acres, it was only allowed to accommodate kindergarten through third grade. Today, Edison School is the Edison Academy of Differentiated Learning.

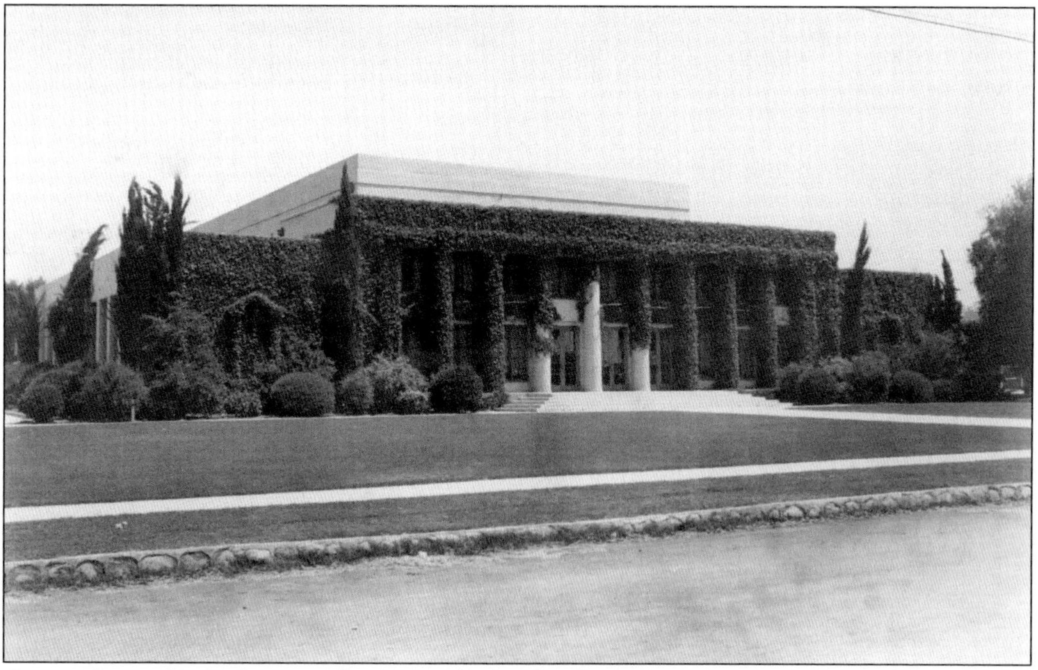

Ontario Junior High, Ontario's first junior high school, was built in 1921 facing J Street opposite Palm Avenue. Vina F. Danks became its first principal in 1923 and remained until her sudden death in 1938; the school was renamed in her honor the following year. This building was demolished in 1974 and rebuilt facing Vine Avenue in 1975.

Nine

Around Town in the Early Days

This chapter offers an opportunity for a modern-day resident to catch a glimpse of what everyday life might have been like for pioneers in Ontario's earliest days. Shown are some early churches, businesses, and clubs organized in the model colony of Ontario, along with various people and places.

Shopping, banking, and other town services are illustrated in this chapter, which provides an opportunity to understand the differences and similarities between the early days in Ontario and the current day. Many will remember the businesses, hotels, and buildings, some of which still exist today, as well as many early landmarks.

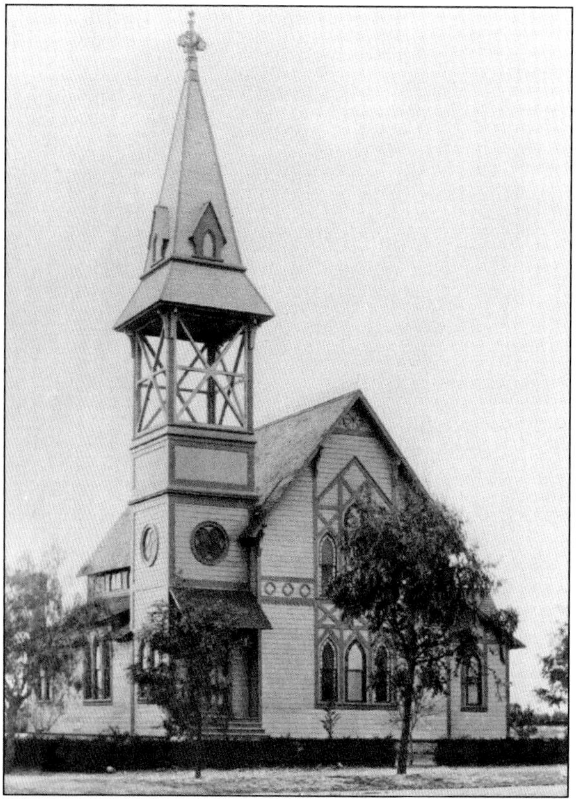

The First United Methodist Church, formed in 1883, is Ontario's oldest church. The first church building (left) was constructed in 1887 on the northwest corner of Euclid Avenue and G Street. Among the more interesting events at the church was one on January 3, 1903, when famous African American educator and civil rights pioneer Booker T. Washington gave a lecture. Sadly, this building burned down on July 13, 1911, and nothing was saved. A new building was erected on the site (below) and served the congregation until 1950, when an entirely new church complex was constructed at its present location, at Euclid Avenue and I Street.

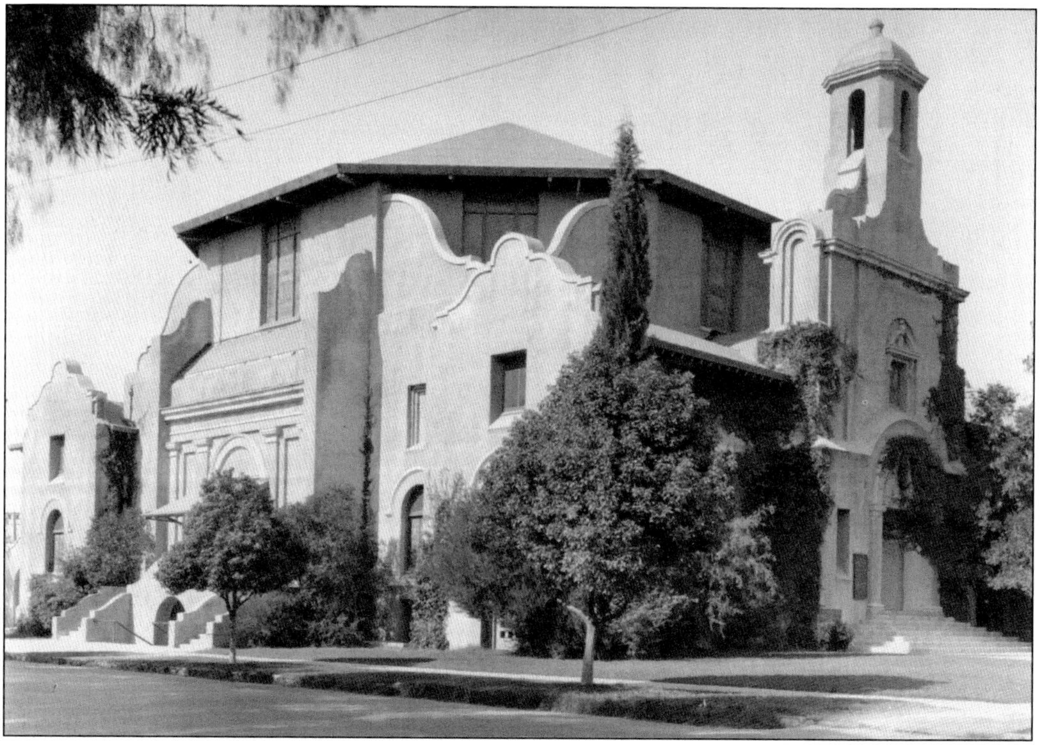

Bethel Congregational Church, Ontario's second church, was formed in February 1885 and was the church attended by the Chaffeys and their extended family. In fact, the church was formed by Anna Waddingham, the sister of Mrs. William Chaffey. The first building was constructed in 1888 at Palm Avenue and A Street (now Holt Boulevard) but was replaced by its current building (pictured), at Euclid Avenue and F Street, in 1913.

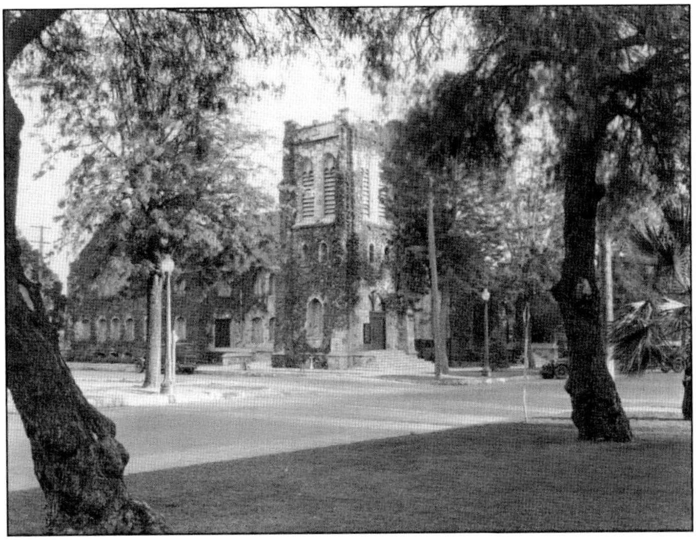

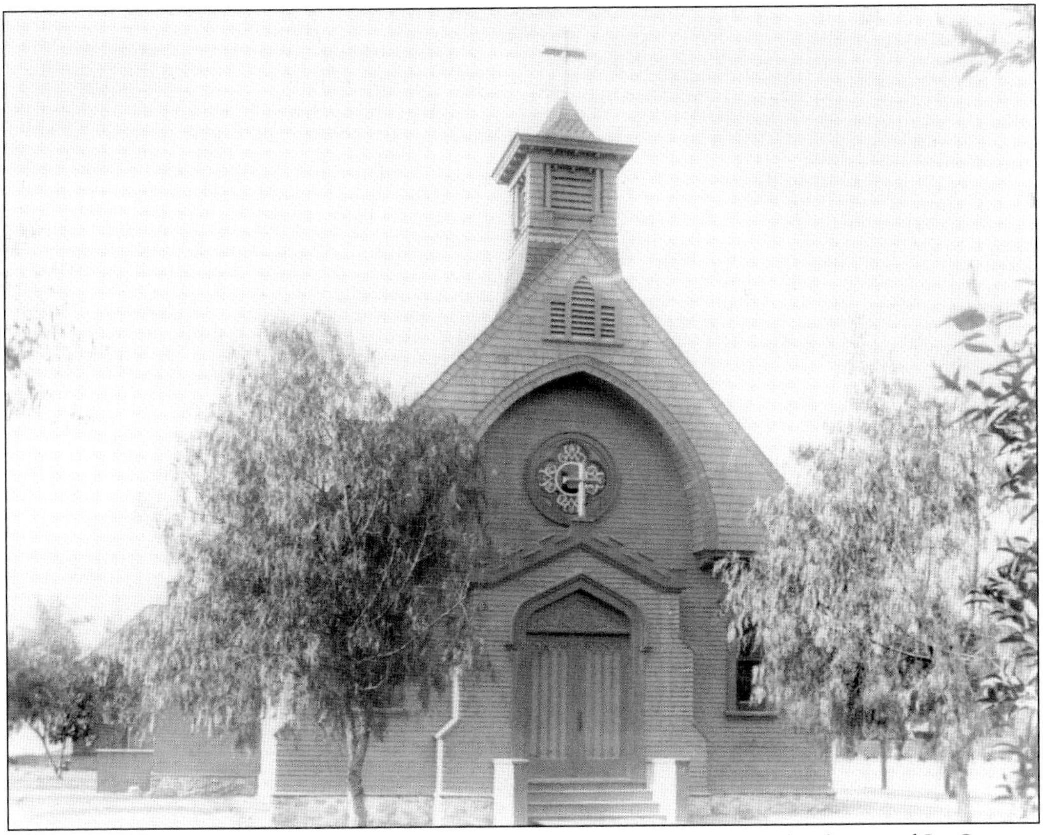

Ontario's first Catholic church (pictured) was built in 1899 and dedicated in honor of St. George, the patron saint of Bishop George Montgomery. Topped with a bell tower with a gilt gold cross, it was designated a mission church until 1905, when Father Andrew Garriga was assigned to the church. By the 1920s, the congregation had outgrown the building, so a new church was built in 1923. The original church was used as a hall until 1956.

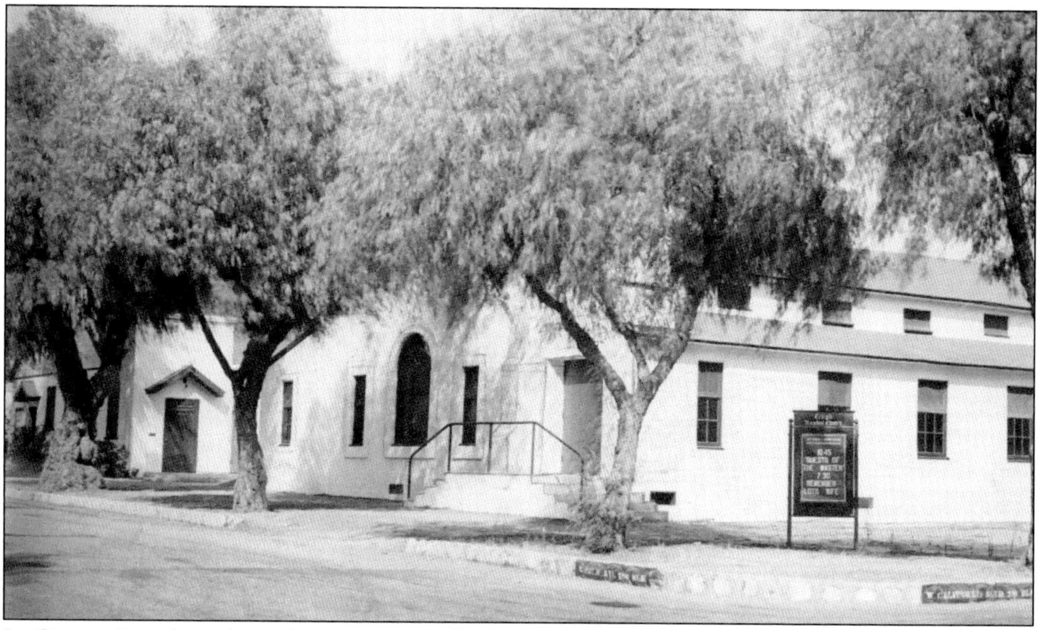

In Ontario's earliest days, there were very few African Americans living in the town, but by the 1920s, this was changing. On June 25, 1922, Pastor Arthur F. Seaton founded Mt. Zion Baptist Church in support of the African American community, and a new building was erected in 1925 on the northwest corner of Sultana Avenue and Nevada Street. As the congregation grew, more space was needed, and in 1978, the church moved to 224 West California Street, into the former Temple Baptist Church building, seen here.

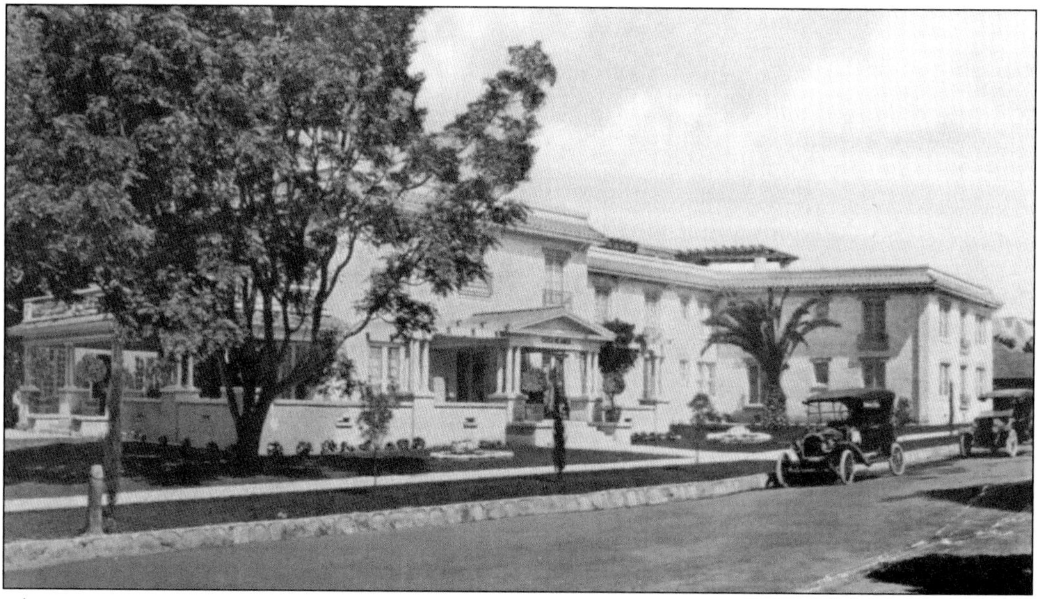

The Casa Blanca Hotel opened in April 1915 at 210 South Fern Avenue. It was a beautiful, two-story, gray brick building in the architectural style of Italian Renaissance Revival. The hotel boasted 42 mahogany-furnished bedrooms with en-suite bathrooms, offered tennis, golf, casino-style gambling, and billiards, and was a favorite of many Hollywood celebrities. Unfortunately, the building had fallen into disrepair by the 1970s and was demolished in 1998.

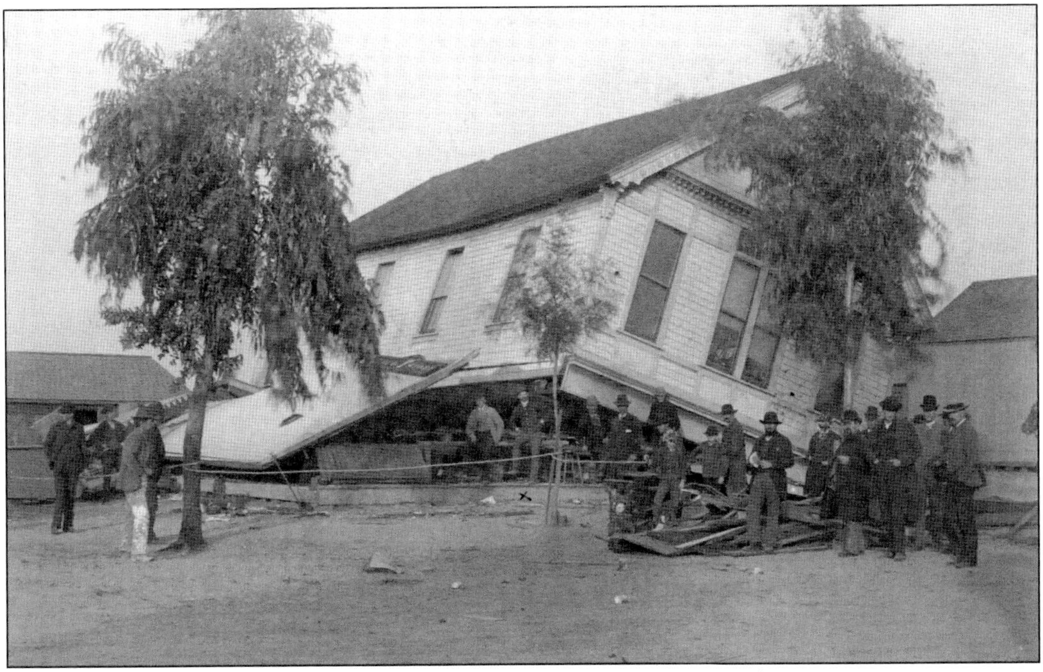

Druggist Henry Rose came to Ontario in 1885 and began construction the next year on a two-story, ornamental building on the west side of Euclid Avenue between A and B Streets. The first floor was used as his drugstore, and the second floor was reserved as a community meeting hall until the great "norther" of 1887. A torrential windstorm kicked up for a few days, and on December 13, a large gust knocked off the building's second story, landing it partially on the lot next door, and reducing the first floor to rubble, as seen above. Rose converted the hall into his drugstore, but after a few years, he decided to build a new structure (below), which still stands today. He sold the old building to the Episcopal Church, which moved it to the southeast corner of Euclid Avenue and C Street. It was demolished in 1960.

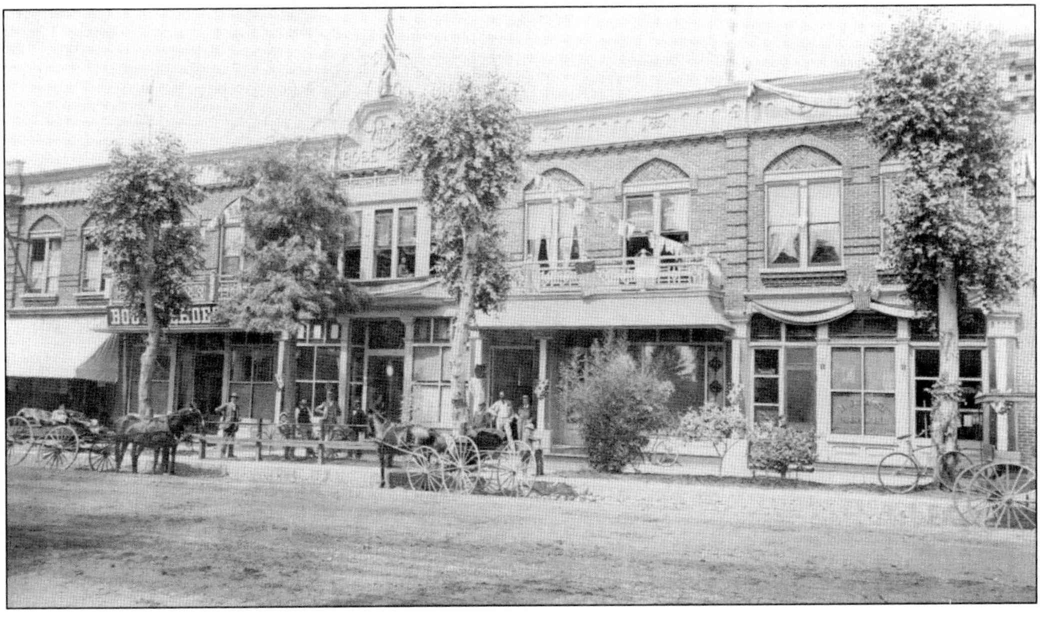

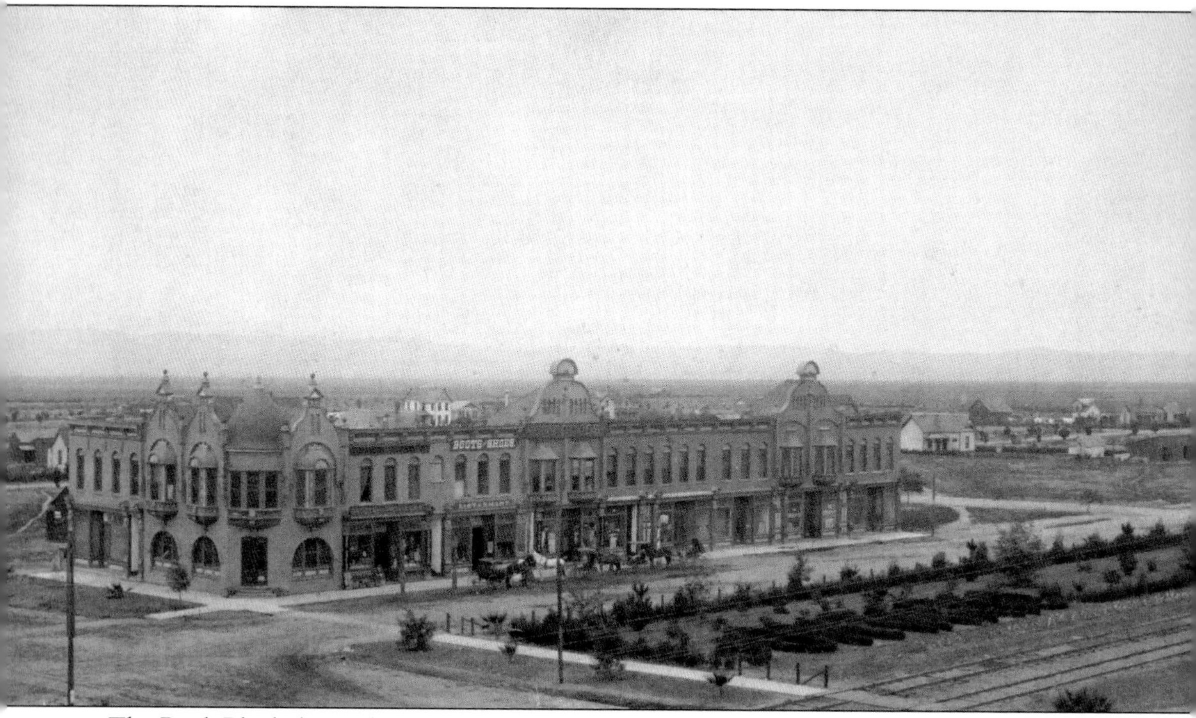

The Bank Block, located on the west side of Euclid Avenue at Main Street, was built in 1887 to house the Ontario State Bank, which opened on September 1, 1887. This bank became notorious when it was robbed by two armed assailants on January 4, 1895, who beat cashier Fred Stamm and locked him in the vault. Stamm's brother George was alerted to open the vault, but he was in Cucamonga Canyon at the time. Fortunately, the mule car was parked at the head of Euclid Avenue, so George hopped on the car and ordered the brakes released. The car made the six-mile trip down Euclid Avenue in only nine minutes, but by then, Fred had been freed from the vault. Later that month, one of the robbers was caught and sentenced to six years in San Quentin. The other robber was presumed dead. The Bank Block, Ontario's first business block, was later known as the Grand Palace, famous for selling furniture and antiques, and burned down in 1986.

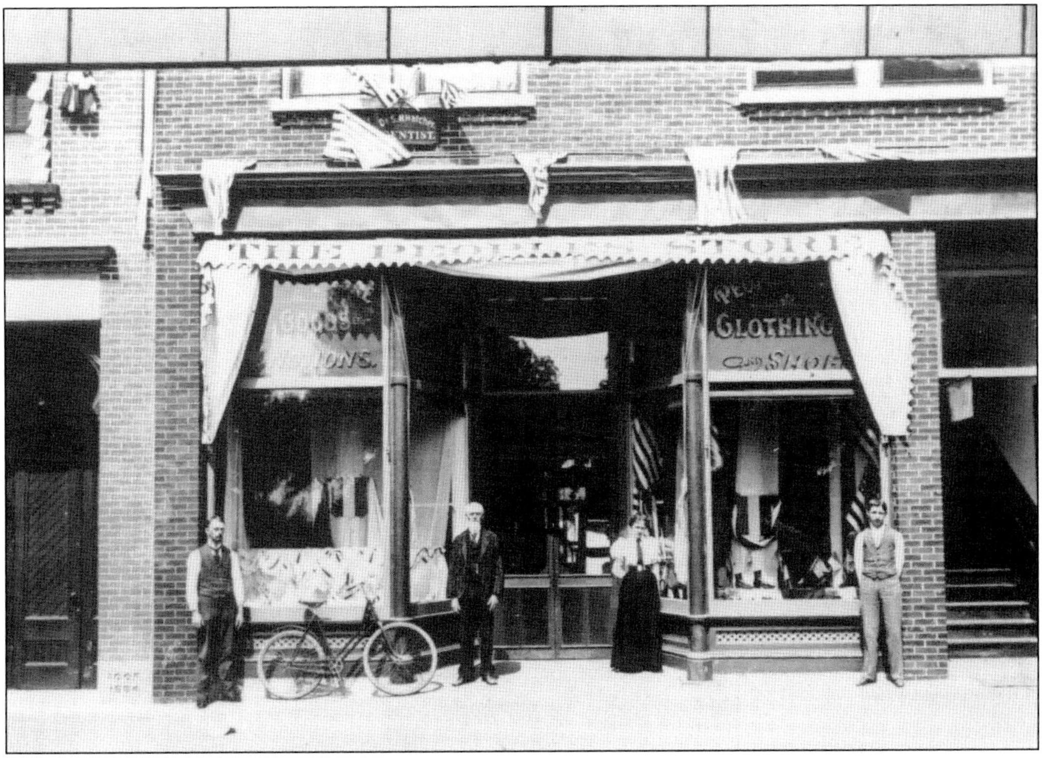

Hickman Philips's mercantile, known as the People's Store, opened in 1890, and in 1895, moved to the west side of Euclid Avenue between A and B Streets. Canadian settlers and brothers William and Fred Fallis purchased it in 1906, just after settling in Ontario. Originally called Fallis Bros., the store was known simply as Fallis' for years, even after the family sold the store to Robert Marver in 1958. Marver ran the business until 1988, and the building was demolished in 2001.

W.W. Smith opened his grocery store (pictured) at 209 North Euclid Avenue on May 17, 1887. One of Ontario's earliest grocery stores, Smith stocked everything from coffee and tea to fresh groceries and canned goods, as well as tableware. Smith retired from his business in 1919 and sold out to Walter Moore, who had recently merged his grocery store with White's Grocery, just up the street at 221 North Euclid.

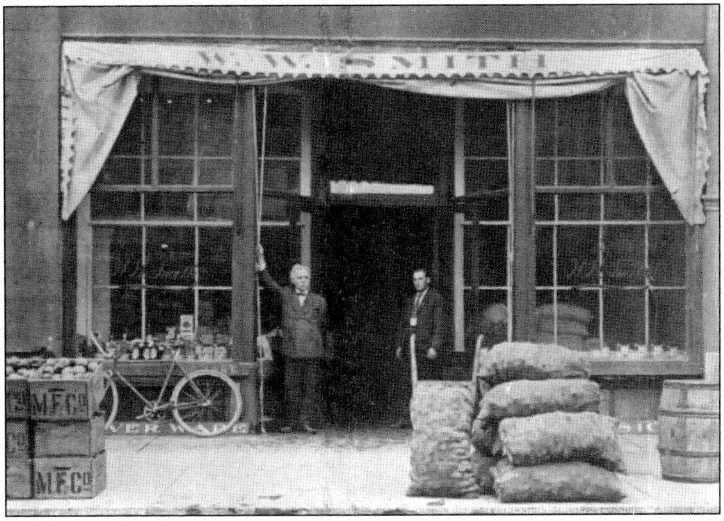

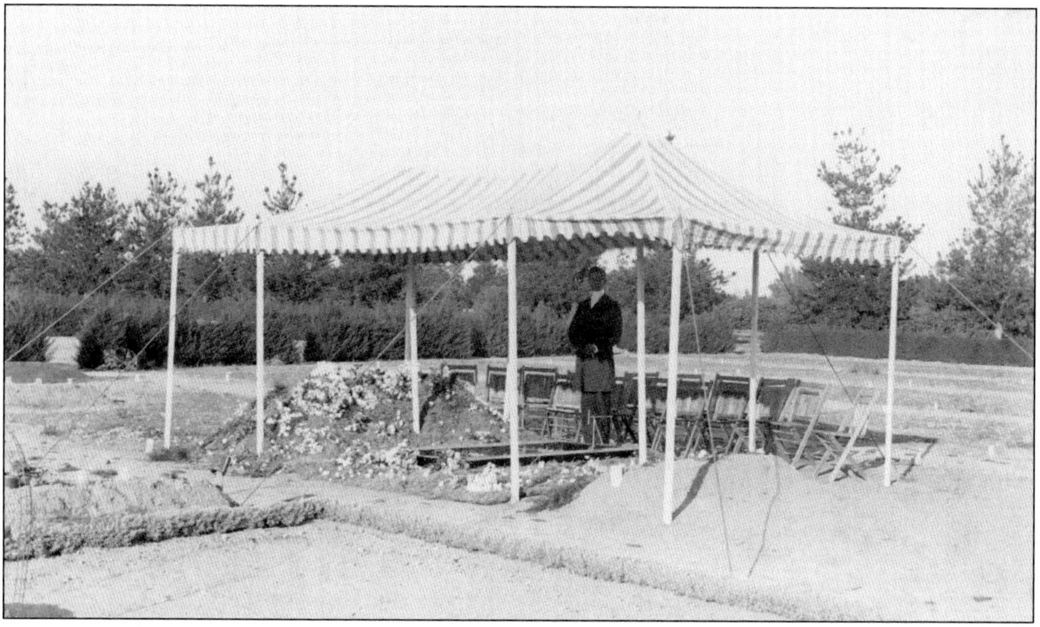

Ontario's only cemetery was established in 1891 at Mountain Avenue and G Street on land owned by Charles Harwood. The cemetery was incorporated in 1892, with Harwood, A.G. Kendall, brothers Herbert C. and John W. Oakley, and their brother-in-law Isaac Garbutt chosen as the board of directors. Many local pioneers are interred at the cemetery. Undertaker Ed Drew is pictured here.

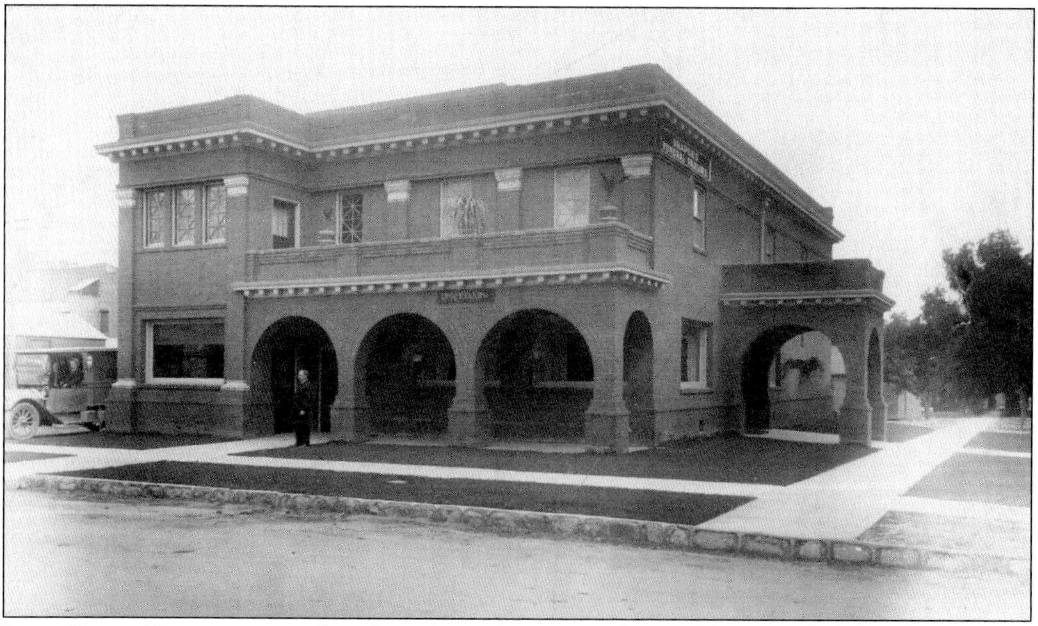

James Birney Draper was another Canadian who migrated to Ontario in 1894, first working as a tailor. In 1898, he purchased an undertaking establishment, but also continued work as a tailor. Originally located at 143 North Euclid Avenue, Draper built this large, two-story brick building at 125 West C Street in 1911. In 1962, Draper Mortuary moved to its current location on North Mountain Avenue, and is still in business today.

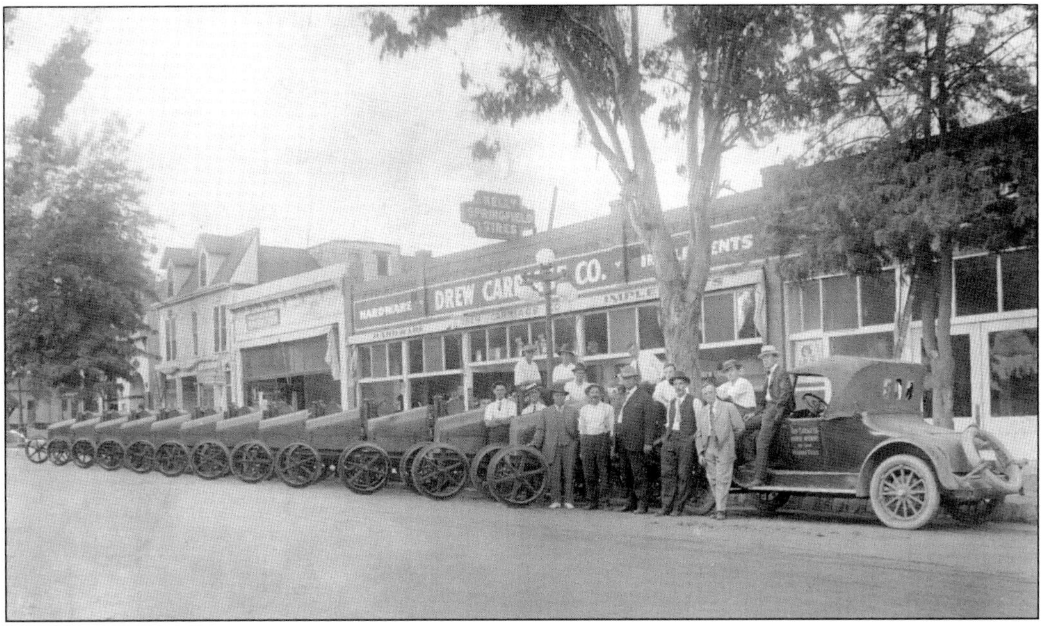

F.A.C. "Fred" Drew came to Ontario from Canada with his parents, Edred and Lydia, in 1884. His father launched an undertaking business, which Fred took over when his father died in 1898. In 1902, he established the Drew Carriage Company at 208 North Euclid Avenue, selling buggies, but he later became a major dealer for International Harvester in addition to selling general hardware. The company remained a family business until it closed in 1984.

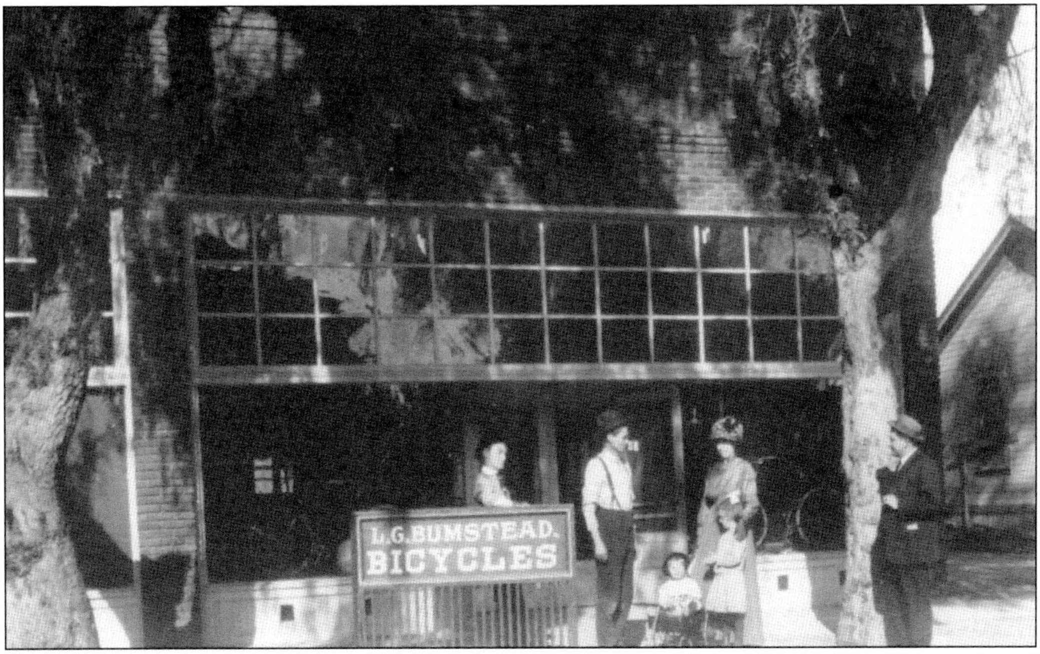

In November 1909, L.G. Bumstead announced that he had purchased E.V. Caldwell's bicycle and sporting goods shop. Originally located at 133 North Euclid Avenue, the shop has moved a few times over the years. Bumstead Bicycles is still in business today and remains family-owned. It is now located on Fourth Street and deals solely in bicycles.

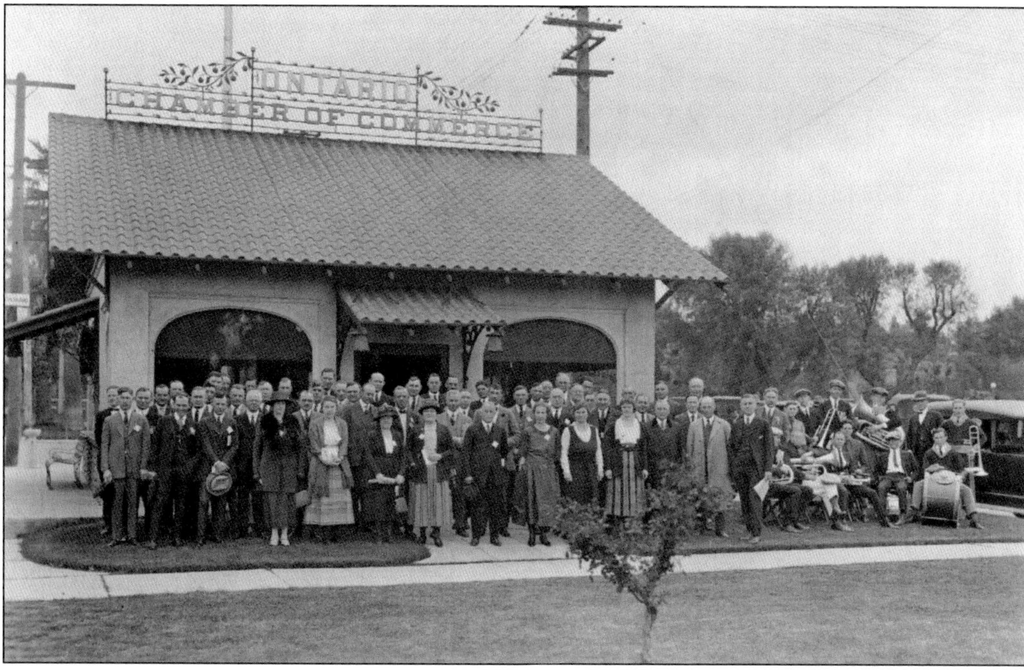

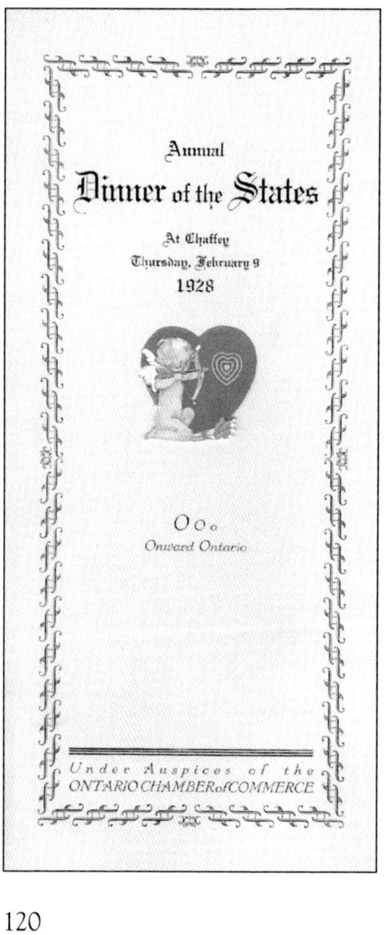

The Ontario Chamber of Commerce dates to 1903, but membership faltered in the early days. The chamber was reestablished on October 14, 1909, with 78 new members who each paid 50¢ per month in dues. In 1910, they constructed a building on the median of Euclid Avenue, seen here, across from city hall. In 1916, the chamber held its inaugural Dinner of the States, an annual member dinner where participants were seated at the table of their home state. To commemorate Ontario's 50th anniversary, the event was held as an outdoor picnic at Fourth Street Park (now John Galvin Park) and was dubbed the All States Picnic. Carl Holmer, Ontario's city manager, pitched the idea of holding the event on the Euclid Avenue median, and in 1939, the picnic was held there for the first time at "the world's longest picnic table." The rest is history.

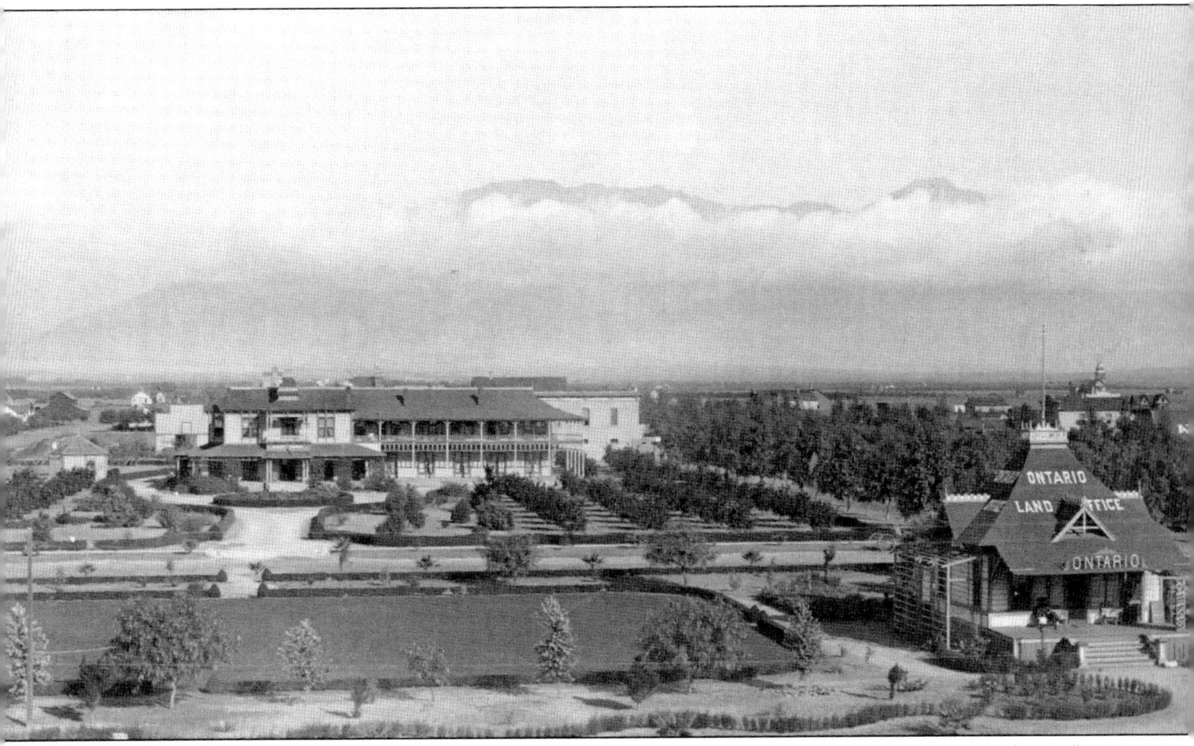

The Ontario Hotel, shown here along with the Ontario Land Office (at right), opened in July 1883. The grand hotel served visitors and potential land buyers. Built by A.W. Boggs of Riverside, the two-story hotel offered 12 rooms. Charles Frankish's Ontario Land and Improvement Company purchased the hotel in 1886 and built an east wing in 1887, which added 24 rooms with verandas and balconies and doubled the size of the dining room. The hotel closed in 1909, and in 1912, Frankish sold the building in order to construct his Frankish Building on the site. The hotel was divided into two sections, with the original section moving to the southwest corner of Holt Boulevard and Campus Avenue to become an apartment house, where it was eventually demolished in 1932. The east wing moved to 208 West Holt Boulevard, where, for years, it was known as the Tre-El-Een Hotel. It was demolished in 1969 to make way for a parking lot.

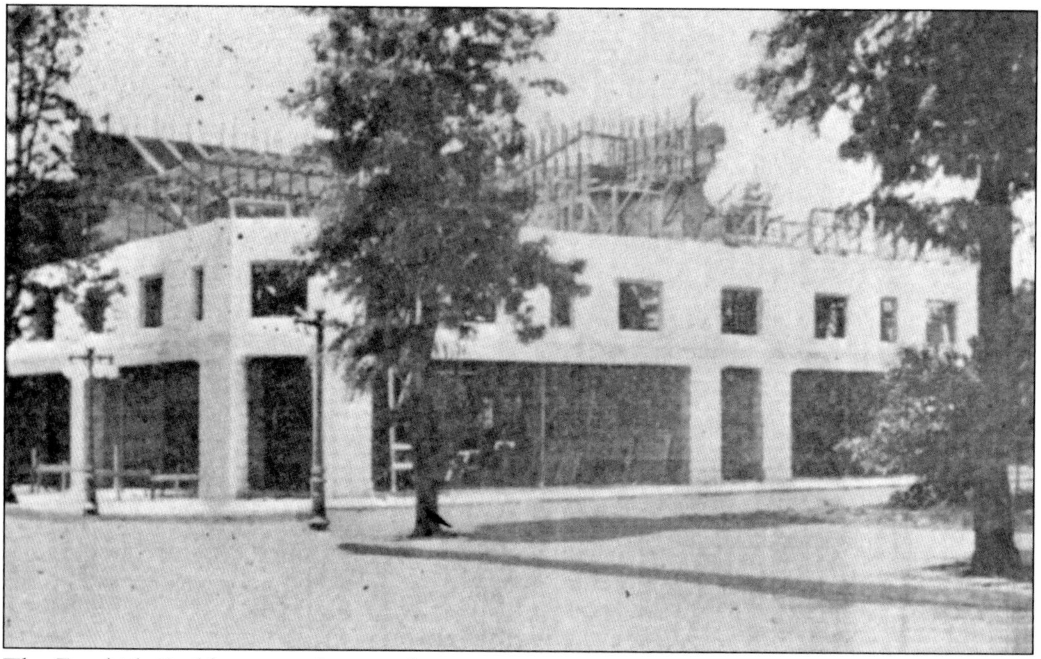

The Frankish Building, seen here under construction in 1914, was completed in 1916. Charles Frankish spared no expense in its construction, designing the main floor for commercial use and the second and third floors as luxury apartments. In the 1940s, it served as the local USO headquarters. It stands today on the southwest corner of Euclid Avenue and Transit Street and was listed in the National Register of Historic Places in 1980.

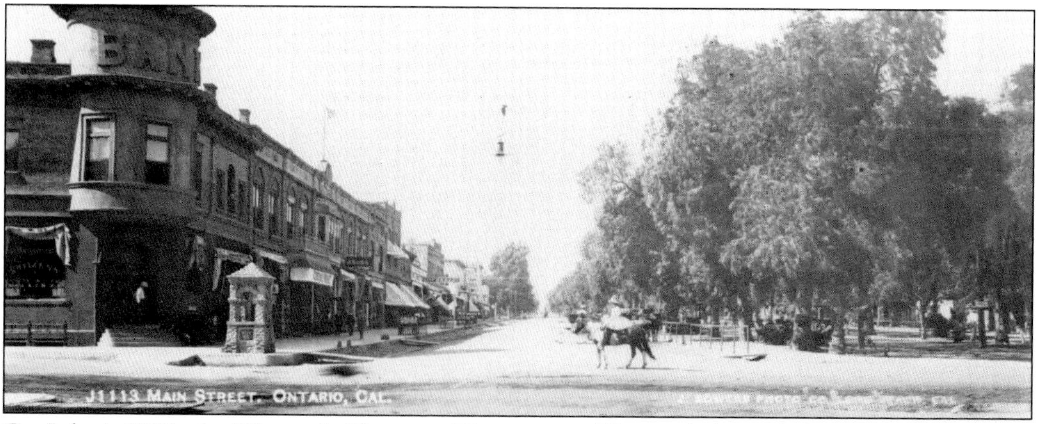

On July 4, 1908, the Women's Christian Temperance Union dedicated their fountain on the northwest corner of Euclid Avenue and A Street, seen here. In October 1915, a Mrs. Marble was struck by a car as she was having a drink at the fountain, prompting it to be moved. It was moved several times over the years, and in 1998, was moved to its present location next to the bandstand on the Euclid Avenue median. This 1909 postcard shows the fountain's original location.

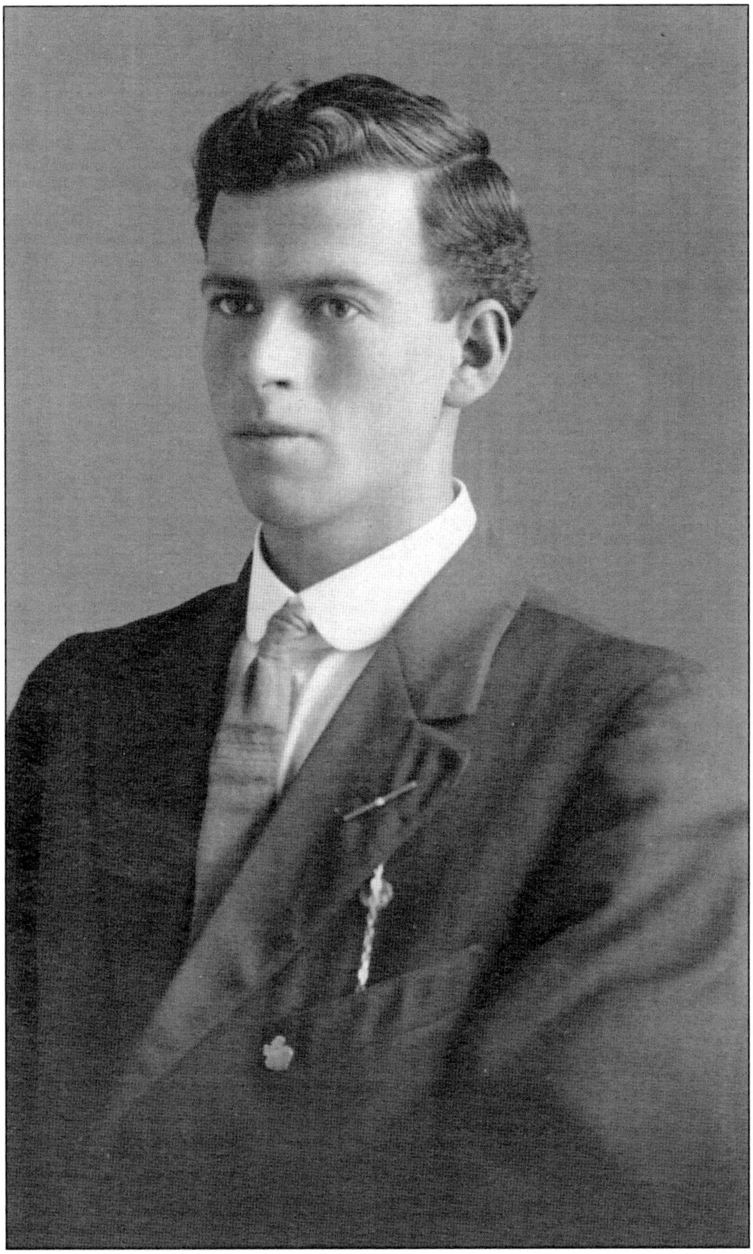

Ralph T. Kingery was born in Springfield, Missouri, on December 16, 1891. He and his family moved to Ontario when he was about 18 years old, and he worked for King Fruit Company before being drafted into the Army in August 1917. Kingery was with the first troops sent overseas after the US declaration of war on April 6, 1917, as part of the 1st Infantry Brigade. He arrived in Europe on Christmas Day, 1917, and was sent to France soon after. The 1st Infantry Brigade was sent to relieve the First Moroccan Division in the Ansauville sector of France on January 15, 1918. Kingery was killed in action by a German shell while in the front line trenches on February 19, 1918, the first soldier from California to be killed in action during World War I. His body was brought home to his parents in Ontario on June 24, 1921, and he was given a military funeral at Bellevue Cemetery.

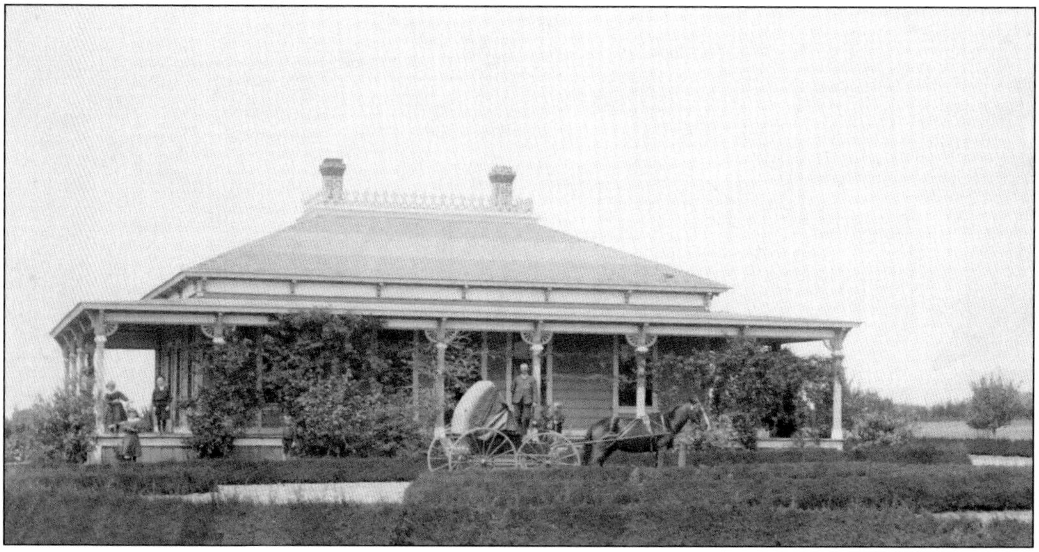

Dr. Elswood Chaffey, one of George Chaffey's three younger brothers, brought his family to Ontario in July 1883, ranching citrus and serving as Ontario's first doctor. He built this handsome ranch home at Euclid Avenue and Fifth Street for $4,000. It no longer stands. Dr. Chaffey was a restless sort, and left Ontario in 1889 for other adventures. After some years moving his family around, he finally settled in rural Mexico, where he worked as a country doctor until his death in 1920.

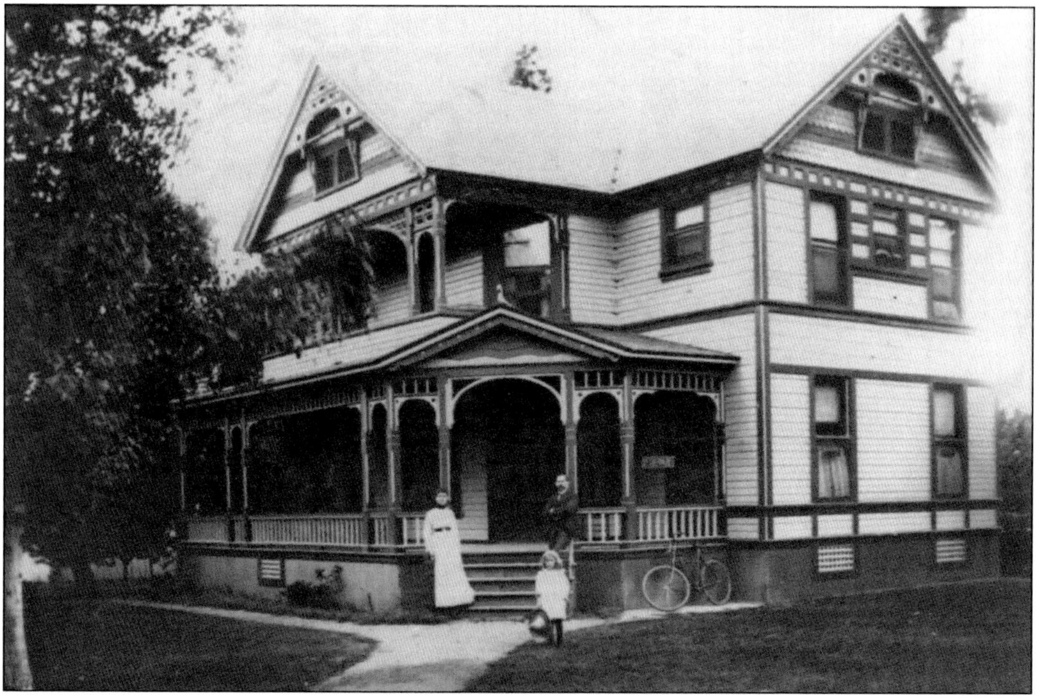

Dr. Orville Ensign was one of Ontario's earliest physicians, settling in the colony in 1888. He built this lovely Victorian home in 1893 in the South Side Tract, at 304 South Laurel Avenue. Dr. Ensign died in 1899, after which the home was occupied by Dr. Christopher Sheppard, a local physician who served the community until his death in 1924. The home still stands today and is listed in the National Register of Historic Places.

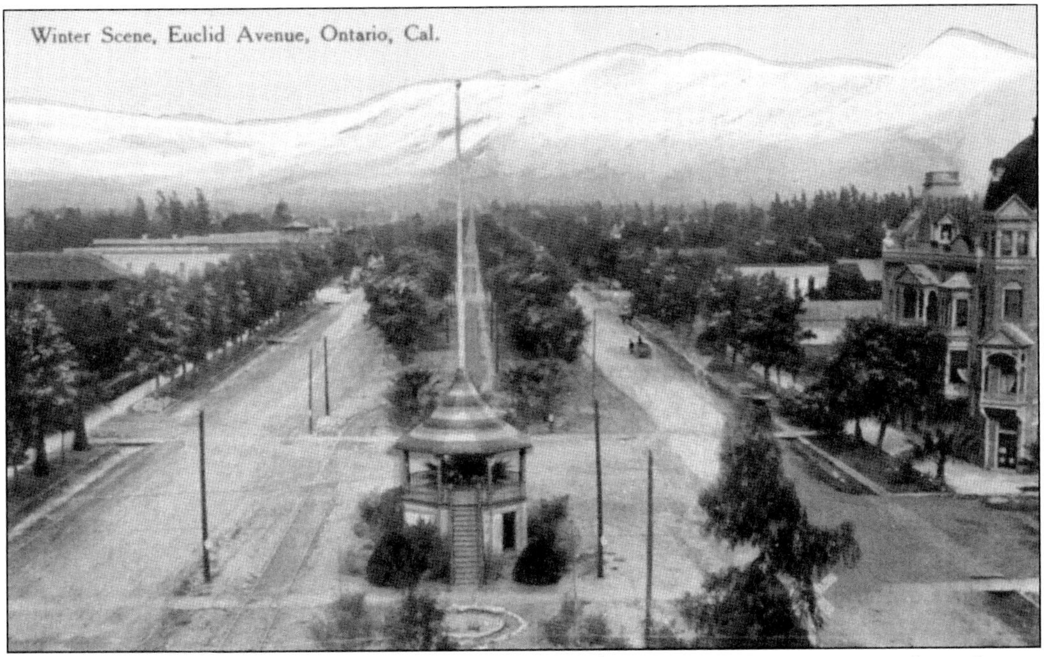

Ontario's bandstand was originally built in 1892 as the two-story structure seen here. It was remodeled in 1905, removing the bottom level. Later, the bandstand was moved to Nugent Park, where it fell into disrepair and was eventually dismantled. In 1997, a replica of the original bandstand was funded by the Kiwanis Club of Ontario. It was rededicated with its new name, the R. Jack Mercer Community Bandstand, on July 4, 2001.

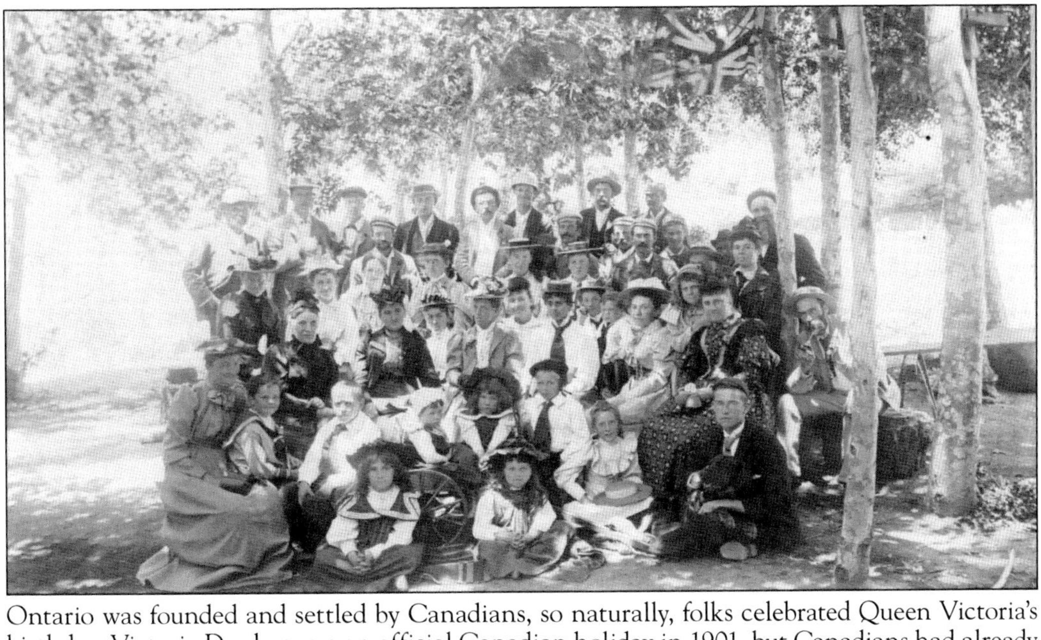

Ontario was founded and settled by Canadians, so naturally, folks celebrated Queen Victoria's birthday. Victoria Day became an official Canadian holiday in 1901, but Canadians had already been celebrating Queen Victoria's birthday for many years. In Ontario, former Canadians celebrated by having a picnic, usually in San Antonio Canyon, as seen here in 1895.

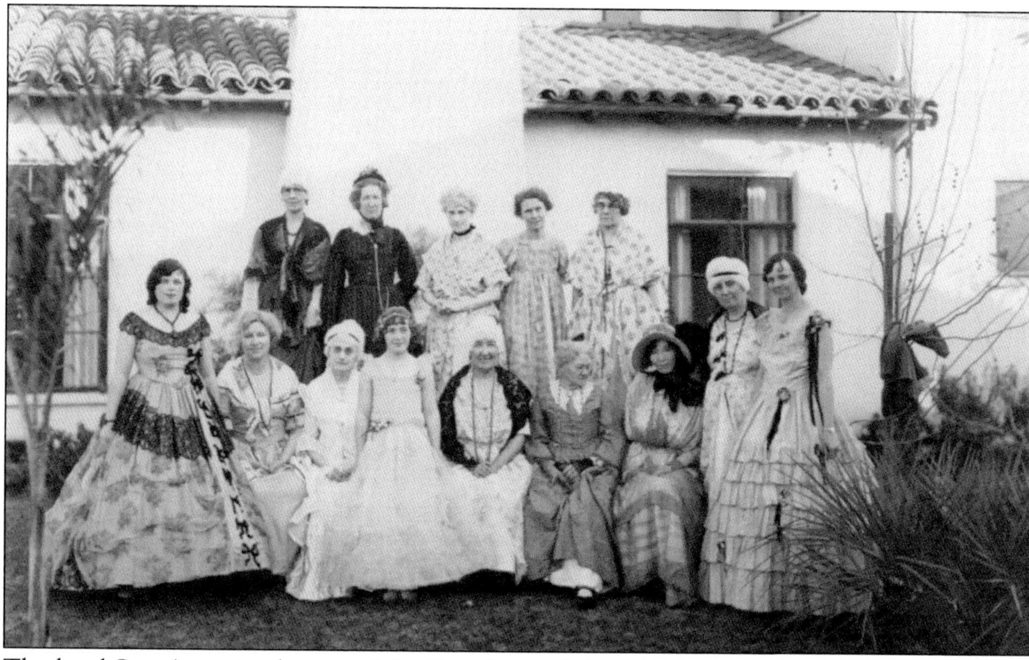

The local San Antonio chapter of the Daughters of the American Revolution was founded in 1910. Members are involved in community efforts to celebrate American history through school speech contests, history contests, and commemorative celebrations through the year. The San Antonio chapter also coordinated the installation of the Madonna of the Trail monument in 1929, which stands at the intersection of Euclid Avenue and Foothill Boulevard in Upland.

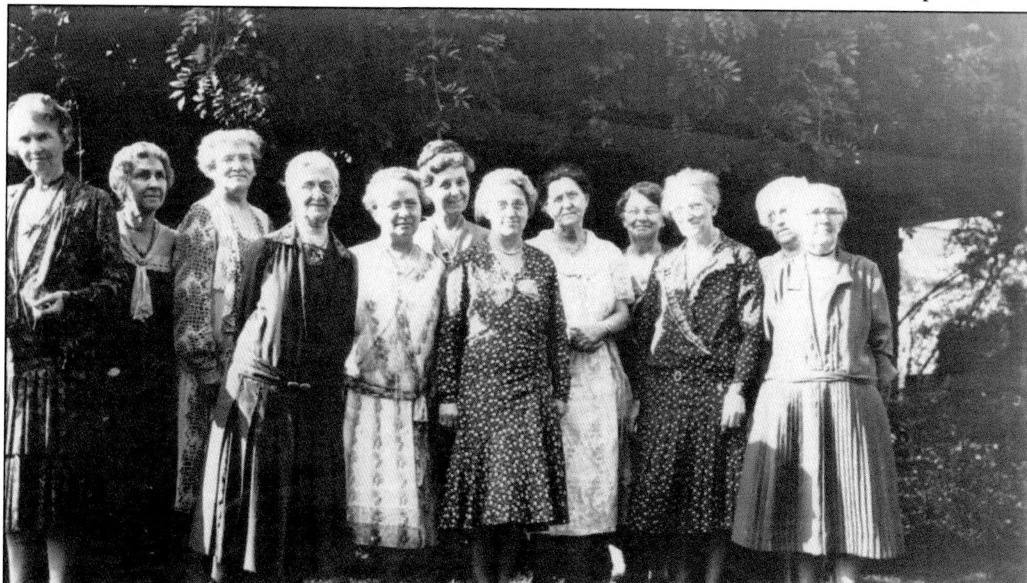

The Friday Afternoon Club is a local literary society that was formed by seven women in February 1896. According to their constitution, the goal of the club is "mutual improvement of its members in literature, art, science, current events, and to promote sociability." The Friday Afternoon Club, Ontario's oldest local club, has also supported community causes and institutions such as the Red Cross, Ontario's public library, and San Antonio Community Hospital.

The Shakespeare Club of Ontario was formed by a group of local women in 1913 for the purpose of studying and appreciating the works of William Shakespeare. Over the years, the club has expanded its purpose to include "the study of literature and contemporary affairs, the development of broader views, and the promotion of sociability." The club has endured for over 100 years and continues to meet twice a month on Friday afternoons.

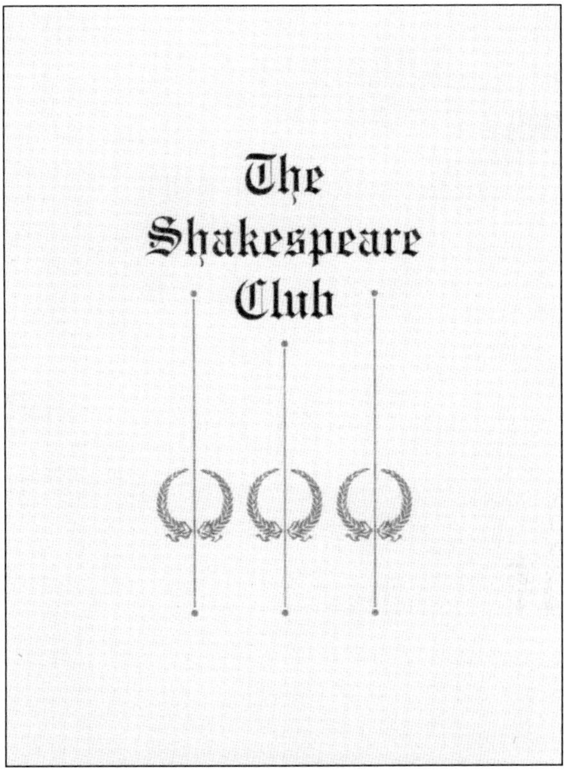

The Grand Army of the Republic (GAR) was a fraternal organization consisting of veterans of the Civil War who served in the Union army, the US Navy and Marines, and the Revenue Cutter Service. Alois Podrasnik, pictured here on the far right, prompted the formation of the Last Man's Club in 1930, when only 12 members of the local GAR remained. This photograph was taken in October 1932.

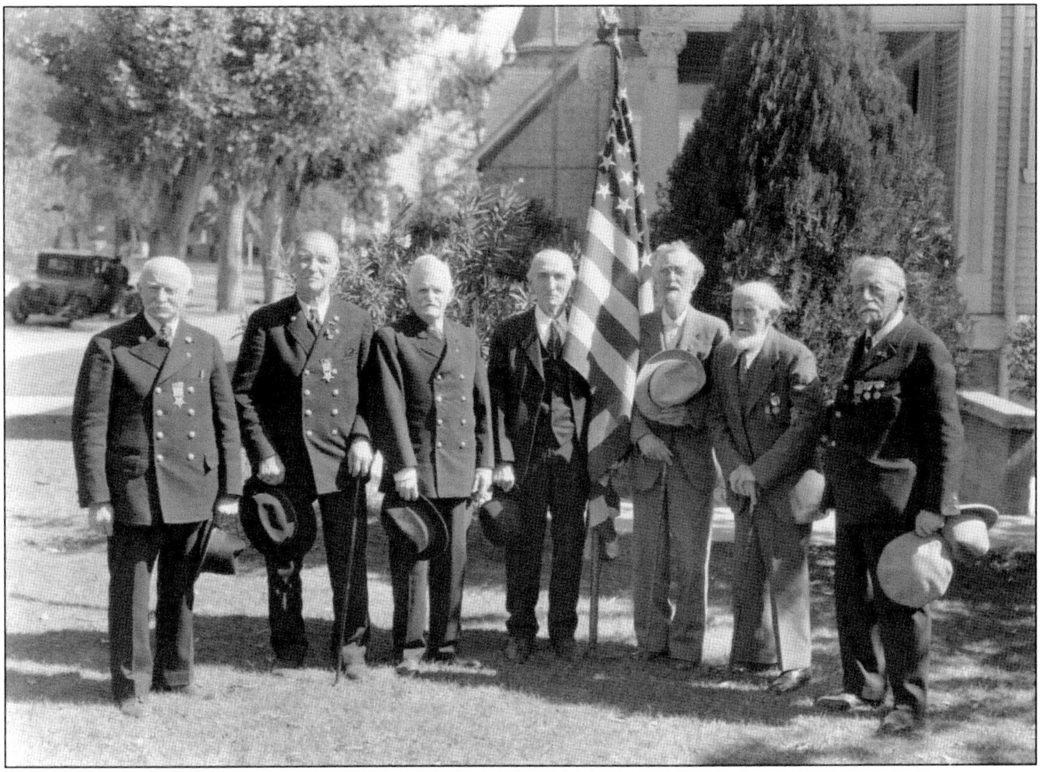